THE POLITICS OF
INDONESIA

Damien Kingsbury

Melbourne

OXFORD UNIVERSITY PRESS

Oxford Auckland New York

OXFORD UNIVERSITY PRESS AUSTRALIA

Oxford   New York
Athens   Auckland   Bangkok   Bogotá
Buenos Aires   Calcutta   Cape Town   Chennai
Dar es Salaam   Delhi   Florence   Hong Kong
Istanbul   Karachi   Kuala Lumpur   Madrid
Melbourne   Mexico City   Mumbai   Nairobi
Paris   Port Moresby   São Paulo   Singapore
Taipei   Tokyo   Toronto   Warsaw

and associated companies in
Berlin   Ibadan

OXFORD is a trade mark of Oxford University Press

National Library of Australia

Cataloguing-in-Publication data:
Kingsbury, Damien.
    The politics of Indonesia.

    Bibliography.
    Includes index.
    ISBN 0 19 550626 X

    1. Indonesia—Politics and government—I. Title.

320.9598

Edited by Lucy Davison
Cover design by Jason Phillips
Typeset by Syarikat Seng Teik Sdn. Bhd., Malaysia
Printed by McPherson's Printing Group, Australia
Published by Oxford University Press,
253 Normanby Road, South Melbourne, Australia

CONTENTS

Preface   v

Abbreviations   viii

1   Introduction   1

2   Traditional and Colonial Influences   17

3   From Independence to 1965   39

4   The New Order Seizes Power   57

5   State-Building, Black Gold, and Economic Achievement   77

6   Signs of Division in Indonesian Domestic Politics   99

7   Political Opposition within Indonesia   127

8   The Role and Requirements of the Media   147

9   Unity in Diversity?   163

10   Human Rights, ABRI, and the Law   176

11   Corruption and the First Family   198

12   Competing Influences   219

13   Looking Ahead: 1998 and Beyond   240

Epilogue: The Fall of Suharto   250

A Review of the Literature   256

References   264

Index   275

For Fiona, without whom . . .

PREFACE

The ideological position informing this work is broadly egalitarian and derives in a generic fashion from the European enlightenment tradition. Culturally, this can be located within a mainstream Australian tendency, which not only includes a mistrust of, and lack of deference for, authority, but also a generalised tolerance of social and political ambiguity. Such a broad ideological and cultural position is at odds with an official or government-sponsored 'culture', such as that of the Republic of Indonesia. However, such a perspective is not entirely out of keeping with many aspects of local culture in Indonesia (including that of the well-spring of Indonesian political thinking, Central Java), and it does provide a critical perspective from which to analyse contemporary Indonesian politics.

An examination of the practice of authority, and hence power, in the Indonesian political system lies at the heart of this study. As such, this book is intended to consider a range of situations that illustrate how the political process works in Indonesia, to whose benefit, and at what—and to whose—cost. It is further noted that, while cultural influences clearly exist, the factor that influences the course of events in Indonesia is not so much cultural identity but how such a cultural identity is interpreted or imposed to suit a particular political advantage and how, as a process of political operation, it is both authoritarian and repressive.

It should be noted that much of the information in this book is based on interviews and conversations with many people, almost all of whom would be compromised if identified. As a consequence, I have been unable to clearly cite all sources of information. This raises two related points, the first being that it is not unusual not to identify all sources of information in a politically sensitive area. The second point is that, while academia is traditionally dismissive of journalism, that craft has a number of aspects that complement academia. That which is most relevant here is the protection of one's sources. Journalists sometimes identify their sources in an intentionally ambiguous or general way, which does not deny the validity of the source or the integrity of the information. In this essay I have drawn on the ethical codes of both academia (in particular, Monash University's Ethics Committee) and of journalism (the Australian Journalists Association/Media Entertainment and Arts Alliance Code of Ethics).

Some political definitions

In any study of political matters, it is necessary to clarify some definitions, and I have largely undertaken to do so throughout the text. However, particularly in relation to distinctions within the broad political structure, I would like to offer a brief clarification of the conceptions of nation, state, state apparatus, regime and government. In the first instance, a *nation* is intended here to mean 'a group of people who understand themselves to have common interests and world views and who usually share a common language'. This may or may not coincide with the *state*, which is the organisational territory under a political authority and which can (or can attempt to) claim or compel the compliance of its citizens to its laws.

The idea of 'state apparatus' implies the functional ability of the state—the means (legislative and institutional) by which it achieves (or attempts to achieve) desired outcomes. Within this text I refer to specific apparatus by their formal names (for example, the armed forces, or ABRI). The idea of a 'regime', which is often used within the context of the Indonesian government (for example, 'the Suharto regime'), literally means the method or system of government, but is usually regarded as a pejorative term for the institution of government; it tends to imply a pre-existing antithesis and is not used here for that reason.

In so far as the text can be construed as antithetical towards its subject, this is based on a conflict between evidence and the values outlined above. The term *government*, which is used throughout the text instead, refers to the political institution that normatively makes and implements decisions for the citizens of the state.

Acknowledgments

I would like to thank the many people who have taken time to talk to me about political issues in Indonesia, who have unstintingly offered insights and analysis, and who have, in a practical sense, helped piece together the multidimensional jigsaw puzzle that is Indonesian politics. For the reasons outlined above, I cannot name those people here.

I would also like to thank Herb and Betty Feith for their encouragement, and Keryn O'Sullivan and Pat Walsh for their critical comments on an early draft of the manuscript. They do not, of course, bear any responsibility for any failings that might be contained herein.

The author and publisher are grateful to the following copyright holders for granting permission to reproduce textual material in this book: Cornell University Press for extract from H. Feith, 'Indonesia', in G. Kahin (ed.), *Governments and Politics of Southeast Asia*, 2nd edn, Cornell University Press, Ithaca, NY, 1964; Centre of Southeast Asian Studies and Harold Crouch for extract from H. Crouch, 'Democratic Prospects in Indonesia', in D. Bourchier & J. Legge (eds), *Democracy in Indonesia*, Centre of Southeast Asian Studies, Monash University, Melbourne, 1994; Political & Economic Risk Consultancy Ltd for extract from PERC, *Country Risk Report: Indonesia*, PERC, Hong Kong, 1997; Ian Proudfoot for extract from I. Proudfoot, 'The Early Indianized States of Indonesia: Religion and Social Control', in J. Fox et al. (eds), *Indonesia: Australian Perspectives*, The Research School of Pacific Studies, Australian National University, Canberra, 1980; Routledge for extracts from M. Vatikiotis, *Indonesian Politics under Suharto*, Routledge, London, 1993; John Stackhouse for extract from J. Stackhouse, 'Anatomy of Australia's First Solo Foreign Affairs Crisis', *Bulletin*, 13 May 1986.

Every effort has been made to trace the original source of all material reproduced in this book. Where the attempt has been unsuccessful, the author and publisher would be pleased to hear from the copyright holder concerned to rectify any omission.

ABBREVIATIONS

ABRI   Angkatan Bersenjata Republik Indonesia (the Indonesian armed forces)
ASEAN   Association of South East Asian Nations
BAPPENAS   Baden Perencanaan Pembangunan Nasional (the National Development Planning Board)
BIA   Baden Intelijen ABRI
CIA   Central Intelligence Agency (USA)
CIDES   Centre for Information and Development Studies
CSIS   Centre for Strategic and International Studies
DPR   Dewan Perwakilan Rakyat (the Indonesian 'parliament')
FBSI   Federasi Buruh Seluruh Indonesia (All Indonesian Labour Federation)
ICMI   Ikatan Cendekiawan Muslem se Indonesia (Indonesian Association of Muslim Intellectuals)
ILO   International Labour Organisation
IMF   International Monetary Fund
IPKI   League of Upholders of Indonesian Independence
KNIL   Koninklijk Nederlands-Indisch Leger (Royal Netherlands Indies Army)
Kopkamtib   Komando Operasi Pemulihan Keamanan dan Ketertiban (Operational Command for the Restoration of Security and Order)
LBHI   Indonesian Legal Aid Foundation
LKB   Institute of Constitutional Awareness
MPR   Mejelis Permusyawaratan Rakyat (People's Consultative Assembly)
NGO   non-government organisation

NII	*Negara Islam Indonesia* (Indonesian Islamic State)
NU	Nahdatul Ulama (Awakening of Religious Scholars)
OPM	Organisasi Papua Merdeka (Free Papua Movement)
PDI	Partai Demokrasi Indonesia (Indonesian Democratic Party)
PKI	Partai Komunis Indonesia (Indonesian Communist Party)
PNG	Papua New Guinea
PNI	Partai Nasional Indonesia (Indonesian Nationalist Party)
PPBI	Pusat Perjuangan Buruhi Indonesia (Indonesian Centre for Labour Struggle)
PPP	Partai Persatuan Pembangunan (United Development Party)
PRD	Partai Rakyat Demokrasi (People's Democratic Party)
PRRI	Pemerintah Revolusioner Republik Indonesia (Revolutionary Government of the Republic of Indonesia)
PSI	Partai Sosialis Indonesia (Indonesian Socialist Party)
PWI	Persatuan Wartawan Indonesia (Indonesian Journalists' Union)
RPKAD	Resimen Para Komando Angkatan (Army Paracommando Regiment)
RUSI	Republic of the United States of Indonesia
SBSI	Indonesian Labour Union for Prosperity
SIUPP	Surat Izin Usaha Penerbitan Pers (Press Publication Business Licence)
SPSI	Serikat Pekerja Seluruh Indonesia (All-Indonesia Workers' Union)
VOC	Verenigde Oost-Indische Compagnie (Dutch United East India Company)

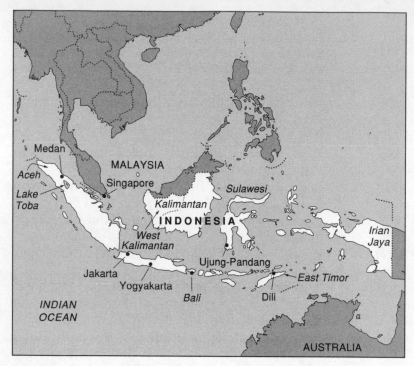

Indonesia and the surrounding region.

1

INTRODUCTION

Dictators ride to and fro upon tigers which they dare not dismount. And the tigers are getting hungry.

Winston Churchill, after a Chinese proverb: 'Those who ride tigers dare not dismount'

A shadow play

It is just after dusk; evening has settled, and the long *wayang kulit* (shadow-puppet) play has just begun under the humid veil of the evening's monsoonal sky. The format is familiar: the ebb and flow of left and right, symbolising the great forces of nature that find balance only in binary opposition. As is conventional for such a play, there is no clear right and wrong, and each character represents both human strengths and weaknesses, which also find balance in life. As befits the form, there are lessons for the audience in appropriate behaviour throughout. The play starts in turmoil, and into this equation, a young *satria* (knight) of humble origins appears, assuming leadership of the right and rising to crush the left.

As the evening deepens, the mystical passing of power is acted out as the *satria* displaces and then disposes of the *panji* (monarch) (Grant 1966, p. 6), whom he believes to have slipped from divine neutrality to supporting the left. The *satria* moves to assume the role of *panji* for himself, casting questioners out of the *kraton* (palace) and relegating opposition from within his own ranks to the periphery. The new *panji* deftly manipulates the right but, in order to ensure his position and believing that potential threats are everywhere, embarks on a reign of terror, descending into routine repression. In the balancing act of the *wayang kulit*, the *panji* justifies his harsh reign by bringing relative order and alleviating the worst of the poverty that afflicts the people under his rule.

1

Yet the *panji*, reflecting the balance between good and evil even within each individual, accrues great wealth for himself, his friends, and his family. This is tolerated for a time as, like the local audience, the main characters know or at least accept that rewards gravitate as if by nature to centres of power. But the balance and discretion that are meant to be the marks of a true *satria* slip away, and the new *panji* is increasingly seen as greedy and blind to the excesses of his retinue. Slowly but surely his power begins to ebb, and with a return to the chaos of his accession, his subjects turn away, in shame, from the crassness of his excesses. Dissent against his rule grows, and with the forces of nature no longer in balance, discord grows among his people.

The *wayang kulit* is a morality play, intended to show the path to goodness and inner peace, and as the night grows long and the first hints of morning appear, the audience tires and grows restless. They know that the play must soon come to an end, yet the final stages of the play drag on. Expecting the *wayang kulit* to provide a salutary lesson in its conclusion, the audience is aware of a range of possible outcomes.

One outcome could be that the old, corrupt, and almost completely blind *panji* will die, causing inevitable turmoil as his succession is resolved. Alternatively, the old *panji* could realise that power is slipping from his grasp and could attempt to save some dignity by acceding to the inevitable, giving his blessing to a new, morally correct *panji*. Another option is that, in his blindness, he will pass the mantle of his position (but not its power) to an inappropriate successor, who will then have to fight to retain it, but who, in the turmoil of the times, may lose it. Yet another alternative is that, having recognised that the old *panji* no longer possesses power, a successor will rise from the ranks of the *satria* and depose him. This successor will perhaps strip the *panji*'s family and friends of their wealth and gradually remove from the *panji* his public claims to dignity and good, delegitimising him as the old *panji* so effectively did his predecessor.

The audience knows there will be other plays on other nights, that the morality tale will continue in a different form, and that, in the great balancing act of life, other forces might emerge—perhaps even the left in a different guise, reborn with a new vision of the future. As the *wayang kulit* moves towards its conclusion, the first rays of dawn appear in streaks of pink and blood red across the horizon.

This fictional shadow play, of course, is a thinly disguised account of the prevailing forces within contemporary Indonesian politics. It draws on Javanese tradition—the well-spring not just for the style of the current president and his government, but also for that of his predecessor and indeed the conceptions that underpin the logic of the Indonesian state. But from an international perspective, which recognises that Indonesia is a state in the world and not an 'empire unto itself', it would probably be more appropriate to sketch the plot of an epic Mafia movie than to appeal to Javanese traditions. Stand-over tactics and corruption, protection rackets, violence, pride, the location of power in the person of the boss, rigged ballots, and the chicanery of naked power all feature in a good Mafia movie, and they are not alien concepts in Indonesian politics either. The main difference between the two, perhaps, is that the Mafia do not work on the scale on which the Indonesian government operates.

This book is an introductory account of the methods, styles, institutions, and influences that comprise contemporary Indonesian political life. The prevailing themes and competitive tensions in Indonesian politics derive from the archipelago's history, its material circumstances, the cultures of its peoples, and the way in which dominant groups and individuals have put their stamp on the course of events. One such theme is the process of development—in which there is tension between Indonesia's majority of poor and its small but extremely wealthy civilian elites —and the role played in that process by corruption. Another theme is the role of the armed forces in the political process, both as the backbone of the Indonesian political system and as a foil to calls for genuine political participation and democracy. Within both of these themes, select individuals, through a system of patronage, play a more important role than they would in many other societies. Yet the forces at work in Indonesian political society cannot be narrowed down to just the will of individuals, the possibilities offered by particular institutions (see Pye 1985; Liddle 1996), or competing visions of a desirable society. Nor does a political economy model alone (see, for example, Robison 1985;

1987) explain the subtleties and nuances of its processes, and cultural issues recur but are not in themselves determining factors. It is a combination of these factors, shifting and varying from one circumstance or moment to the next, that makes a study of Indonesian politics at once engaging and complex.

Any analysis of Indonesia's politics and economy should take a multidimensional approach. In the first instance, not only is a political economy approach useful in recognising the usual array of economic interests represented at a political economy level, but it also allows an examination of the direct manner in which politics has been manipulated to achieve specific, often narrowly defined, economic outcomes. That is, in a conventional political economy, it is common to see dominant economic interests bringing influence to bear on government or achieving representation through government to achieve political outcomes beneficial to those interests (see Robison 1985; 1986; 1990; 1997; Robison, Hewison, & Higgott 1987). It is also common to see subservient economic interests competing (perhaps less successfully) for political representation in order to redress economic imbalance. In Indonesia, control of the political process allows a small minority direct access to economic benefit, while structurally the vast majority are economically excluded.

This situation is partly driven by, and partly reflects, a conception of political authority that originated in Java's pre-colonial past, in the colonial restructuring of Javanese political society, and in the reification of political values selected from these two periods and often reconstituted as contemporary Indonesian political life. In one sense, this reflects the construction of a particular political culture, in which non-participation is commonplace, if not accepted. In another sense, however, it also reflects the imposed politicisation of culture (Anderson 1965; 1972; 1990; Pemberton 1994). Acting as adjuncts to such cultural politics are the institutionalisation of these cultural forms—through the Sanskritised (courtly, pre-modern) *Pancasila* (the Five Principles, which are the prevailing ideology), for instance—and the imposition of particular institutional structures. These include the 1945 Constitution, the subservience of the parliament to the office and person of the president, the hobbling of the party system, the lack of separation of powers between the executive and the judiciary and the formal political role of the armed forces, including the police and various 'intelligence' (secret army and police) organisations.

The relevance of, and interest in, the politics of Indonesia derives from a number of factors, the most pressing being Indonesia's increasing importance as a political, economic, and strategic influence in South East Asian affairs, and hence in world affairs. This relevance is increased by what is a generally poor understanding of Indonesian politics outside Indonesia, if one ignores a handful of scholars and specialist publications.

With a population of just over 200 million, Indonesia is the world's largest predominantly Muslim country and the fourth largest country in absolute terms, which alone gives it considerable significance in world affairs. Indonesia is also one of the world's primary oil-producing countries. But perhaps more importantly, as eastern Asia's economies command international economic attention, Indonesia has a pivotal role in the region's affairs, especially as a consequence of its economic collapse from mid-1997. Indonesia's neighbours live in its strategic shadow, with varying degrees of comfort. All are aware that Indonesia's present internal focus could change, given the country's potentially volatile political climate, which could have implications for its external perceptions. The Association of South East Asian Nations (ASEAN) is a central organisation with regard to Asian affairs, and Indonesia is by far the most dominant nation in that grouping.

Also within the wider context, the end of the cold war and the consequent changes to what, in international *Realpolitik*, are considered acceptable forms of political behaviour have required Indonesia to take some notice of external concerns. Having spent the past five decades as a relatively independent state, and recalling the traditions (particularly of Javanese history) in which the *panji/rajah/sultan* has semi-divine status, Indonesia has had to begin to recognise that it is just one country among many nations and not entirely a law unto itself. While the Indonesian government has occasionally recognised foreign impact, particularly on its economy, it has also often disregarded expressions of international concern about economic issues and, more commonly, issues of political participation and human rights. Foreign influence is a concept that many 'nationalists' in Indonesia's government have trouble coming to grips with. The political structures, institutions, and practices of Indonesia reflect what has been interpreted as a distinctly 'Indonesian' way, and the political elites of the country are having difficulty in reconciling those existing political forms with increasingly loud calls for reform, both from within and without. Indonesia has gone a little way towards recognising this material reality with regard to its economy. This only underlines the fact that, as much as the Indonesian government might try to maintain its inward, Java/Jakarta-centred focus, Indonesia is not the centre of the world and is susceptible to external political influences.

Internally, Indonesia is characterised by a complex, often contradictory, and potentially explosive political mix. The tensions are various and, in most cases, long standing: between devout and nominal Muslims; between Javanese and outer islanders; between the country's 200-plus separate cultures; between the government (backed by the armed forces) and pro-democracy groups; between the various factions within both the armed forces and the government; and, not least, between rich and poor. These tensions have been subsumed by the official Indonesian concept of 'unity in diversity'. This notion reflects both a syncretic Javanese approach to resolving contradictions and the Javanese notion of *halus* (smoothness, refinement), in which appearances are everything and reality is of secondary importance. Yet this form of idealised behaviour (typical of Javanese high culture) is riven by barely suppressed tensions, which in the last years of the twentieth century have increasingly found violent expression.

After the economic debacle of the Sukarno years (in particular 1958–66), Indonesia's economy developed considerably over the following three decades, and average standards of living increased. In particular, starvation, which was all too common in the early 1960s, was generally eradicated, and literacy levels rose. Indonesia was also, importantly, remarkably politically stable, albeit as a consequence of an imposed military order. But the economic growth that Indonesia enjoyed was patchy, with economic slumps puncturing periods of growth, and the source of that growth has been inconsistent, especially as a consequence of large fluctuations in the price of oil. Further, the distribution of this wealth has been extraordinarily uneven, which has had two consequences. The first has been that, for most people, standards of living have not improved in line with economic growth or, in many cases, even risen above Indonesia's minimalist poverty line. This is particularly noticeable in the outer islands, but stark examples of continuing poverty can also be found in rural and urban Java. The second consequence is that, even where standards of living did improve, the beneficiaries were still faced with the images and reality of a much wealthier class, who often live in very close proximity. This then begs the question of why some people should benefit so clearly, indeed so excessively, from the country's economic growth while others do not benefit much at all. Such questioning often leads to envy, not to mention resentment of a political system that condones and even encourages such disparities. That the greatest wealth is often generated through corruption or nepotism is further galling. There is, then, scope for significant political challenge, yet much of Indonesia's political stability has come at the cost of having a government that is only nominally representative, if that. Active political life—particularly dissent—is regarded with suspicion (if not as a crime), and political dissent is often repressed through violent means. There is no scope for economic redress through the official political process, and this only increases resentment, pushing more and more people to seek solutions outside the officially condoned framework, in turn calling forth greater repression.

The 'dual function' of Indonesia's armed forces, dissent, and repression

To maintain political 'stability', Indonesia's armed forces—Angkatan Bersenjata Republik Indonesia (ABRI)—have adopted what they term *dwifungsi*, the 'dual function' of defending the state and helping to administer it. In this sense, ABRI acts as a kind of 'super-police', formally incorporating the police as a branch of the armed services, with a responsibility to maintain 'law and order', to quell dissent, and to participate in the day-to-day affairs of government. In the late 1980s, ABRI's role in government, especially at the policy level, began to diminish, in part reflecting a falling out between the majority of ABRI and the president. Yet this did not accurately reflect ABRI's continuing strength, its tradition of operating independently of the president in many respects, and its role in helping shape the post-Suharto period. ABRI also continued to perform its minatory function, and without its support Suharto would have been unable to maintain office. Towards the end of his reign, the majority of ABRI might have no longer liked Suharto, but it was in the longer term interests of the organisation, if possible, to see him gently shifted from office. ABRI wished to maintain public respect for the office of the president, as it intended to have a sympathiser 'elected' to the position in the period after Suharto's inevitable political or personal demise and it would need for that office to retain its putative legitimacy.

In large part, ABRI's *dwifungsi* and the predominant debate between factions within ABRI and the president not only reflected the closed environment of official Indonesian political discourse, but it also showed up ordinary people's lack of access to the political process. Since the early 1970s, Indonesia has had regular 'festivals of democracy', but the formal opposition has been politically hobbled by various means. The candidates for the offices of the president and vice-president were predetermined, elected by acclaim by a body of people the president had a large say in appointing, rather than being formally voted into office. Even with only the nominal support of ABRI, the president was effectively omnipotent, appointing his own Cabinet and balancing competing political interests as he saw best. He sometimes chose to consult with ministers or advisers, and sometimes he chose to ignore them; he tended to treat all in a patronising manner. The Indonesian 'parliament', the Dewan Perwakilan Rakyat (DPR), was effectively powerless, and the president was, in the final analysis, beholden to no one but himself. This may have meant that he was beyond the pressure of interest groups, at least in so far as he was able to balance their competing interests, but it also meant that the president was free to pursue his own interests with little regard for the consequences.

Between the attractions of development and the threats of ABRI, this situation resulted in a relatively stable if sometimes brittle political structure. But after three decades in power, there was a widespread and growing belief that it was time for a change and that many ordinary Indonesians would like some say in the direction of that change. This was expressed by, and found reflection in, the increasing popularity of what can be loosely termed 'pro-democracy' groups, including official and unofficial political parties, trade unions, and non-government groups. Such expression certainly reflected Indonesia's better educated and more independently minded middle class, but it also reflected—especially in rural areas and small towns—the views and aspirations of the country's *wong cilik* ('small people', peasants and manual labourers). The aspirations of these various groups were almost palpable, but while they have enjoyed an increasingly high profile in the last decade of the twentieth century, they have also suffered numerous government/ABRI-organised set-backs and, in reality, appeared a very long way from achieving fundamental change.

Thrown into this mixture were issues of a compromised judiciary, whereby the courts reflected political wishes more often than the rule of law. Further, the law—such as it is interpreted for a range of purposes—is only applicable in so far as ABRI or the police are prepared to enforce it. If they choose not to bring a witness to court, he or she simply does not appear and the judge is powerless to do anything about it. If the judge passes a sentence unpopular with either ABRI or the government, the case is appealed until a more amenable judge can be found. Beyond this direct interference by ABRI and, to a lesser extent, by government bureaucrats in the judicial process, Indonesian law is based on traditional law (*adat*) and the judicial canons passed on by the colonial Dutch, the prime intention of which was to maintain order among a potentially hostile population. Poorly codified and subject to political influence, the law in Indonesia most often reflects the wishes of the most politically powerful in any given case and is not widely perceived to be a useful means of achieving justice. Although the judicial system is seriously in need of being overhauled—and, indeed, Suharto promised to do this soon after achieving office in 1968—this task has been ignored in large part because the current system continues to serve the interests of the political and economic elites so well.

Then there are the separatist movements in Aceh and Irian Jaya, and the still burning problem of Indonesia's occupation of East Timor, which has a separate history and legal background from Indonesia and which is still recognised by the United Nations as being illegally occupied. Perhaps the least well known of these trouble spots, Aceh in northern Sumatra was for centuries a wealthy sultanate in its own right. It was one of the first parts of the archipelago to accept Islam and has retained a stronger commitment to it than most other parts of the region. The Acehnese were among the most strongly opposed to Dutch colonial rule, succumbing only after many years of bloody conflict and never fully accepting their incorporation into either the colony or the subsequent modern Indonesian state. As a consequence, there has been a sporadic guerilla campaign waged in Aceh against the central government for decades.

Although a part of the Dutch East Indies and claimed by the fledgling Indonesian state, Irian Jaya was not a part of the original peace settlement between the Netherlands government and the Republic of Indonesia, being occupied by Indonesia in 1963 and formally incorporated in 1969. The formal armed resistance of the Organisasi Papua Merdeka (OPM—Free Papua Movement) can be dated from 1969, a conflict that has at times threatened to spill over into neighbouring Papua New Guinea. The OPM's campaign for independence does not threaten the central government but continues to receive impetus from profound economic inequality, racial and cultural discrimination, the often heavy-handed treatment meted out to the province's indigenous people by the armed forces, and continuing resentment over not being genuinely consulted over incorporation.

Probably best known of the recalcitrant provinces is East Timor (*Timor Timur* in Indonesian), which during the process of decolonisation from Portugal was invaded by Indonesia in late 1975 and incorporated soon after. The main opposition came from Fretilin, which has continued to wage a low-level guerilla campaign against the government, in the hope of one day achieving an internationally brokered settlement. East Timor has been a serious handicap to Indonesia's international standing and may yet succeed in gaining some form of autonomy from the government in Jakarta.

Construction of the state

These areas—provinces if you accept East Timor's incorporation—are at the sharp edge of opposition to the central, Jakarta-based government and reflect a long-standing tension in the construction of Indonesia as a unitary state. It is common to refer to or think of Indonesia as a 'nation', but even more so than most postcolonial states, Indonesia is constructed by pulling together the often disparate remnants of a former European (in this case

Dutch) colony. The idea of a 'nation' implies a shared set of values, but none can be said to have existed before the construction of the Indonesian state (Ricklefs 1993a, pp. 50, 147; Ricklefs 1993b, p. 10). According to Clifford Geertz, Indonesia's 'essentialist element' is 'extremely unhomogeneous'. This, he says, is true for most new states, in which competing traditions are gathered into a concocted political framework (Geertz 1993, pp. 244–5). Originally intended as a federation, in which each province would contribute equally to government of the whole, Indonesia has become a centrist state based on Jakarta and reflecting idealised, or manufactured, Central Javanese conceptions of appropriate political and social behaviour. Needless to say, many non-Javanese have been less than satisfied with this arrangement, and even many Javanese view the reconstruction of their precolonial culture for contemporary political purposes as inappropriate. The colony itself was never conceived of as a united region but rather as an administrative institution over diverse islands, and this further complicates both the theory and practice of Indonesia's unity.

Perhaps the most important tools of Indonesian government since the late 1960s in terms of discouraging major challenges has been the subsuming of political aspirations to the cause of 'development'. Suharto himself has claimed the title of 'father of development', indicating just how potent this idea is in Indonesian political society. The term 'development' is used in Indonesia, and many other countries, to mean economic growth, implying some degree of sharing of that increased wealth. From the early 1960s, when inflation was rampaging out of control and starvation was a real and widespread problem, until the late 1990s, Indonesia managed to record generally good rates of economic growth, average incomes increased, and starvation resulting from poverty and mismanagement had become effectively non-existent, although malnutrition was still a problem in some regions and especially among the very poor.

The government has also ploughed money back into development projects—education in particular and, to a lesser extent, public health campaigns. Few Indonesian citizens were likely to starve, and their children are more likely to be literate than are their parents. By the early 1990s, there were also many signs of a growing and prospering middle class, if the consumption of motorcycles and television sets is any indication. However, much of the wealth generated by the country since the 1960s has been skimmed off, helping to construct a new class of 'super-rich', which has engendered very considerable resentment. Even the relative wealth of the middle class was not fairly distributed, and the quality of life of most Indonesians, particularly outside Java, was only marginally better than it was in the 1960s, and certainly not in proportion to the wealth their regions have helped generate.

Among Indonesia's most wealthy citizens are members of the country's long-established Chinese community. Long disliked—they are pejoratively called *cukong* ('boss')—much public resentment is directed towards Chinese businesses and people, and they have often been the focus of attacks and even rioting. Most Chinese are not Muslim, further alienating them from large numbers of formal Muslim Indonesians. Complicating the position of the ethnic Chinese in Indonesian society are the close links between a small number of super-rich Chinese business people and Suharto and his family. This brought together anti-Chinese sentiment with the desire to oppose Suharto, to end corruption, and to see a greater redistribution of wealth. Nowhere has this sentiment been more strongly expressed than within the formal Islamic community.

The role of Islam

Islam has been a significant influence in the area now known as Indonesia since the fourteenth century, having been brought to the archipelago by Arab traders and others fleeing the Portuguese occupation of the Islamic trading state of Malacca (on what is now the Malaysian Peninsula). Towards the end of the nineteenth century and into the twentieth century, Islam became the focus of the movement against Dutch colonialism, though Islam has developed into various streams since then and continues to lack political unity. The trend towards a more widespread acceptance of Islam gathered momentum in the wake of the suppression of the Indonesian Communist Party (PKI) in 1965–66, after which it was dangerous not to be aligned to a formal religion. Into the 1990s, Islam has increasingly become a symbol of piety and of anti-Western or nationalist sentiments. Restrictions on displays of Islam initially imposed by the government to repress what it regarded as activist religious sentiment—such as women wearing the *jelbab* (nun-like headdress)—have been lifted. Indonesia's Islamic community, in particular that of Java, is divided between formal (*santri*) and nominal (*abangan*) Muslims. The latter incorporate traditional elements of Javanese mysticism but have also shown greater political flexibility.[1] The former, sometimes referred to by *abangan* as 'pseudo-Arabs', tend to align either with the Islamic dominated Partai Persatuan Pembangunan (PPP, or United Development Party) or with the nominally apolitical Nahdatul Ulama (NU, or Awakening of Religious Scholars). Under Indonesia's restrictive political laws, the PPP was but a shadow of the organisations that originally comprised it.

Of the non–party-political Islamic organisations, two organisations were created in 1912 in response to doctrinal differences. These were the Muhammadiyah (or followers of the prophet Muhammad) and the Sarekat Islam (Islamic Association), which was more militant and internally factionalised along political and religious lines. The Sarekat Islam was suppressed by the Dutch, although its influences remained (with one faction forming the core of the PKI). The Muhammadiyah was founded by predominantly urban, modernist *santri* Muslims who saw it as necessary to purge Islam of syncretic or Hindu–animist Javanese influences. Muhammadiyah is a predominantly social and educational organisation. In the late 1990s, it claimed about 28 million members across Indonesia. In response to the founding of the Muhammadiyah, more conservative, rural-based *santri* Muslims formed the NU in 1926. It has a following of about 30 million, mostly in East and Central Java. The NU had been involved in the political process since the founding of the state, but in 1973 Suharto forced NU to join with three smaller Islamic parties to form the politically ineffective PPP. The NU withdrew in 1984 to concentrate on social and religious issues, although it still exercises considerable political influence.

Throughout Indonesia's history, there have been a number of Islamic inspired or influenced rebellions against the central

---

1 Java's *abangan* formed the basis of the PKI, as well as the Indonesian Nationalist Party (PNI). Because of their nominal rather than formal religious affiliation, they are significantly less associated with the *santri*-dominated United Development Party (PPP).

government, as well as riots against the government and ethnic Chinese, and in his early years in power, Suharto limited Islamic political aspirations. However, since the late 1980s, Suharto has encouraged Indonesia's Muslims, partly to counter his rift with ABRI. In 1990 he founded the Ikatan Cendekiawan Muslem se Indonesia (ICMI, or Indonesian Association of Muslim Intellectuals); while originally a Suhartoist vehicle, ICMI has become increasingly independent. Islam is in a revivalist phase in Indonesia and is now less an escape from temporal concerns for uneducated Indonesians than it is a means of asserting an ethical and political identity.

The pro-democracy movement

Apart from the PPP, the other official political party is the Partai Demokrasi Indonesia (PDI, or Indonesian Democratic Party). Since 1974 the PDI has, in effect, been a tool of factions within ABRI, rendering it politically ineffective. However, in 1993 the daughter of Indonesia's founding president, Achmad Sukarno, Megawati Sukarnoputri, was elected as chair of the PDI, in effect as its leader, and for three years the party grew both in stature and as a real political force. Some even believed that it might present a credible 'democratic' alternative to Suharto, especially after he left office. However, in mid-1996 a government-sponsored faction of the PDI ousted Megawati and appointed a more government-friendly leader. Soon after, protesters wearing PDI T-shirts, supported by the military, invaded the PDI headquarters and ousted Megawati's supporters, leaving a number dead and others injured. This move sparked a serious riot in Jakarta.

The riot was blamed particularly on an unofficial political party, the Partai Rakyat Demokrasi (PRD, or People's Democratic Party), which was likened to the banned PKI. The PRD was a small organisation run by a handful of students. A number of its leaders were gaoled, while others went underground following the post-riot crackdown. In the period following the riot and the crackdown on the PRD, there was considerable political tension in Indonesia, with a sense that events were escalating towards some sort of climax. In the first half of 1997 and in early 1998, there were a number of seemingly unrelated riots across Indonesia. However, most observers agreed that each riot reflected not only the increasing political tensions within Indonesia, but may also have been orchestrated to further the interests of different factions as they jockeyed for position ahead of Suharto's inevitable leaving of office.

More directly related to the government and a cause of considerable political tension, corruption continues to be a (probably *the*) major political issue. Although corruption is endemic in Indonesia and can be found at every level of government service, it has caused most public concern when manifested among the friends and family of President Suharto. However, until 1998, these individuals appeared increasingly blind to the anger being caused by their domination of the Indonesian economy, and this brought the government into increasing conflict with large sections of the armed forces, as well as pro-democracy groups.

Beyond domestic concerns with corruption, Indonesia is an increasingly significant player in the world economy. As such, it is encountering conflict between the conventional financial accountability of foreign investors and world markets, on the one hand, and the monopolies, scams, and shonky deals of some of the country's wealthiest business people, on the other. The tug-of-war between Indonesia's more circumspect economic planners and the wealthy elites has ensured that economic policy has charted an indirect course, and this has inevitably hampered Indonesia's economic growth. However, economic growth did take place, until mid-1997, at levels that were quite respectable by developing country standards. Most of the country's growth in the 1990s was fuelled by foreign investment rather than domestic productivity, indicating that at least part of the international business community believed Indonesia was sufficiently on the straight and narrow path, or at least offered a secure business climate. However, this economic bubble burst in the second half of 1997, leading to effective economic collapse by the beginning of 1998.

The various tensions that arose as a consequence of so many competing claims was reflected in a Byzantine political framework, at one level intensely traditional and recalling many of the mystical aspects of the old *kratons* (courts) of the pre-colonial sultans and the rajahs before them. The traditional, almost exclusively Javanese symbols and methods of gaining, maintaining, and exercising power have found a new lease of life in post-colonial Indonesia. On another level, though, Indonesia is a modern state, constrained by, or at least aware of, modern conventions such as international borders, the separation of powers between the executive and the judiciary, an internationally susceptible economy, and universalist claims to democratic representation, freedom of expression, and more broad civil and political rights.

Operating in the tension between these political forms are internal political intrigues the likes of which are rarely seen. Some observers have likened the politics of Jakarta to those of the former Soviet Kremlin, in which appearances rarely betrayed reality and symbolism abounded. For every political event in Indonesia there is usually a handful of different theories about its origins. The shifting of a political appointee, a protest or riot, or even a statement or speech by a political player, even the president himself, is nearly always interpreted as reflecting deeper concerns or machinations. Questions about who is in, who is out, and who is jockeying for position within the 'palace' politics of Jakarta are cause for endless speculation and much theorising, though little informed comment. Even seasoned observers of Indonesian politics find themselves caught in a maze, or more accurately a *mandala*, sometimes hearing the distant calls of others, but rarely gaining an overview. In the middle of it all, however, is the president, and it is at this 'exemplary centre' that contemporary Indonesian politics finds its focus, if not always its source.

In the following pages you will encounter power plays, makers and winners of fabulous fortunes, and losers cast out of the palace, sometimes to plot their revenge. You will come across deal-making for both wealth and empire, factional loyalties and betrayals, jealousies and intrigues, and finally there will be violence, both symbolic and real. The rewards of winning and the cost of losing can be—and in Indonesia are—very high.

2

TRADITIONAL AND COLONIAL INFLUENCES

Starting in Java

It has been maintained by observers both within and without Indonesia that its modern political form owes much to traditional influences. The impact of Dutch colonialism was also significant in shaping modern Indonesia, not least by effectively defining its modern borders. Any assessment of Indonesia's 'traditional' influences, though, must look primarily to Javanese tradition, as it is from Java that the modern state receives most of its political cues. The empire that had most influence on the region that now forms Indonesia, the Majapahit, was based in Central Java. Indeed, it is not uncommon for Indonesian nationalists to portray Indonesia as a continuation of the fourteenth-century Majapahit empire that, in exaggerated accounts, claimed suzerainty over the area effectively comprising the modern state as well as the Malay peninsula, and extending to the vassalage of further flung regions.[1]

It was also in Java that the Dutch made their first and most important colonial base in what was to become the Dutch East Indies, the foundation territory of the modern state of Indonesia. And Java continues to possess close to 120 million of the total Indonesian population of 200 million (although perhaps only 85–90 million are ethnic Javanese). Java is unarguably the dominant influence in modern Indonesian life, and it is Java's 'traditions' that have been largely adopted as the traditions and values of the post-colonial state. It is important to note here that the 'traditions' of

---

1   The actual area in question was probably limited to Java and some nearby coastal regions, with a more nominal tribute being paid by other nearby states and cordial relations being conducted with states even further afield.

Java that contribute to the modern state are problematic. Apart from the reconstruction of 'official' Javanese culture under the Dutch, the New Order government has incorporated and re-invented much tradition for its own political purposes (Pemberton 1994).

The Javanese, along with most other Indonesians, are of Deutero-Malay ethnic stock, having migrated in successive waves from mainland South-East Asia and southern China from around 4000 years ago. (The other main group is the Proto-Malay group, which includes the Dayaks of Kalimantan and the Bataks of Sumatra.) These immigrants to Java tended to practise wet rice culti-vation in the island's valleys. Java's hot, fairly even temperatures, consistent and heavy rainfall, and preponderance of rich volcanic soil were well suited to wet rice (*sawah*) agriculture. It is this, and the settled habitation it engenders, that helps explain the relatively early development of a complex culture, compared with the far less productive and more migratory dry-field (*ladang*) rice grow-ing of the other islands. The inhabitants of Sumatra also adopted *sawah* rice farming, developed sophisticated cultures, and had considerable contact with foreign influences. However, the Suma-tran civilisations were less able to sustain themselves in a regular pattern of growth and, despite flourishes of imperial control, were ultimately less influential in the region that was to become Indonesia. Drawing from the productive hinterland, towns were established, and small monarchic states developed. Metals, mostly bronze but also some iron, began to be worked from around 2000 years ago, which also marks the first contacts with Indian traders and the beginning of Java's (and Sumatra's) Hindu influences.

Religious and other cultural influences

Animism, or spirit worship, was the first predominant religious form, and this continues to exert considerable influence over much religious practice and, in a diffused sense, aspects of Javanese culture. One important aspect of this animism is that it has shown itself to have potential for syncretism—that is, it can be blended with other religious forms. Because of this long-standing syncretic tradition, Javanese culture has been identified as having a strong spiritual base. Another consequence of this syncretic tradition is that the Javanese are popularly believed to be a 'tolerant' people, in that they easily accept, or incorporate, that which is different. Without assuming that the Javanese are significantly more or less tolerant than most other peoples, it is useful to note that their tolerance functions best when what they are required to accept can be identified or explained within a pre-existing logic. That is, tolerance for other religions is accepted if they are able to be syncretised or interpreted as a reflection of what is already known. For example, European political practices are interpreted as variations on Javanese practices of power. Similarly, tolerance of non-Islamic religions is, generally, acceptable if those religions can be interpreted within the Islamic monotheistic framework (Anderson 1965, pp. 4–6). Having said that, the question of tolerance is often overstated and is often confused with a 'politeness' that may hide hostility.

Javanese culture is also popularly regarded as having a high awareness of this politeness and an associated deference through communicated forms, such as language and deportment, although this perhaps reflects relatively fixed and non-reflexive, hierarchical power structures. These derive from pre-colonial and colonial Javanese life, and from the cultural and political dominance of Javanese elites, and the late-colonial and post-colonial reinvention of aspects of Javanese culture for overtly political purposes. Such refinement of communication is not always, or even often, reflected at more common social levels and is relatively uncommon among many village peasants and the urban poor. In this sense, communication finds itself divided between a normative, aristocratic form and a normatively vulgar, common form.

The idealisation of politeness is a part of a broad, formally desirable behavioural form of *halus* ('smoothness, refinement'). Being 'Javanese', in an officially sanctioned sense, also has a specific normative meaning, including personal control, appropriate responses, particular preferences, a rigid etiquette, and to feel 'certain quite distinctively Javanese (and essentially untranslatable) emotions—"patience," "detachment," "resignation," "respect"' (Geertz 1993, pp. 52–3). While pertinent, this observation identifies an 'ideal' Javanese 'type', which presupposes within Javanese society an endorsement of such values, not to mention their universal attainment. It also does not account for the pervasive influences of the outside world, which have been making a rapid impact on the fabric of Javanese life, especially since the 1970s. As

Geertz notes, even within Javanese society there is no universal cultural 'type': 'We must, in short, descend into detail, past the misleading tags, past the metaphysical types, past the empty similarities to grasp firmly the essential character of not only the various cultures but the various sorts of individuals within each culture' (Geertz 1993, p. 53). Further, if this Javanese 'type' is held by social elites to be desirable, it retains negative implications for the treatment of those people who do not directly conform to such standards, including less refined peasants and urban workers, and those who consciously reject such type-casting. That is, patterns of behaviour thought by some to be 'cultural' can be understood by others to be 'political'. In the day-to-day reality of common Javanese life, the ideal of *halus* is often not achieved, or even attempted. But it does serve as a model of public behaviour that complies with the political interests of Indonesia's elites. Interestingly, the dark side of *halus*—of inwardly focusing frustrations, anger, or other negative emotions—is the concept of *amok*. The state of *amok* is when repressed tensions explode to the surface and the individual concerned engages in wildly harmful behaviour, often resulting in death, including his or her own. This goes some way towards explaining the sometimes angry responses of Indonesian political leaders when their sense of smoothness and refinement is tested.

Within the traditional Javanese context, the metaphysical was seen to form a nexus with external forms of behaviour, both reflecting and enhancing each other through a continuum. Java's religious history is closely intertwined with—and for many, perhaps most, people still informed by—the abovementioned animism, which predates the more formal religions of Java (Hinduism, briefly Buddhism, and then Islam) (Geertz 1960; see also Vatikiotis 1993, p. 100). While such influences remain in Central Java among some of the *abangan* population, a clearer example of this animism can still be found in central Bali, which avoided the obscuring influence of Islam. The people of Bali are Hindu. The adoption of Hinduism by the Balinese was closely related to the introduction of Hinduism to Java and was reinforced by Javanese Hinduism with the collapse of the Majapahit empire and the retreat of Majapahit elites to Bali in the late fourteenth century. The Hinduism of Bali, however, is a far cry from the Hinduism of India and is, in large part, a sop to Indonesia's *santri* (formal)

Muslims, as all Indonesians must profess an officially sanctioned ('monotheistic') 'world' religion: Islam, Hinduism, Catholicism, Protestantism, or Buddhism. To not do so opens one to charges of being a 'primitive' (*orang yang belum beragama*, or 'person not yet possessing religion', implying that one will eventually do so) or, worse, an atheist and hence a 'communist'.

In part, then, Javanese religious commitment derives from a range of sources—which in many cases overlap—and in part from an official political requirement to profess a sanctioned faith. In trying to create and maintain a world in keeping with their desires, with mythologised ideals, and with the official cultural requirements of state, the Javanese are no more or less spiritual, no more or less polite, and no more or less concerned to communicate openly than people from other parts of the world. If there is a tendency towards spiritualism among the Javanese, or among other Indonesians, then it is of the type that finds parallels in other societies that have only relatively recently moved from widespread illiteracy and feudalism[2] or colonialism into 'modernism' and industrialisation.

The Javanese are constrained, in particular by their political and material circumstances. The tendency to internalise anger, frustration, and indeed happiness (though exceptions to this are common) is based on the historical construction of Javanese political society, in which outward manifestations of emotion were regarded at best as uncivilised or at worst as a threat to the political status quo. This tendency towards the normative qualities of internalisation, politeness, deference, and respect finds reflection in Java's dominant mythology, as portrayed in the 'Javanised' Hindu stories of the Ramayana and Mahabarata (Anderson 1965). To reconcile real circumstances with normative responses, it has not been uncommon for Javanese to bend circumstances to reflect an ideal by portraying surface appearances as reality (Vatikiotis 1993, p. 22), feigning indifference to annoyance, suppressing anger, and constraining strong outward expressions of happiness. This complex

---

2 The term *feudalism* here implies a vassal–lord political and economic relationship, although it is not intended to exactly replicate the European model, which was exclusively based on land ownership and tillage for service or impost, and which necessarily implied the almost complete local compartmentalising of the state (Pirenne 1936, pp. 146–60). Some compartmentalising, under local military or business figures, does occur in Indonesia.

aspect of Javanese culture reflects an ability to incorporate and synthesise what are perceived, especially by outsiders, to be contradictory conditions. In this manner—within a contemporary context for example—the New Order government claims to represent a working democracy, even though it has been one of the least democratic states in the world for four decades. This situation is rationalised by employing the synthetic medium of the *Pancasila*, in particular the adjunct 'government by consent guided by deliberation'. This submerges the apparent contradiction beneath a deep layer of formal appearance.

The influence of wet-rice agriculture

This preoccupation with matters of form (which are intended to reflect substance) may be partly explained by returning to Java's material circumstances. As noted, the settlement of Java quickly gave rise to a 'hydraulic' or water-dependent society, the economic base of which was wet-rice agriculture. This gave activities an inward focus (Ricklefs 1993a, pp. 16–17). This 'inwardness' reflected the immediate, localised, and fixed concerns of wet-rice agriculture, and can be identified in a number of ways. For example, despite living on an island located among many other islands, the Central Javanese (and Balinese) traditionally tend to locate inland in the valleys and plains below the island's volcanic mountain ranges. The sea was, and often still is, regarded as the home of often malignant spirits, and the coastal regions are still commonly believed to be dangerous.

The wet-rice agriculture system that is common throughout eastern Asia contributed significantly to the political forms that arose there (see Wittfogel 1957; Missen 1972, pp. 51–2, 97–104). In simple terms, large-scale irrigation and the requirement of organising large numbers of workers enhanced the creation of centralised states, while peasants who relied on the fixed and initially labour-intensive cycle of wet-rice agriculture were unwilling or unable to move easily, and were thus vulnerable to domination by a military elite. This military elite extracted surplus value from the peasants it dominated, and its leaders established themselves as hereditary rulers. This gave rise to powerful and complex political structures, which being both centralised and relatively stable, took on an autocratic political form. Court life was separate from village life, except through the payment of taxes or tribute, and through recognition of political association (loyalty). Such political systems were oppressive and closed to modification, other than through direct challenge (Goodenough 1970, p. 58). There were some reciprocal arrangements built into such a structure (Ricklefs 1993a, pp. 121–2), but on the whole peasants had to look elsewhere—to religion and aesthetic cultural forms—for personal fulfilment.

Another effect of this relatively stable agricultural form was that it provided the foundation for the development and later incorporation of officially endorsed religious structures. From around the second century, there was a formal shift from the administrative disorganisation of animist religious practices to the hierarchical organising principles of the politically sanctioned (though variously syncretised) Hinduism-Buddhism (which was most fully established between the eighth and tenth centuries) and Islam (which became established from the fourteenth century) (Caldwell & Utrecht 1979, pp. 8–10; Grant 1996, pp. 4–8). The region of Central Java in the Yogyakarta–Surakarta–Kartasura area[3] and to the near east—the most fertile and productive on the island—supported what were Java's most powerful rulers: the Sailendras,[4] the early Mataram, the Majapahit, and the late Mataram. As probably the first great sea power of the region—lasting from the seventh century until its decline in the thirteenth century—the Buddhist coastal state of Srivajaya on the Palembang river in southern Sumatra challenged the land-based Javanese states for greatest regional authority. From the ninth century, the Sailendra dynasty merged with that of Srivajaya, relocating to Palembang and reinforcing that state for a further 200 years. However, at least partly because of the sedimentation of the river access, Srivajaya's fortunes declined and the state fell into disrepair, preceding the rise of other sea powers, including Malacca. While the authority of Srivajaya declined, succeeding Javanese rulers continued to prosper.

3　This area is known as *kedjawa*, or the 'real Java'.
4　Interestingly, the Sanskrit name *Sailendra* derives from the imperial title 'King of the Mountain', which was used by the rulers of the ancient Indianised state of Funan, located approximately in the region of modern Cambodia.

Conceptions of power

One consequence of Java's autocratic political forms and its animist tendencies was that conceptions of power were developed partly to explain and partly to rationalise early political circumstances. In a society in which the desires of his subjects had only a minimal bearing on the responsibility of the monarch, conceptions of political power lost all but the most abstract sense of there being a relationship between cause, effect, and ethical responsibility. Combined with a volcanic geographic environment that was indifferent to the fate of the people living in its shadows, the political forces at work in the lives of ordinary Javanese were not conditional upon jural consent but simply *were*, in much the same way that the sun rises in the east and sets in the west. An animistic conception of power, then, linked the power exercised by a monarch with the power of nature and did not incorporate any idea of popular participation.

Within this sort of political environment—that is, an environment produced by traditional Javanese political culture, where power is abstracted from the influence of ordinary people and simply *is*—the issue of power does not raise the question of legitimacy (Anderson 1972). This formulation is still ascribed to by a number of Indonesian political observers and analysts in Jakarta. According to this conception, power derives from a single, homogeneous source. Given this, the idea of power does not include ethical questions, such as whether power is being exercised for good or evil purposes. According to Ben Anderson, in traditional Javanese thinking it would be meaningless to claim the right to rule on the basis of differential sources of power—for example, to say that power based on wealth is legitimate, whereas power based on force is illegitimate. In a traditional Javanese sense, power is neither legitimate nor illegitimate and is 'without inherent moral implications as such' (Anderson 1972, pp. 1–8; see also Moedjanto 1993; Proudfoot 1980). In this sense, the holder of political power within a traditional Javanese context is free not only from reliance on popular political participation but also from the need to defend or legitimise political decisions.

To further complicate the traditional Javanese idea of power, there is no single translation of the word 'power' in Javanese, the closest equivalent being *kasekten*, which incorporates ideas of power, legitimacy, and charisma. This interpretation is based on an idealised traditional conception and accords with a number of aspects of Weber's conception of charismatic and traditional authority. However, *kasekten*, as a conception of power, underwent significant change during the colonial period and during later contact with European political values, as its logic was fundamentally challenged and, along with its practitioners, its rationale defeated: 'Contemporary Javanese political culture is therefore a heterogeneous, disjunctive and internally contradictory complex of traditional and Western elements, with a lower degree of internal logic and coherence than in the past' (Anderson 1972, section 5.8; see also Zainud'din 1975, p. 97). For example, a reflection of such heterogeneity is the ambiguous, official post-independence ideology of the *Pancasila*, which is strongly enforced but the meaning of which is interpreted by the president according to practical and changing circumstances.

One interesting aspect of traditional Indonesian culture that is implicitly rather than explicitly reflected in Javanese political behaviour (and which finds echoes in contemporary Indonesian politics) is the Hindu-Buddhist conception of the *mandala*. A *mandala* is a circular figure symbolising the perceived universe, and in political terms it is a useful means by which to understand the pre-modern idea of the state. In modern terms, the state is an organised political community under one government within recognisable borders. But in a number of pre-modern and, in particular, Asian societies, the state differed primarily in that it had no clearly recognisable borders and had an organised political community only at the centre. The centre of authority and administration was clearly delineated, but power became increasingly diffuse the further away one was from the centre. Consequently, at the boundaries, the state faded into an area of ambiguous political control until finally merging with the realms of a competing power. That is, within the political notion of the *mandala*, the state is 'strongest at its center and recedes in distance' (Anderson 1972, p. 30; see also Geertz 1993, p. 223; Lowry 1996, pp. 9–15). At the centre of the state was the monarch, who was the pinnacle of the state's power.

Since the Javanese conception of power that dispersed towards the periphery was 'fluid and unstable, always ready for dispersal and diffusion, interstate aggression necessarily becomes a basic assumption about interstate relations' (Anderson 1972, p. 31). This 'doctrine emphasised the cult of expansion . . . as the dynamic factor calculated to disturb the equilibrium of inter-state relations. A state's belligerence is in the first place directed towards its closest neighbour(s)' (Moertono 1981, p. 71). If the *a priori* enemy of the state is its closest neighbour, Java is happier in a dominant rather than equal (or power-sharing) role within the wider contemporary state. Beyond Indonesia's state borders, secure only in the modern statist sense, Indonesia is most likely to be more aggressive towards neighbours than distant nations. This might, in part, explain the historical ambiguity of Indonesian–Australian relations, as well as military hostility towards Malaysia during the *Konfrontasi* (Confrontation) of 1963–66 and towards East Timor, as well as the country's regional rebellions. Jakarta's interest in East Timor in 1975, of course, derived from the possibility of a potentially influential (and hence potentially threatening) Leftist state within the archipelago. However, Indonesian interest in what was then Portuguese Timor officially dated back to the constitutional debates of 1945 (see Feith & Castles 1970). Further, if, in a 'mandalic' view of the state, power recedes the further one is from the centre, East Timor continues symbolically to represent a point of dispersal of central power, from which other outlying regions could take a cue. The Indonesian government has repeatedly acknowledged East Timor's potential to threaten the cohesion of the state in this way. The view that closest neighbours may be the recipients of primary 'belligerence' was confirmed when it was confidentially expressed to me by senior Indonesian officials that Indonesia expected its nearest neighbours (in this case Malaysia) to treat it with proportionately greater respect than more distant states. It might also help to explain the tight military control exerted over recalcitrant Indonesian provinces. Within the intra-Indonesian context, this extension of the mandalic state rests on the basis that the state is most 'pure' closest to the centre—in this case Jakarta or Central Java—and that the distant provinces are more inclined to spin out of the Javanese orbit. Implicit in this conception is the idea that Indonesia is therefore not a state in which all parts are equal, but rather it suggests that Indonesia is a reinterpretation of a Javanese empire.

Related to this mandalic conception of the state is the idea that, personifying the state, the president finds a parallel with former *panji*/rajahs/sultans. That is, if the state is most diffuse at its periphery and most concentrated at its centre, then the core of the centre is the office of the monarch. The office of the monarch was exemplified by the person of the monarch, thus making the person of the monarch the centre and source of power, authority, and legitimacy. Similarly, the office of the president is at the centre of Indonesia's administrative structure, with authority, legitimacy, and at least nominal power being held by the person of the president. Sukarno adopted this posture, particularly from the late 1950s until political circumstances began to slide from his grip after October 1965, while Suharto, also towards the end of his rule, increasingly did so. But like earlier monarchs, both presidents had to balance the competing forces that comprise the *kraton* (palace) or the body politic. In the end, for Sukarno the stakes were raised too high and the polar opposites became too extreme for him to be able to survive. Suharto's primary advantage in his final years was that, although the stakes were high, the polar opposites were neither as extreme nor as evenly balanced, making his transition slightly less than the all-or-nothing transition of the Sukarno era. In Java, elements of the past are never very far away, although making a distinction between authentic and reconstructed tradition becomes increasingly difficult as history blurs into official myth and the categories slide into propaganda.

The arrival of Islam

The arrival of Islam within the region of the archipelago, in the last instance travelling the same sea routes from India as had Hinduism and Buddhism, occurred over a period of centuries but received its greatest boost from the flourishing of the city-state of Malacca on the Malay Peninsula from the early fifteenth century. Malacca's ruler accepted Islam in 1414, and as the port city came to dominate regional sea trade and occupied much territory over the rest of the century, it helped spread Islam throughout the region. The spread of Islam throughout the archipelago was assisted by two events. In 1511 the Portuguese conquered Malacca, displacing both many local Muslim traders, who moved to rival trading centres such as Aceh, and, perhaps at least as importantly, ensuring that Muslim trading ships travelled to other ports, including those on the northern Javanese coast (the *Pasisir*). In Java itself, there was increasing disaffection with the tributary system adopted by the Hindu Majapahit empire, which since the late fourteenth and early fifteenth centuries had been in a state of decline. A coalition of Muslim *Pasisir* trading states gathered against the Majapahit, and its decaying structure collapsed under their combined force.[5]

The spread of Islam was, however, uneven throughout the archipelago. Northern Sumatra, first exposed to Islam, and western Java were among the most strongly influenced, while most of the rest of Java gradually accepted Islam in combination with existing animist and Hindu traditions. Thus was born the *abangan/ santri* split, which has recurred as an important theme in Indonesian politics to this day. In part, the less formal *abangan* interpretation of Islam can be attributed to the mystical Sufi version of Islam, which made its way from India to the region. But perhaps the traditional resilience and syncretism of pre-existing Javanese animist beliefs are more responsible for the distinction between those who profess a formal Islamic belief and those who are more nominal. In those regions that Islam did not penetrate, such as Bali, traditional Hindu-animist traditions remain, while Protestant and somewhat fewer Catholic Christians were converted by Dutch and other missionaries from animism, often resulting in a Christian-animism.[6] In the last-colonised provinces, animism remains a dominant religious form, although not formally accepted by the government, which requires people to profess Islam, one of the two noted forms of Christianity, or Hinduism or Buddhism.

The rise of Islam as a political force in Java was at its most developed during the period of the Mataram empire. Mataram can be traced back to the Hindu kingdom of the seventh century, flowing and ebbing over the following centuries and reaching its final peak as an Islamic sultanate in the sixteenth and seventeenth centuries, when it dominated all but the western edge of Java, as well as the nearby northern island of Madura. At this time, the sultanate of Aceh was at its most powerful, dominating the western end of the archipelago, while the sultanate of Ternate, a small island in the Maluku (Moluccas) group, dominated the east. The

---

5 One consequence of this was the removal of the remaining Hindu court to Bali, which nominally retains the Hindu religion.

6 Christianity has shown itself very capable of developing its own forms of syncretism, in South East Asia but more obviously in Latin America. This may reflect what some have suggested are the syncretic origins of European Christianity.

rise of Mataram might have continued unchecked but for the fact that the period of its ascendancy coincided with the arrival of the Dutch.

Until well into the period of Dutch colonialism, the basic unit of social and political life for the vast majority of Javanese (and others of the archipelago) was the village. Being a small and relatively closed unit, the village encouraged mutual participation, decision-making through consensus, and a disinclination to air grievances publicly. Given that the vast majority of the population lived in villages and that moving from villages to cities in substantial numbers is a relatively recent phenomenon, it is not surprising that many village customs live on. Indeed, villages find a poor replication in the *kampongs* (small clustered communities or neighbourhoods) of the cities, in which there is an attempt to establish some sense of the local community that was known in the villages from which most of their inhabitants or their parents came.

One consequence of this village influence on Indonesian life is that there is a well-developed notion of the value of the collective, as opposed to the particular worth of the individual. It is an overstatement to suggest, as some have, that in village life the community is all and the individual nothing, as many villages do include competing groups or individuals. But in a close social environment, in which participation and mutual assistance were often the difference between success and failure, the greater good usually took precedence over the desires of an individual. This aspect of traditional life finds a particularly clear reflection in the Indonesian political system, which both officially and unofficially regards conceptions of individualism and the rights of the individual as having little correspondence with the 'traditions' of the state. It almost goes without saying that, as the embodiment of the political community, the state can and does impose its will at the expense of individuals or smaller collective groups. It is also convenient for a government that is intolerant of dissent or opposition to identify itself as the embodiment of the state in order to suppress individual or small group claims in the name of the greater collective. There appears to be a genuine, though logically misguided, belief among at least some members of the government elite and bureaucracy, as well as the armed forces, that the state itself has an existence independent of its people and that it can have 'rights'.

The influence of the Dutch

The influence of the Dutch on Indonesia's political development is important in two respects. In the first instance, through the colonial experience, the Dutch geographically and politically defined the region that was to become Indonesia. The Dutch also restructured the ruling elites to serve their colonial interests, helping to reinvent and reimpose, beyond traditional limits, the privilege of the elites, the influence of which remains. The impact of Dutch colonialism on Java was at one level relatively superficial, with the Javanese managing to preserve much of their cultural integrity despite the occupying power. But at another level the impact of the Dutch could not help but be profound, giving rise to a notion of the state based on the colonial Dutch East Indies, as well as influencing the political framework of Java.

Overland trade routes with the 'orient' were effectively closed, first as a consequence of Mongol invasions and then, in the fifteenth century, following the rise of Turkish Islam in the Middle East. As a result, the newly emerging naval powers of Europe— Portugal and Spain, and later Holland and England—began visiting the archipelago from the sixteenth century. Their primary goals were to seek spices and other tradeable goods, and to establish routes to and from China and the Pacific. In 1602 the Dutch United East India Company (Verenigde Oost-Indische Compagnie, or VOC) was established, initially based at Banten on the western edge of Java, although in 1619 the Dutch seized Yacatra, renaming it 'Batavia',[7] on the north-west coast of the island. From here they could trade with the other islands and further afield, as well as counter the strategic Portuguese stronghold in Malacca, which the Dutch captured in 1641.

The development of Dutch political influence and later control of Java is complex, but suffice to say that Java was quickly recognised as a potentially rich colonial 'resource'. Although the Dutch had some technological and military advantages over the Javanese, the primary method of political and military control by the Dutch was to play off royal Javanese households against each other or to exploit divisions within them (Ricklefs 1993a, p. 147; 1993b). Those royalty who sided with the Dutch or agreed to Dutch terms remained intact and continued to exercise rule over vast

---

7 Batavia was named after an early Germanic tribe, the Batawi.

tracts of the island; those who did not were subjugated. Even though the royal houses of Java remained, the Dutch were the real power behind the various thrones.

The economic system employed by the VOC relied on a monopoly of trade, and it coerced cash-crop (*preanger*) bonded labour on coffee and sugar plantations throughout those parts of the archipelago that it controlled. But because of corruption, mismanagement, piracy, and changing patterns of trade, the economic fortunes of the VOC steadily declined, and when the company's charter expired on the last day of 1799, it was not renewed (Caldwell & Utrecht 1979, pp. 14–15; see also Geertz 1963, ch. 4).

Following Dutch support for the American War of Independence, and as a consequence of the Treaty of Paris in 1784, by which that war was ended, the Netherlands' South East Asian 'preserves' were opened to free trade. Great Britain took advantage of this situation and occupied the island of Penang off the north-west coast of the Malay Peninsula in 1786 and the island of Singapura (Singapore), off the peninsula's southern tip, in 1819. Following Holland's subjugation during the Napoleonic Wars, Great Britain occupied and administered the East Indies from 1811 to 1816. The consequent Anglo-Dutch Treaty of 1824 reflected the growing Dutch hegemony in Java and Sumatra, and the British control over the Malay Peninsula, formalising the situation and requiring the British to vacate the footholds it had gained in Sumatra, while the Dutch abandoned Malacca on the Malay Peninsula. The effect of these changes was to formally partition the Malay world along the Straits of Malacca and (from 1912) through northern Borneo, effectively defining the borders of the postcolonial states of Indonesia and Malaysia.

In 1830, following economic and military catastrophes in Holland, and the devastating Java War of 1825–30 (which was waged by the charismatic son of the Sultan of Yogyakarta, Prince Diponegoro), the Dutch raised the Royal Netherlands Indies Army (Koninklijk Nederlands-Indisch Leger, or KNIL). It was largely manned by outer islanders and was used to quell uprisings in other parts of the archipelago. The KNIL later constituted a significant basis for outer island opposition to the government of what was then the new republic, both as a reason for opposition as through the role it played in the opposition. But probably more importantly in the short term, the Dutch also introduced the *cultuurstelsel* (literally 'culture system', but more accurately 'forced cultivation system'), a more systematic, methodical, and widespread form of the *preanger* system (Geertz 1963, ch. 6). Under the *cultuurstelsel* Javanese peasants were obliged to grow commercial crops for the government on one-fifth of their land, although in reality it was often two-fifths or more. Further, though earlier Dutch (and British) administrations had attempted to limit the power of the *prijaji*, or traditional aristocracy, their rights were not only restored but also reinforced under the *cultuurstelsel*, rewarding both Dutch and *prijaji* supervision of the system with a percentage of profits. It also introduced government more directly into the affairs of villages, which had previously been left relatively untouched. By the mid-nineteenth century the Javanese ruling classes were increasingly subject to supervision or interference from Dutch officials. This detached the *prijaji* from ordinary Javanese society and removed the restraints that *adat* (traditional law) imposed on them: 'Indeed, it was a prime aim of Dutch rule to employ the "traditional" prestige of the aristocracy in the cause of cheap administration' (Ricklefs 1993a, pp. 121–2). To this end, what had been a relatively stable, if lop-sided, relationship between Java's traditional elites and its peasants was further developed to the benefit of the elites. This exaggerated status of the elites was made all the more tense and brittle by their lack of real power. Their status and their intolerance of criticism has carried over into modern Indonesian interpretations of the methods and extent to which power can be 'legitimately' employed. While the elites under Dutch colonialism lacked real power, the post-independence elites made up for this shortfall by securing the services of the army, which at the senior levels tended to merge with and become a part of the country's political and economic elite.

A second consequence of *cultuurstelsel* was the removal of the association between labour and reward. Most individuals in most societies have a reasonable tendency to want to do as little as possible for as much reward as possible, and in Indonesian society this tendency is marked. At the bottom end of the scale, it is not uncommon to find people being paid very little for doing effectively nothing, while at the top end it is not uncommon to find other, more fortunately positioned people raking off considerable sums of money for doing very little. This is not to suggest that there are not some very hard-working Javanese, as there are, particularly those working on farms or in fields, or those who are forced to work hard by being employed in factories or similar enterprises for long hours and very low levels of pay. There are also some very diligent business people and there are even good performers within Indonesia's bureaucracy, this latter institution being almost universally maligned for slackness, inefficiency, and corruption. But the business of business can amble along at an easy, sometimes somnolent pace, and in part at least, this reflects the long-standing view that there is little point in working too hard if there is no significant reward for one's endeavours. The separation of labour and reward is also, arguably, reflected in contemporary corruption, although this also derives from the example set by the elites in claiming the rewards of office and, obviously, from the need to top up low levels of pay.

The third effect of the *cultuurstelsel* was that it impoverished the Javanese economy at a time when it could have established a base for later economic development. Though it was feudal (see footnote 2), pre-colonial Java was not a poor island by world standards at the time, and the Netherlands certainly grew rich by exploiting it and the neighbouring islands. Indeed, the modern Netherlands only exists in its current degree of prosperity as a direct consequence of the wealth it extracted from the East Indies. Although, if left in Java, such wealth might not have been well distributed (and nor might its economy have been as well developed), there is little doubt that reinvestment in the colonies from the profits extracted by the Dutch during this period would have provided Indonesia with a far more solid economic footing (and significantly less debt) on which to have embarked as an independent state. That such reinvestment was not the purpose of colonialism to start with does not detract from this point. But between 1856 and 1865, the *cultuurstelsel* system was abandoned and was increasingly replaced by private capital. Thus the scene was set for more thorough colonial economic exploitation in the latter part of the nineteenth century and the first four decades of the twentieth century (Caldwell & Utrecht 1979, pp. 18–22).

While Dutch political hegemony was well established in Java and much of Sumatra by the nineteenth century, its control over the wider archipelago was not fully achieved until the early twentieth century. Aceh in northern Sumatra maintained its political integrity until deprived of British protection in 1871, with the Dutch attacking in 1873 but with Aceh holding out until 1908. Bali was occupied in 1906, and eastern Nusa Tenggara, inland Kalimantan, and Sulawesi were effectively ignored until being 'pacified' between 1900 and 1910 (Grant 1996, pp. 16–17). The period before Europe's Great War represented the peak of European colonialism, with European powers scrambling for the last scraps of territory that had not already been brought under one or other of their powers. Already ensconced in the East Indies, the Netherlands moved to complete its regional political and military hegemony. This completion of Dutch domination over the East Indies had a number of consequences, one of which was to transport indigenous troops from one area to assist in repressing the peoples of another. This had the effect of spreading the old, simple Malacca-based trading language of market Malay. The increased trade between the islands also furthered the development of this language, and already the most common language to be used between ethnic groups, it increasingly became the lingua franca of indigenous Dutch East Indians wishing to communicate with each other, providing the disparate ethnic groups with their first sense of common identity.

At around the time of the completion of Dutch hegemony in the East Indies, the colonial authorities also introduced what was called the 'Ethical Policy' in response to humanitarian indignation in the Netherlands and a decline in the well-being of the local population. The impact of this policy was most significant in the area of education. The policy had the benefit of training indigenous peoples to assist in the rapidly growing primary sector of commercial cropping (sugar, coffee, tea, and, in the outer islands, tobacco and rubber), and the mining of tin and drilling for oil. One main consequence of the rise in educational levels among indigenous peoples was the growth and influence of Western educated local people. These individuals began to question and rebel against the North East Indies government when it implemented a legal caste structure, which provided a distinction between Dutch, mixed-race, and indigenous Indonesians. Thus was born the beginnings of Indonesia's independence movement.

Drawing in particular on an elaborated interpretation of the Srivajaya and Majapahit empires of Sumatra and Java, Sukarno later argued that Dutch colonial occupation had been little more than an interruption in Indonesian history. However, pre-colonial connections throughout the archipelago were weak and often hostile. There was no pre-Dutch 'Indonesian' unity, while the political traditions of Java that have been posited as 'Indonesian' were reconstructed through the Dutch in an authoritarian parody of traditional style to suit Dutch colonial needs. Even the name 'Indonesia' is foreign in its etymology, being 'pseudo-Hellenic' (Anderson 1991, p. 120).

Despite some changes in form, the Dutch administration within the East Indies before the Second World War retained a paternalistic ethos and continued to be both unitary and centralised in its political structure. The Japanese occupation of 1942–45 did little to alter this structure (and perhaps enforced it). As a consequence, these political characteristics of paternalism, unitarianism, and centralism deeply influenced the new republican government, not only throughout the 1950s and especially after the proclamation of 'Guided Democracy' in 1958, but also into and throughout the New Order government of Suharto after 1966.

The Japanese interlude

One notable influence of the Japanese, beyond reinforcing a paternalistic, centralist ethos, was that, although they were repressive, ruthless, and to a considerable extent disorganised, they did establish organisations that would play a key role in the establishment of the republic. For propaganda purposes, the Japanese brought together the major Islamic organisations, notably Muhamadiyah and NU, under the umbrella group Masyumi, which later became a significant political player. They also trained Indonesian youths in Islamic and nationalist military units to both police the colony and assist in fending off expected Allied attacks. By 1943 there were over 35 000 men in the Javanese auxiliary army alone (Feith 1964, p. 198). This organisation—the Volunteer Army of Defenders of the Fatherland (Tentara Sukarela Pembela Tanah Air, or 'Peta')—was to become the basis of the revolutionary army and later the foundation of ABRI. One of the impacts of Japanese training of the auxiliary army was to encourage young Indonesians to believe that people of the 'East' could militarily defeat people of the 'West' (Mangunwijaya 1992, p. 6). Another impact of the Japanese military influence, described as 'fascist' in character,[8] was the introduction into Indonesia's incipient armed forces a notion that society could and should be controlled, and that the armed forces should be allied with government in closely directing and controlling Indonesian society.

The Japanese coopted proto-nationalist leaders, for both propaganda and organisational purposes. Despite Japanese ruthlessness —few of the 300 000 Indonesians deported to work in labour camps returned—these leaders cooperated because it held some hope of final independence. The Japanese also promoted the use of market Malay as a national language and began to open senior administrative posts to Indonesians.

Under mounting pressure from nationalist leaders, but probably more in an to attempt to forestall Allied military advances in the Pacific, the Japanese announced the establishment of an Investigating Committee for the Preparation of Independence in March 1945. It began work in August of that year under the leadership of pre-war nationalists Sukarno and Hatta. On 17 August 1945, two days after Japan surrendered, Sukarno and Hatta proclaimed the Republic of Indonesia, of which Sukarno was to be president and Hatta vice-president, with an advisory Central National Committee of 135 members. The republic received almost immediate widespread support in the former colony. By the end of September it had obtained arms from surrendering Japanese soldiers, with which it was aware it would have to battle the Dutch and possibly the Allies in the period after the cessation of hostilities with Japan.

Seeking identity

The first Constitution of the Republic, referred to as the 1945 Constitution, was proclaimed at that time. It was (and remains) a short and in many respects ambiguous document, the intention being that it would allow the president considerable scope for decision-making. The 1945 Constitution vested primary authority in the person of the president, who selected a Cabinet and directed the affairs of state. The Constitution was changed in 1949

---

8   David Bourchier has also argued that the political forms that took root in Indonesia,
     especially in the New Order period, derived from Japanese 'organicism', although
     they were also strongly influenced by European 'organicism' (that is, fascism)
     (Bourchier 1996).

and again in 1950 to vest authority in the Cabinet, with the prime minister being the senior office holder. This change coincided with the 'parliamentary democracy' period of 1949–57. However, following the move towards Guided Democracy from 1957, the 1945 Constitution was re-adopted in 1959 in a final act of abandoning the authority of parliament, the party system, and democratic processes. It is the 1945 Constitution that prevails today.

The impact of the Dutch on the development of modern Indonesia was significant, and the occupation of the Japanese was a catalyst, as it was throughout so much of Asia in the years following 1945. But it was in the traditions of Central Java that the modern state of Indonesia increasingly sought conceptual and symbolic guidance, and by which it continues to be most strongly influenced. The Indonesian government maintains, in both subtle and obvious ways, not only that Indonesia is centred on middle Java, but also that the values at the core of Indonesian political thinking—the values that comprise 'Indonesian culture'—derive from Java's rich, predominantly spiritually oriented past. That is, where there are fundamental and unresolvable contradictions, what is referred to as Javanese thinking will recall syncretic solutions; where there is a desire to speak out, Javanese thinking will impose *halus*, or deferential behaviour; where there is a complaint about official corruption, Javanese thinking will recall the natural accrual of wealth to power; where there are complaints about centralism, Javanese thinking will recall the *mandala*; and where there is concern about the sometimes unbridled exercise of power, Javanese thinking will recall that power requires no justification.

Yet despite the rich spiritualism that is alluded to in Javanese tradition, the hard reality of life in Central Java and Jakarta was, and remains, that people were and are still moved by concerns more material, immediate, and prosaic than those suggested by claims to, and of, a rich spiritual tradition. They can be, and were, polite and rude by turns, brusque and friendly, concerned with form and necessity, and lately transfixed by the more culturally crass attractions of television at least as much as by religion or tradition. Depending on the region, the muezzin's call to prayer is as much ignored as it is respected, while the malls and markets of the larger cities increasingly betray aspirations to, or a fixation with, consumerism, with a concomitant loss of interest in matters that do not correspond to that materialism. Others were simply more concerned with the material circumstances of their lives: whether they and their families would have enough to eat; whether their food would be nutritionally suitable; whether they had access to health care; or whether they could provide the basic necessities that would allow their children access to education. Many, perhaps most, managed to rise above the weighty material constraints, at least until the crisis of the late 1990s. But many did not, or were not sure of being able to do so.

This is not to deny the multiplicity of Javanese cultural forms or the authentic (*asli*) echo of Java's spiritual traditions in contemporary Javanese society, but is rather a comment on the flexibility of culture—a shared world view—to respond to changing circumstances. Indonesian politics implies a particular culture, and this officially defined culture is used to justify or rationalise a range of political responses. It is a culture that, in the final analysis, derives from Central Java, and it is interesting to note that the cultural forms upon which it is based are not static but dynamic. Indonesia generally and Java in particular have been undergoing dramatic, almost radical, economic and social changes since the 1970s, and the behaviour of ordinary Javanese has changed in line with that. There are always traces of the 'old Java' in the new, but the 'old Java' is slipping into redundancy, the efforts of the government to reinvent and reinstitute culture in an official capacity (Pemberton 1994) notwithstanding. The gap between rhetoric and reality, in Indonesian politics, is a wide one.

3
FROM INDEPENDENCE
TO 1965

Competing conceptions of the modern state

While Indonesia, as a state, has a clear association with the former colony of the Dutch East Indies, it is important to remember that the Dutch treated the colony as a group of essentially separate 'subcolonies' linked to the administrative centre of Jakarta. This was especially the case with Irian Jaya, or West Papua, which remained a separate colony until Indonesia's occupation in 1963 and formal incorporation in 1969. Further, the creation of the state based on the former colony did not take into account the degree of resistance to Dutch rule or to incorporation into a wider administrative structure. Nor did it reflect aspirations to a more local form of independence, such as in Aceh in northern Sumatra, which helps account for varying degrees of anti-Javanese sentiment and outright rebellion over the period of Indonesia's history as a state. The idea that the Indonesian state is based on the former colony does not account for the incorporation of East Timor, although one influential school of thought in Indonesia's formative period (nominally led by Sukarno) took a larger view of the geography of the Indonesian state. It incorporated not only the whole Dutch colony and Portuguese (East) Timor but also the Malay peninsula, northern Borneo, and even the Philippines. As it transpired, this conception of the Indonesian state was not to be, although the state as it now exists is larger than many imagined it would have been, particularly among those regionalists who still aspire to local autonomy or independence.

Yet while there remains considerable regional identification throughout Indonesia, there is also a strong and increasing identification with the concept of the Indonesian state as it currently exists. This has largely been brought about by the standardisation of a common, if synthetic, language—Bahasa Indonesia (Anderson 1990, pp. 123–51)—and the imposition of a 'national' culture (see Atkinson 1987; Tsing 1987, pp. 196–200). The efforts of both the Sukarno- and the Suharto-led governments further assisted in cementing the idea of Indonesia in the minds of ordinary Indonesians, both through their rhetoric and through a range of government-sponsored development programs. This national culture, however, strongly reflects aspects, often reconstructed, of the political culture of Central and Eastern Java. The aspect of Indonesian culture that relates to the recognition and exercise of political power derives from a confluence of a Central Javanese understanding of power, its modification under Dutch colonialism, borrowings from the Western tradition of the nation-state, and the exigencies of the survival of both the nation-state and its elites. This political structure was then effectively imposed on the state as a national ideology.[1]

It is not unreasonable to claim that of the various unifying elements, the single greatest unifying factor in Indonesia is language, despite the fact that more than 200 languages and dialects are spoken by Indonesians. Market Malay provided the basis of a national language, which was adopted by nationalists in the earlier part of the twentieth century. The language of traders and merchants throughout the archipelago since at least the fourteenth century, its use was expanded through the posting of indigenous KNIL soldiers in different parts of the colony. Not only was market Malay often spoken throughout the archipelago (a variation of it was the predominant language in much of Sumatra, for instance), but it was also relatively simple for newcomers to learn and use. In its earlier period it also brought with it a relatively egalitarian value system, which particularly suited revolutionary nationalist interests. Perhaps most importantly, though, market Malay did not carry with it the stigma of being imposed by Java (the predominant language of which is quite different, being more highly structured and far more hierarchical than market Malay), even though it was from Java that market Malay derived its political force. Market Malay in its adopted form is officially referred to as 'Bahasa Indonesia' (Indonesian language).

---

1   John Pemberton (1994) discusses Javanese tradition and culture, and the construction of the Indonesian state from a particularly critical perspective.

Not only was Bahasa Indonesia the primary means of communication between nationalists and others throughout the archipelago, and hence a common bond, but it was also the vehicle for a range of nationalist ideas that would probably have otherwise foundered at linguistic borders. It was through the national language that the idea of nation was developed where none had existed previously. It was also through the national language that education, and propaganda, took root in establishing a common history or set of shared experiences—regardless of the fact that much of this sense of history sprang at least as much from imagination as it did from historical facts. Since the adoption of Bahasa Indonesia as the national language, a range of new words (some of Javanese origin, others from Dutch or English) have been added to give the language a distinctly 'Indonesian' flavour (as opposed to the very similar Bahasa Melayu, the national language of Malaysia). Many of those words are political in character and, etymologically, are composites of other words. Since independence, the Indonesian government has shown a real passion for inventing new, composite words. Under Sukarno, with his somewhat idealised view of international socialism, the style of such words borrowed heavily from what was then the Soviet Union. In art and architecture, this borrowing from the old Soviet Union was further reflected in many national monuments that were created in the 'social realist heroes-of-the-revolution' style. Yet while Sukarno's government and the old Soviet Union have passed away, the use of this style of language (and architectural and artistic 'social realism') remains. Beyond language, Ben Anderson has also accredited the development of printing technology and the growth of literacy with helping forge a sense of nationalism or, in the case he puts, an imagined nationalism (Anderson 1991).

This imagined shared history, particularly of the struggle for independence, is continually reinforced throughout Indonesia, with one of its most noticeable manifestations being street names. No matter where one goes in Indonesia, streets and especially the major thoroughfares reflect the names of Indonesia's historical figures or more significant heroes, particularly from the period of the revolution, but also later military and political figures. As a consequence, one can find the names of Javanese military heroes from the revolutionary period (1945–49) in East Timor and Northern Sumatra, as well as within Java itself. Military divisions also received historical names, with perhaps the best example being the Diponegoro Division, named after the Javanese prince who led a rebellion against the Dutch from 1825 until being captured in 1830, and in which Suharto served, being appointed commander in 1957.

Pancasila and the 1945 Constitution

The method of common communication and even a shared, or imposed, sense of common history mean little if there is no consensus about the nature of the state. In that sense, Indonesia has been both successful and unsuccessful. A national ideology, the *Pancasila* (Five Principles), has been created, and there is an adherence to the 1945 Constitution. Although the *Pancasila* and the 1945 Constitution are not the only problematic issues in Indonesian politics, together they constitute official Indonesian ideology and are the foundation stone of the Indonesian political system.

The five principles of the *Pancasila* are social justice, a just and civilised humanity, belief in one god, Indonesian unity, and government by deliberation and consent. However, the wording of the *Pancasila* has changed since it was first enunciated. For example, government by deliberation and consent was originally interpreted to mean the people's sovereignty, while unity was interpreted as nationalism. These interpretations are not necessarily contradictory, but they do allow considerable scope for the derivation of meaning. Further, regardless of the wording (or their English interpretations), the meaning of the *Pancasila* has been quite differently interpreted by both the Sukarno-led governments, which depicted it as leaning towards nationalism and socialism, as opposed to the Suharto government, which has opted for a semi-feudal and capitalist patrimony. The principles have also been interpreted differently during each period of government. In simple terms, the *Pancasila* is so vague that it can be held to mean whatever the government of the day says it means or wants it to mean. For example, belief in one god has been interpreted to mean that all Indonesian citizens must espouse one of five nominated religions that allegedly recognise one god. They are Islam, Buddhism, Catholicism, Protestantism, and Hinduism, yet neither Hinduism nor Buddhism believe in a single deity (the government argues that Shiva represents a supreme Hindu deity). Indonesia's many animists, who worship various local spirits and who usually know nothing of Hinduism, Protestantism, or Catholicism, are categorised as Hindus, Protestants, or Catholics for the purpose of the exercise. More importantly, however, 'government by deliberation and consent' is a blanket term that allows for all manner of political forms, the most notable of which is autocratic rule. And 'unity in diversity' is a typically Javanese syncretic concept that incorporates logical contradictions that are represented as having been resolved, yet which more accurately ignores or represses such contradictions. But because the *Pancasila* is the foundation stone of the Indonesian state, it cannot be questioned, and alternative interpretations of its meaning (though they exist) are not countenanced. Thus the variable but rigidly applied meaning of the *Pancasila* is one of the fundamental problems of Indonesian politics.

The other fundamental problem revolves around the 1945 Constitution. The 1945 Constitution was the first proclaimed but was always intended to be a short-term document aimed at helping to establish the state, to be replaced with a more thorough document at a more opportune time. It was indeed replaced, twice, although its replacements were themselves also short-term documents, anticipating the creation of a more complete and representative document. However, because the 1945 Constitution places considerable power in the hands of the president, and because it is both short and ambiguous, it is highly interpretable and has been construed to mean many different things since it was reintroduced by Sukarno to help usher in the period of Guided Democracy. Like his predecessor, Suharto also viewed the 1945 Constitution as a suitable vehicle for a strong presidential rule. And as with the *Pancasila*, strict adherence to the 1945 Constitution is required of all Indonesians. Yet the set of principles to which Indonesians are required to adhere has shown itself to be indistinct and politically malleable.

Moving towards Independence: 1945–49

While the Republic of Indonesia had been proclaimed on 17 August 1945, it was clear from the outset that such a unilateral declaration would still need to be 'negotiated' with the former colonial power. Not surprisingly, given the manner in which the Second World War had been fought, the Netherlands government and the governments of the Allies initially regarded the establishment of the Republic as an instrument of Japanese warfare—which, from the Japanese perspective, was correct.

Allied, mostly Australian, troops had been involved in 'mopping up' campaigns in the eastern islands in the final months of the war and, upon the cessation of hostilities, moved to take authority from the defeated Japanese. Within weeks British troops had begun to land in Java, and Dutch troops began to return soon after, assuming the role they had occupied before the war. At the same time, local units loyal to the Republic had begun seizing arms from surrendering Japanese. In technical terms, as the prewar administrative power, the Netherlands held the 'legal' claim to sovereignty over the archipelago, while in practical terms it was the British and Australian troops who initially occupied the region and accepted the surrender of the Japanese. But the Republic also proclaimed its sovereignty, with its troops also occupying some areas. In this situation, in which authority was claimed by two armed and politically opposed groups, fighting inevitably broke out, particularly in Java and Sumatra, first with the British and then, as they handed over authority, with the Dutch.

Within the Republic, any authority that had been vested in the old aristocratic elites who had worked with the Japanese was quickly ceded to younger nationalist leaders. There were political and administrative changes within the structure of the republican government to make it more effective, and recognising the different sources of nationalist sentiment, there was a call for the establishment of political parties. Of the major groups, one was Masyumi (Consultative Council of Indonesian Muslims), which was led by both wartime Masyumi members and newer members. Another was the Partai Nasional Indonesia (Indonesian Nationalist Party, or PNI), which was led by many of the older leaders of the PNI established by Sukarno in 1927 and who were active under the Japanese administration. Finally there was the Socialist Party (PSI), which had a strong youth wing. The Indonesian Communist Party (PKI) was also re-established, and a number of smaller parties and political organisations, often nationalist-communist in orientation, also sprang up[2] (Feith 1964, p. 200).

---

2   Most of these were later merged into an expanded PKI (Feith 1964, p. 202).

One of the moderate socialist leaders, Sutan Sjahrir, as head of the Cabinet, agreed to negotiate with the Dutch, as did his successors. But there was considerable opposition to negotiation, both from the Republic's regular army and from the irregular military units over which the government had little control. As a consequence, the period from 1945 to 1949 was marked by both negotiation and fighting, with negotiation tending to be pursued by the government of the day and opposed by the Opposition, almost regardless of who held power and who was in opposition. The Dutch military forces were stronger in the cities and surrounding areas but had little influence in the hinterland. By the middle of 1947, the Dutch had 150 000 soldiers in Indonesia and, with the negotiations failing, launched a full-scale attack on the Republic. The United Nations Security Council pressured the Netherlands to settle, while within the Republic the more radical, anti-negotiation socialist Amir Sjarifuddin[3] headed the Cabinet.

In August 1948, Musso returned from a twenty-year exile in the Soviet Union and welded together the fledgling Republic's left-wing parties into an expanded and significantly more influential Communist Party, which he headed. Sjarifuddin's Cabinet was replaced by a moderate Masyumi–PNI coalition, and in response, a group of second-tier leaders in the PKI at Madiun in Central Java announced a revolt against the Sukarno-Hatta government in September. Hindley recounts that the Madiun communists panicked when they believed the new government would move to disband local communist-led armed units (Hindley 1964, p. 21). The Republic's army attacked the rebels, and Musso, Sjarifuddin, and a number of other senior leaders were killed in the following weeks, all of which constituted a severe blow to the PKI. The 'Madiun affair', as it was called, was regarded by the Republic's regular army as treachery during hostilities with the Netherlands. It marked the beginning of a distrust between ABRI and the PKI, which culminated in the events of 1965–66.

A second major attack by the Dutch from December 1948 resulted in military successes on the ground but also in increasing pressure from the United Nations and particularly from the USA,

---

3 Sjarifuddin announced in 1948 that he had been a secret member of the PKI for the previous thirteen years. As it transpired, a number of ministers in his and later Cabinets were also secret members of the PKI (Hindley 1964, pp. 18–20).

through its postwar Marshall Plan, to resolve the dispute. In November 1949, the Netherlands agreed to a settlement in which fifteen outlying, Dutch-created states would come together with Java and Sumatra in a federated Republic of the United States of Indonesia (RUSI). The creation of the outlying states accurately reflected local conditions and loyalties, as well as the Netherlands' conception of its colony as comprising a number of smaller colonies rather than being a large, unified colony. But the manœuvre did not enjoy total support in the outer islands and was clearly a means by which the Netherlands would continue to exercise control over the region. Given the disparate nature of the archipelago, it was an unworkable structure if the state was to remain intact. The Republic was also required to assume the Netherlands East Indies' debt of 4300 million guilders, of which 1291 million guilders (US$339 million) was external debt repayable in foreign currency (Feith 1964, p. 203). From the very beginning, Indonesia's economic position was compromised, a situation that was exacerbated in the following decade by questionable economic decision-making and management, and which pushed the state to the brink of self-destruction.

Liberal Indonesia: 1949–57

On 27 December 1949, Sukarno was sworn in as president of RUSI, while Hatta was chosen as prime minister. The Cabinet included ministers from Masyumi and PNI, as well as non-party ministers and five ministers chosen from the federal states. The first significant change was the abandonment of the federal structure, partly because it was unworkable, partly because it was a result of the aforementioned creation of Dutch divisionist policies, and partly in keeping with the unitarian ambitions of the Jakarta-based government. A primary characteristic of Central Javanese political tradition, enhanced by the Dutch, was the notion that power is necessarily centralised, as noted by Moertono (1981). Being at the forefront of the revolution, the Javanese increasingly took it upon themselves to lead the new state. Their claim to be at the centre of the new republic was further enhanced by the fact that Java was also the location of the Netherlands' administrative centre of Batavia (later Jakarta), and that the Javanese had by far the biggest population of the islands' ethnic groups. This situation was warily accepted by the outlying regions. However, while this aspect of its political form was at least temporarily settled, many of post-independence Indonesia's other attempts to reconstruct a stable political form were not (Geertz 1993, p. 224–5).

Sukarno's vision for the state as manifested in government policies was not universally accepted, particularly as it focused both power and economic resources in Jakarta, and thence Java, at the expense of the wider archipelago. Within Java, formal *santri* Muslims had their Islamic aspirations largely ignored, while the ideologies of the pro-nationalist groups were scattered, often in tiny clusters, across the political spectrum. Divisions in Indonesian politics, therefore, date back to the first years of the struggle for independence. In order to address these divisions, and to develop a state ideology that not only drew on traditional political forms but also incorporated modern political concepts, Sukarno included a clearly defined version of nationalism into his conception of politics. Sukarno's nationalist aspirations for Indonesia were shared by many intellectuals and by the newly emergent armed forces, but among the peoples of the former Dutch colony, there was at least as much to separate as to bind. Further, the economic and political development that Sukarno hoped to oversee was necessarily imposed, incorporating conceptions that did not always reflect existing cultures. The attempt by Sukarno and other leading nationalists to create and develop a new state, then, had to rely on an appeal to a common identity. According to John Mayall, 'Nationalism is widely used to disguise the alien and external nature of the modernising process, and its role as such and as the ideology of domination is repeatedly pointed up by repressed groups' (Mayall 1978, p. 41).

As a consequence of at least some of its artificiality, all was not well with the nationalist project. Under the Republic as it fought the Dutch up until 1949, there were splits over strategies, in particular over possible compromise settlements. Further, there was division over the briefly imposed RUSI, which was a federated rather than a unitary state. From 1950, reflecting an earlier rejection of compromise with the Dutch as well as the secular nature of the new state, there was a fundamentalist Islamic rebellion, known as the *Dar'ul Islam* (Nation of Islam) rebellion in West Java, South Sulawesi, and Aceh. In this case, the rebellion was based around irregular Islamic military units that had been fighting since the

Japanese occupation and later against the Dutch. These militant Islamic groups had always been outside the control of the central government and were unwilling to bow to central government directives after 1949, especially after earlier 'treachery'. The prime example of such 'treachery' was the fledgling government's acceptance of the compromise Renville Agreement in January 1948, in which, to attain a qualified independence, the Republic conceded territory it had lost in 1947 to the Dutch. As a part of the agreement, the republican government conceded West Java to the Dutch on the condition that the Siliwangi Division based there could be removed to Central Java. However, this left behind independent Islamic guerillas in West Java, who continued their own campaign against the Dutch, proclaiming it a *jihad* (holy war). By December 1948, the Islamic guerillas, under Kartosuwirjo, proclaimed the Negara Islam Indonesia (Indonesian Islamic State, or NII). Kartosuwirjo announced that the Republic had ceased to exist and that the NII was the true embodiment of the revolution. After Indonesia gained practical independence in 1949, the *Dar'ul Islam* movement continued to defy the central government, at times extending its influence into Central Java and over Aceh and much of South Sulawesi. The *Dar'ul Islam* rebellion probably had most impact in the period from 1957 until 1961, at least partly in reaction to the growing influence of the PKI in government. It also received a significant boost when rebels in South and Central Sulawesi joined the movement in 1952 and 1958 respectively, having been in their own state of rebellion since 1950 (initially in response to internal military tensions in South Sulawesi since the late 1940s). The South Sulawesi rebellion collapsed in 1961, in response to a government amnesty. With the capture of Kartosuwirjo in 1962, the movement in West Java was militarily wiped out. The *Dar'ul Islam* revolt had been Indonesia's longest sustained rebellion.

The *Dar'ul Islam* revolt had never threatened the cohesion of the state of Indonesia in the way that the PRRI–Permesta rebellion of 1957–58 did. However, even into the late 1990s, there were signs that the values that engendered it were still strongly held: primarily a desire for an Islamic state (or, in the outer regions, independent Islamic states) and a distrust of the central government in Jakarta. The most noticeable of these indications was a series of riots in Sumatra and Java from 1995 through to early 1998. The riots were primarily aimed at the local ethnic Chinese communities, who were predominantly Christian and Buddhist but who, more importantly, also dominated the local economies. A number of people were killed in these riots and damage to property was widespread. It was suggested by some that these riots were at least partly inspired by political manœuvrings in Jakarta, both to destabilise the government, to cast political Islam in a poor light, and to use the Chinese as a scapegoat for serious political and economic problems. Such suggestions had credence in so far as Islam was increasingly being regarded as the only viable alternative to the New Order style of government. Also, some of the country's wealthiest business people, who had close links with the president, were ethnic Chinese, and the attacks were seen by some as being both direct and symbolic. In Aceh Province, a descendant Islamic separatist movement was also continuing a low-level guerilla campaign against the government.

While the commitment to liberal democracy in the years from 1949 until the late 1950s was less than total, there was a practical adherence to pluralist democratic forms. At that time:

power was in the hands of the parties. Parliament was an institution of some authority, and the power of the chief extraparliamentary political actors, President Soekarno and the army, was effectively limited. It would be an exaggeration to say that the political leadership of the period was fully committed to the principles of constitutional democracy, but there was certainly a serious attempt to contain political life within the body of rules laid down by the existing constitution (Feith 1964, p. 204).

In 1952, NU left Masyumi, establishing itself as a political party in its own right. This division in the Islamic vote reflected deeper tensions between Indonesia's Islamic organisations and how Islam was viewed, particularly in Java. Despite the Islamic parties' stated desire to create an Islamic state, they remained a part of the liberal political system. One consequence of the Republic's commitment to a multi-party system was the regular rise and fall of coalition governments that divided over a series of issues. This constant division, lack of political stability, and tendency to compromise obstructed forward economic planning. The biggest economic problems between 1949 and 1957 revolved around a number of issues. Destruction caused by the Second World War and the struggle for independence from the Dutch, along with the crippling debts that the republican government agreed to take over, put the fledgling state at a disadvantage from the outset. Infrastructure was limited and production of most goods grew slowly if at all. Beyond that, foreign investment was limited particularly by the gradual undermining of Dutch economic power, which occurred especially through the granting of monopolies and liberal credit facilities to private Indonesian companies. This compounded otherwise unsustainable budget deficits, while protecting local businesses at the expense of the export market or, alternatively, promoting exports that damaged local businesses. As the sometimes chaotic events of the 1950s began to unfold, tensions grew between two broad groups within the political system, who Herb Feith has referred to as 'administrators' and 'solidarity makers' (Feith 1962).

Even from the earliest days there were major political difficulties. In 1952, the Republic was shaken by the 'October 17 affair', in which a group of army leaders attempted to force Sukarno to dissolve the parliament. The political consensus that had marked the development of policies until that time began to fall apart, with the party's positions becoming polarised. On one hand, there was Masyumi, the socialists and the two small Christian parties (Protestant and Catholic); on the other side were the PNI, the PKI, and several smaller parties. In 1955, a coalition Cabinet of the PNI, NU, and smaller nationalist and Islamic parties, led by Ali Sastroamidjojo, pushed for greater 'Indonesianisation' in the areas of importing, banking, and shipping. The consequences of this nationalist policy on economic life included escalating inflation and corruption, and an exchange rate that further hampered exports.

In 1955, the army refused to accept the Sastroamidjojo Cabinet's appointment of a new chief of staff, and as a consequence of this lack of confidence, the Cabinet fell. A change of government to a Masyumi–Socialist–NU coalition offered a reversal of economic policy, which reduced prices and settled the exchange rate, but which also damaged much indigenous business. Political differences hardened, and by the time of the elections of December 1955, political bitterness (including a marked split between Masyumi-supporting *santri* Muslims and the PNI-supporting *abangan* Muslims) had become extreme. Political consensus was effectively dead; government bureaucracy had divided along partisan lines, and increasingly there was a view that an alternative political system had to be found (Feith 1964, pp. 204–7). By 1956, foreshadowing what was to come, Sukarno was already talking about the need for Guided Democracy.

In December 1956, matters worsened, highlighting the division between both the centre and the periphery of the Republic, between Javanese and non-Javanese Indonesians, between former revolutionary soldiers and former members of KNIL who were incorporated into the Indonesian army, and between the two broad political groupings. Bloodless coups were enacted in the three provinces of Sumatra, where newly established councils headed by local (often former KNIL) army officers claimed power, rejecting the central government and accusing it of excessive bureaucracy, over-centralisation, neglect, corruption, and being too tolerant of the PKI. Fuelling this discontent in practical terms was Java's declining share of the export trade despite its being the main recipient of government and private expenditure. To effect their rejection of the new Sastroamidjojo-led government, the officers channelled exports directly to world markets, which, along with extensive smuggling often sponsored by army units, deprived Jakarta of foreign exchange. While the North Sumatra Council was overthrown from within, the Central and South Sumatra councils remained intact. In March 1957 a similar bloodless coup gave power to an army-led council in East Indonesia (Sulawesi, the Moluccas, and Nusa Tenggara). The outer islands thus came to most strongly represent Masyumi–socialist interests, while the centre reflected PNI–NU–PKI characteristics.

The dissident leaders in the outer islands called for a return to consensus politics, based on a political reunion between the Javanese Sukarno and the Sumatran Hatta. Sukarno responded by repeating his idea of Guided Democracy, to be supported by an advisory 'National Council' representing a range of 'functional groups' (*golongon karya*) including workers, peasants, the army, business, and so on. These 'functional groups' would later be echoed in the 'functional groups' brought together by ABRI in 1964, which, under its abbreviated name, 'Golkar', was to become the political vehicle for Suharto's New Order government. The PKI, which (along with the PNI) strongly supported Sukarno, gained forty-five seats on the National Council, although none in the Cabinet.

Of all the events of the 1950s, perhaps the most important and far reaching in its consequences was the effective nationalisation of Dutch property in 1957, which was formalised in 1958. This nationalisation of Dutch interests was ostensibly in response to a failed United Nations bid to settle the outstanding problem of the incorporation of Dutch New Guinea into the Republic, as well as to end Dutch 'economic imperialism'. The process of nationalisation of Dutch interests had the combined effect of halting foreign investment in the Republic and cutting shipping within the multi-island state by the Dutch-owned shipping company KPM (Koninklijke Paketvaart Maatschappij), which had provided about three-quarters of transportation between the islands. The economy, saddled with debt from the outset, and plagued by unstable government and almost no economic policy, slid further and further. The crisis was mounting

Guided Democracy: 1958–66

When the Sastroamidjojo Cabinet resigned in March 1957—the seventeenth Cabinet since 1945—parliamentary democracy was finally abandoned and Sukarno's Guided Democracy was adopted in modified form. Along with Guided Democracy came martial law, on 14 March, strengthening the position of the army's central leadership under its chief of staff, Major General Abdul Haris Nasution. This provided legal grounds for army intervention in civil affairs and laid the groundwork for ABRI's 'dual function' (*dwifungsi*) of both protecting and helping to run the state. The Indonesian army had never confined itself to a purely military role, being particularly active in the affairs of the fledgling Republic during the period of the revolution. From 1949, ABRI had formally accepted the sovereignty of the civilian government, but this formality belied a continuing belief within the army that it was the guardian of the state, both in security affairs and in the broader political environment. To that end, the army ran a parallel administrative structure to that of the state, from Cabinet level through to local administrative regions and down to villages. This system has been identified as deriving from, and being similar to, the military system initiated by Japan during the war, through which civil society was increasingly regimented and militarised. In particular, there continue to be parallels between wartime Japan and Indonesia's armed forces. The similarities range from the creation of village or sub-district military commanders (*goshi* and *komandan rayon militer*) all the way through to a wives' organisation (Fujinkai and Darma Wanita), the officially sanctioned and imposed ideology (*yamato damashii* and the *Pancasila*), and the politico-military role of the armed forces (*gunsai* and *dwifungsi*) (Mangunwijaya 1992, pp. 12–15). When the army finally asserted what it regarded as its rightful role in the affairs of the state, its structure for implementing that role was already firmly in place.

The move towards Guided Democracy from 1957 was in some senses an attempt at political stability, and it was marked by what Sukarno maintained was his faith in achieving or understanding popular sentiment, or *mufakat*. *Mufakat* is based on the consensual model of political arbitration. Consensus in this context is not defined by the open airing of differences of opinion, but is marked by conformity to group norms, with an emphasis placed on the observation, absorption, and imitation of the behaviour of one's seniors. Individually oriented behaviour is frowned upon (Willner 1970, p. 261). In this sense, what constituted consensus was not general agreement on an issue as a consequence of discussion, but consensus based on anticipation of a required code of behaviour. Within the traditional Javanese political framework, such a code is ultimately defined by the uppermost reaches of a hierarchical power structure. Hence, 'a number of influential Indonesian political leaders have remained averse to decision-making procedures that involve voting. They are convinced that these stimulate disharmony and make differences explicit, crystallizing points of view to an extent where they are too hard to be mellowed or melted down into a common synthesis through further discussion' (Kahin 1964, p. 599). This Javanese derived aversion to 'disharmony' has remained a consistent theme in Indonesian politics, particularly in relation to the 'disharmony' caused by non-government political groups and the media. But Sukarno's belief in his grasp of *mufakat* (and indeed Indonesian unity based on an 'exemplary' Javanese centre) was misplaced. Increasingly Indonesian politics was a balancing act, with Sukarno in the middle.

Alienated both politically and economically from the central government, Sumatra and Sulawesi raised themselves in revolt, in what was called the PRRI–Permesta rebellion. Local military leaders staged the series of aforementioned bloodless local coups against civilian authorities between December 1956 and March

1957, establishing revolutionary councils. The military was supported in the coups by business people and in many cases ordinary people in the outer islands, who were already dismayed by the government's economic policies generally, by the channelling of wealth from the exporting outer islands to importing Java, and finally by the move towards nationalisation. The Sulawesi-based Permesta (Perdjuangan Semesta, or Overall Struggle) rebellion was formally proclaimed on 2 March 1957. One of the first moves of the councils was to engage in open and direct trade with Singapore, Hong Kong, and other international centres. Bruce Grant described the rebellions as a 'revolution of economists and colonels' (Grant 1996, p. 34). The proclamation of martial law by the Indonesian government in March 1957 only exacerbated regional tensions. When Dutch interests were nationalised in December 1957, the move assisted the rebellious movements by limiting their sea contact with Jakarta

On 10 February 1958, after the call for a new, less Left-oriented Sukarno–Hatta led government in Jakarta went unheeded, rebellious officers in Padang, West Sumatra, demanded full autonomy and proclaimed the PRRI (Pemerintah Revolusioner Republik Indonesia, or Revolutionary Government of the Republic of Indonesia). With the proclamation, the leaders of the councils had demanded that the Cabinet installed by Sukarno resign and be replaced by a new Cabinet under either Hatta or the Sultan of Yogyakarta, with attendant changes to financial arrangements with the outer islands. On 15 February, with no change in Jakarta, a revolutionary government was proclaimed at Padang in Sumatra. The PRRI invited other rebel groups outside Java to join it in opposing the Jakarta government and to accept its authority. The Permesta group complied, but the whole of South Sumatra, already embroiled in the *Dar'ul Islam* revolt, remained aloof from this further conflict.

When the challenge was thrown down by the PRRI–Permesta movement, Sukarno, then in Tokyo, was hesitant to move militarily. However, army commander General Nasution and air force commander Suryadharma were not so hesitant and declared war on the rebellion. Opposing what was increasingly seen as a Left-leaning government, especially after Sukarno's invitation on 21 February 1957 to the PKI to join his government, the USA and the United Kingdom provided covert support to the rebels (with a United States B-26 aircraft being shot down by government forces, proving the association). However, within two months ABRI had crushed the PRRI rebellion and moved on the rebels in Sulawesi, defeating them three months later. The division of the army between the Javanese-based 'loyalists' and the PRRI–Permesta rebels ensured that outer islanders would henceforth play a less significant role in the officer-base of the army, which has since become Javanese dominated (MacFarling 1996, pp. 153–7). The defeat of the rebels was also the primary method by which the army formally included itself as an indispensable player in Indonesia's decision-making process, being able to more fully assert its claim to a role in affairs of state. This assertion was widely accepted, not least by Sukarno, and ABRI was thereafter popularly regarded as the saviour and guardian of the state, a role it did not shy away from comprehensively adopting.

While the army formally included itself in government, the PKI also increased its standing, both as an independent political party and within the government. Despite being a communist party (and one with links to the Chinese Communist Party), the PKI was perhaps surprisingly democratic in its public position on the structure of Indonesian politics. The PKI congress in September 1959 stated: 'For the progressive development of Indonesia, PKI will continue to fight against the danger of military dictatorship or individual dictatorship, and at the same time to defend and extend democracy. But in case a military or individual dictatorship cannot be prevented . . . the duty of every Communist will be to fight it with all his strength' (Hindley 1964, p. 287). While the PKI generally supported Sukarno, it was not uncritical of him. It expressed 'extreme regret' over the dissolution of the DPR in March 1960 and was openly in favour of new general elections, from which it believed it would do well (Hindley 1964, pp. 287–8). As with other communist organisations, the PKI grew by appealing to popular sentiment regarding issues of economic equality, especially among the *abangan* Javanese, and through 'front' organisations of special interest groups.

Acknowledging the growth of the PKI during this period, Sukarno endorsed socialist and later communist ideologies for their economic egalitarianism, their potential to act as an organising principle for revolution (which Sukarno viewed as ongoing), and their contribution to social development. The ideologies of the Left also enabled Indonesia to more closely identify with a number of other post-colonial states. Along with his support of nationalism and religious practice, Sukarno coined the term *Nasakom*, incorporating and syncretising the 'ideals' of *nasionalisme, agama*, and *komunisme* (nationalism, religion, and communism). It was, in practice, a grab-bag of political ideas. In 1964, towards the end of Sukarno's tenure, Clifford Geertz, quoting Lamartine, identified this political eclecticism as a jumbled catalogue, an unfinished revolution that no one knew how to complete (Geertz 1993, pp. 221–2). In such a confused political context, with already low levels of economic development and little infrastructure within a rapidly declining economy, it is not surprising that Indonesia under Sukarno was politically unstable.

As Indonesia's economy declined and its political structure became more untenable, Sukarno increasingly adopted the forms and symbols of traditional Java. A. R. Willner identified Sukarno's style as similar to that of traditional Javanese rulers: claiming titles and deeds not directly earned, avoiding direct political criticism, arbitrating conflicts, and balancing factions. Like his successor, Sukarno manipulated, negotiated and bargained, bestowed and withdrew approval and appointments, and pre-empted the probable responses of his supporters and of other leaders and contenders for power. And there was, significantly, an 'absence of concrete and specific provisions for succession, which served to heighten the jockeying among contenders for his favor' (Willner 1970, p. 249).

By 1965, the government under Sukarno had almost completely lost control of the economy. In that year, the general rate of inflation had reached 500 per cent, and the price of rice, which was in short supply, had risen by 900 per cent. The budget deficit had risen to 300 per cent of government revenues, and if foreign debt repayments for 1966 were to be made on schedule, they would have amounted to almost the total of the nation's export income (Crouch 1988a, p. 204). Then Sukarno's health appeared to begin to fail. With the process of succession left unresolved, the country's two biggest political players, ABRI and the PKI, viewed each other with increasing suspicion. A showdown appeared increasingly inevitable.

4

THE NEW ORDER SEIZES POWER

The events of 30 September and 1 October 1965

The style of the present government, and perhaps the government to follow it, was largely predicated on its method of achieving power. On 30 September 1965, at the height of chaos under what was to become termed the 'Old Order' government of Sukarno, the Indonesian Communist Party (PKI) allegedly attempted to stage a coup in which six senior generals were killed. The alleged coup attempt was put down by forces still 'loyal' to the formal military hierarchy under the command of General Suharto. Over the next several months, being caught both unprepared and unarmed, the PKI was crushed by the army, with 300 000–400 000 members, suspected sympathisers, and victims of long standing local feuds being killed. Some have estimated that up to a million and a half political deaths occurred over the period 1965–70 (Defence of Democracy Groups 1985, p. 4). The crushing of the PKI, and the consequent assumption of authority in 1966 and ousting of Sukarno from the presidency in 1967, ushered in the New Order government of Suharto, formally proclaimed in 1968.

The practicalities of the shift from Sukarno to Suharto were thus reasonably straightforward. But there is considerable disquiet about the motives and internal manoeuvres involved in the events. The view popularised by the New Order government is that the affair was a PKI plot against the government. According to this official view, the killing of the generals was the result of an 'attempted coup' that failed to win popular support and was subsequently put down by loyalist forces. The PKI might have been involved, but the scenario that it was primarily a PKI-planned event seems unlikely and makes more sense as a rationalisation for the massacres that followed, as well as for the army's final demolition of its old enemy, the PKI. It is also useful to note that the most practical method of determining who has successfully staged a coup is to look at who has achieved office as a consequence of the events in question.

What is known about the 'coup' or 'attempted coup' (as it is popularly although incorrectly called) is that a middle level officer, Lt Colonel Untung, led a small group of soldiers and air force personnel and, on the night of 30 September 1965, kidnapped six of the Indonesian army's leading generals, killing three in the process. Kidnapping senior figures to persuade them to a different course of action and then releasing them was not uncommon during the revolutionary period, and that might have been the Untung group's original intention. But the resistance of the three generals, which led to their deaths, reconfigured that plan, leaving Untung and his group with few options.

The dead and surviving generals were taken to the Halim air force base, just south-east of Jakarta, where the remaining three were killed and their bodies dumped in a well. One general, Abdul Haris Nasution, escaped his abductors, although his daughter was shot in the process of his attempted abduction and one of his aides, a lieutenant, was captured and killed with the generals. The army maintained, at the time, that the bodies of the officers had been mutilated, which has been said to have further inspired the consequent feverish violence. But these claims are not supported by photographs of the bodies on display at the ABRI museum at Bukit Tinggi in West Sumatra. Although taken from a distance, the photographs do not indicate that the bodies had been mutilated, and certainly not in the manner in which they were said to have been (such as having the eyes and genitals cut out). Considering the Javanese Muslim respect for the dead, these stories of mutilation created a sense of public outrage over and beyond that of the murder of the generals. However, like much of the official version of events—which does not necessarily correspond to anything resembling provable fact—such stories appear to have been designed with a particular political purpose in mind. One such story, which has never been established and which serious historians rarely mention, is that at the time the PKI was about to receive shipments of arms from China in order to create an independent 'people's' military force. The PKI was close to China, as was Sukarno, and there was discussion about the establishment of a PKI-based 'fifth force'. However, this does not imply the establishment of a militia intended to challenge or replace the army. Ian MacFarling argues that the PKI's campaign to establish a 'fifth force', which was supported by Sukarno, 'had the potential to reduce the Army's monopoly on weapons and the management of violence in the name of the Republic' (MacFarling 1996, p. 70). It may be that Sukarno and the PKI were moving towards balancing the army's internal security role, but it had certainly not come about by the time of the alleged attempted coup, nor during the period of PKI persecution.

What is known, however, is that tensions between a majority faction of the army and the PKI had reached almost hysterical levels by 1965. The PKI was gaining more and more influence in Sukarno's government, and the armed forces were required to compete with what they had previously considered to be an untrustworthy organisation. Policy differences between the army and the PKI were numerous:

- PKI members claimed they were the true revolutionaries, but the army had played the primary role in the revolution.
- The PKI wanted military training for the civilian population, but the army did not want civilian military training.
- The PKI wanted to rely on 'the people' for political mobilisation, but the army wanted to exercise greater administrative control.
- The PKI was in favour of *Konfrontasi* (Confrontation) with Malaysia, but the army was against it.
- The PKI opposed Western 'imperialism', but the army was more friendly towards the West.
- The PKI wished to give more power to trade unions and peasant organisations, but the army wanted to restrict their influence.
- The PKI looked to communist countries for economic inspiration and self-sufficiency, but the army looked to Western aid.
- The PKI wanted to reduce army representation in the government, but the army wanted to reduce PKI representation in the government.

(Hindley 1964, pp. 286–97)

Apart from their sense of historical hostility, there was almost nothing of substance on which the PKI and the army agreed. Yet as now, the position of the armed forces was not universal, and there were many in the services, particularly in the air force and navy, who were either communists or sympathetic to them. Further, a reduction in the living conditions of lower level soldiers in the period of the *Konfrontasi* with Malaysia from 1963–66 had exacerbated tensions within the army, particularly between lower level soldiers and the senior generals.

It is possible, though not certain, that Untung had the tacit endorsement of at least some senior members of the PKI when he and his co-conspirators decided to abduct the senior generals. But the subsequent announcement of 'revolutionary councils' ahead of elections seems like an *ad hoc* decision rather than a careful plan. For example, almost all those named by Untung as a part of the revolutionary council denied knowledge of the plot, and the PKI —three of whose members were named as being involved in the plot (along with other political parties)—were militarily unprepared for the action. It therefore seems odd that its leaders would commit the party to this move against the generals, although perhaps they were panicked by the developing circumstances.

A more realistic version of events, which does not endorse the 'coup' theory and which was propounded by Untung in a radio broadcast on 1 October 1965, was that some junior pro-Sukarno officers moved against the generals as the generals were planning their own coup against President Sukarno. In August 1965 Sukarno had fallen sick, raising the spectre of his death and the ensuing competition between the PKI and the army for control of the presidency. The proposed date for the generals' coup was Armed Forces Day (5 October), when large numbers of troops loyal to the generals would have been in Jakarta. By 1965 Sukarno had moved closer to the PKI, particularly to balance the growing influence and power of the armed forces. The senior leaders of the army had long been deeply hostile towards the PKI, and by this stage, many were only marginally more enamoured of Sukarno. The generals almost certainly had the tacit support of the USA in toppling the militantly non-aligned (and increasingly pro-China) Sukarno and bringing Indonesia into closer contact with the West.

In assessing the events leading up to (and on) the night of 30 September, it is easy to believe that some of the junior officers who supported Untung informed the very top levels of the PKI of the plan, drawing them, as major political players, into it. However, given the PKI's lack of preparation for a 'coup', it seems that only the party's most senior leaders and its 'Special Bureau' (intelligence), which maintained contact with the armed forces, knew of the Untung plan. The PKI most probably decided to go along with the Untung statement—that the abduction of the senior generals was an internal army affair—so that it could benefit if events turned its way but could deny responsibility if they did not.

Did Suharto know?

There is also the persistent view that Suharto himself knew of the Untung/PKI plan to kill the generals (Wertheim n.d.; see also Institut Studi Arus Informasi 1995). Suharto had known Untung well.[1] He also knew another coup leader, Colonel Abdul Latief, who perhaps more than coincidentally visited him when Suharto took his son, Tommy, who had just suffered minor burns, to hospital on the night of 30 September. Suharto was excluded from the inner circle of the army's most senior officers and, indeed, had been at odds with Nasution, but had also had responsibility for executing Sukarno's plan to occupy West Papua (later Irian Jaya) militarily. As such he could well have been considered a potential, if not actual, sympathiser in the plot against the generals. Or, as some have suggested, he could himself have been involved in the plot against the generals. If he did have foreknowledge of the events that were about to transpire, Suharto did nothing to prevent the abduction (and consequently the deaths) of the generals, which in such an extreme context means he was at least nominally in favour of the plan. But it is also possible that he did not know of the plan, which would clear him of being implicated in its execution.

Regardless, Suharto immediately seized power once the plan began to unfold. Of all the top generals seized or almost seized by the plotters in Jakarta that night, Suharto was not among them, though Latief obviously knew where to find Suharto. Major-General Suharto was then head of Kostrad (Army Strategic Reserve Command), which had its headquarters facing Jakarta's Merdeka Square. Troops who were ostensibly loyal to the coup occupied three sides of the square, but the Kostrad headquarters were not blocked. Further, troops from the two battalions that

---

1   Suharto had known Untung in Central Java and in the West New Guinea campaign, and had attended Untung's wedding in 1964.

occupied the square in support of the 'attempted coup', battalions 454 and 530, were under Kostrad and hence Suharto's command. Once returned to 'loyalty', these two battalions were later used to thwart the 'coup' leaders.

It is therefore difficult to prove that Suharto was definitely involved in the affair or that he was its mastermind, as suggested by Wertheim, but it is equally difficult to prove that he was not involved or unaware of the plot against the generals. For every ten scenarios that appear to be conspiracies, nine are usually explainable in terms of accident or fate, although that does still leave a number that are indeed conspiracies. Whether the events of 30 September and its aftermath involved Suharto or not will probably never be known. Those who might have provided an answer to the question of Suharto's involvement or foreknowledge (and, indeed, of who else might have been behind the affair) have since died or been executed (as recently as 1986) (Defence of Democracy Groups 1985; Waddingham 1987; see also Crouch 1988a, pp. 97–134). In any case, the events that unfolded after the night of 30 September are clear enough, and by themselves indicate the lengths to which Suharto would go to secure for himself his country's top position.

After the death of the generals, the movement launched on 30 September briefly appeared to stall, giving Suharto time to rally 'loyal' soldiers, to talk many of the rebellious soldiers at Merdeka Square (including those at least nominally under his command) into laying down their arms, and to eventually launch an attack against Untung's supporters at Halim, to which Sukarno had travelled. It is worth noting the poor logic of the New Order government's claim that the 30 September movement was an 'attempted coup': the abduction was intended to *protect* Sukarno, and he was eventually implicated in the events. One can launch a coup against a government of which one is the head, but one cannot, of course, launch a coup against oneself. Sukarno never called the events an 'attempted coup' or used Suharto's preferred term *Gestapu* (30 September Movement); rather, he referred to them as *Gestok* (the 1 October Movement), thereby being ambiguous about whether he was referring to the Untung group or to the movement launched on 1 October by Suharto.

Some believe that Sukarno knew of the move against the generals beforehand, or that he had approved the move. The leader of the PKI, Aidit, was also at Halim that day, having spent the night there, therefore implicating the PKI in the affair, although he may have been taken there rather than gone of his own accord. Aidit's presence at Halim provided the pretext to unleash the massacre of PKI members, supporters, and others.[2] It is difficult to adequately outline the slaughter, but the killings were so extensive in Java and Bali in particular that rivers were said to be clogged with bodies. No one knows how many people died in the terror of 1965–66, with estimates ranging from 100 000 to over a million, although 300 000–400 000 seems realistic. Not all, or even most, of those killed were communists. Many were suspected communists or sympathisers, members of organisations linked to the PKI, or simply victims of old grudges and score-settling. The United States Central Intelligence Agency described the killings over the period in the following way:

In terms of numbers killed, the anti-PKI massacres in Indonesia rank as one of the worst mass murders of the twentieth century, along with the Soviet purges of the 1930s, the Nazi mass murders during the Second World War, and the Maoist blood-bath of the early 1950s. In this regard, the Indonesian coup is certainly one of the most significant events of the 20th century, far more significant than many other events that have received much greater publicity (CIA, as quoted in Schwartz 1994, p. 20).

The terror of the time has remained with Indonesians old enough to remember it, and it continues to sit, like some horrific night-mare, as a backdrop to contemporary events. No one in Indo-nesian politics wants to disturb this blood-lusting beast, lest it awaken and again consume so many so remorselessly.

The shift of power

In Javanese tradition, the metaphor for the transition of power from Sukarno to Suharto is that of capturing the 'castle' and hence capturing the empire that it controls, along with the charisma of office that is transferred from the previous ruler. By 1965 Sukarno was losing his grip on power, and by effectively putting down the Untung plan Suharto seized practical political

---

2   There are a number of accounts of what happened on 30 September and 1 October 1965 and why, the version here being a synthesis of a few of them. For further accounts, refer to Crouch 1988, pp. 69–157; Anderson & McVey 1971; Wertheim (n.d.), Hindley 1967; Mortimer 1971.

control, first of Jakarta, and then of Central Java and other pro-Untung strongholds (Geertz 1993, pp. 222–3). Sukarno had been widely regarded as a charismatic leader,[3] in the politico-religious Javanese tradition (Anderson 1990, p. 83). However, in the period following 1965–66, Sukarno's charisma rapidly waned, especially as he was increasingly identified with the 'attempted coup' leaders, while that of Suharto rose, if less ostentatiously, as power was transferred.

The political events between 1 October and early the following year were marked by manœuvrings in which Sukarno attempted to shore up his crumbling power base through the Cabinet. He was beset by an increasingly belligerent armed forces leadership, which encouraged public demonstrations and a sense of chaos in Jakarta's streets. Sukarno's attempts to save his position through Cabinet appointments, which included some PKI members, only served to further alienate much of the already hostile military leadership. In practical terms, Sukarno gave almost *carte blanche* to Suharto to 'restore order' in a letter of 11 March 1966, which was referred to as 'Supersemar'. It is widely believed that senior military officers pressured Sukarno into signing the letter of 11 March 1966, while Sukarno believed that by signing the letter he could buy time in which to restore his political fortunes. Quite the opposite was the case. The day after the letter was signed, Suharto formally banned the PKI. Four days later, after Sukarno refused to dismiss Cabinet ministers distrusted by the army leadership, the army arrested them. The signing of the letter by Sukarno marked the effective transition of power from the president to the general. Consequently, the 'charisma' of leadership as it pertained to Sukarno was transferred in accordance with 'the natural order of things', as leadership and then the presidency itself was 'transferred'—or taken[4] (see Weber 1964, p. 366). Sukarno is said to have acknowl-

---

3   Max Weber proposed that charisma (as an idealised type) and economy are mutually incompatible notions, although charisma and acquisition are not. Weber noted that 'the charismatic party leader requires the material means of power. The former in addition requires a brilliant display of his authority to bolster his prestige. What is despised . . . is traditional or rational everyday economising' (1964, p. 362).

4   Again, as Max Weber notes, charismatic authority tends to be routinised: 'It cannot remain stable, but becomes either traditionalised or rationalised, or a combination of both' (1964, p. 364). While Sukarno tended to 'traditionalise' his authority, Suharto's orientation has been towards rationalisation.

edged that Suharto came to exercise effective power, following the tradition of 'one of the older generation who willingly gives up his life to one of the younger generation who reluctantly takes it' (Supomo 1980, pp. 571–2). If that was the case, the acknowledgment was very reluctant, with Sukarno fighting a rearguard action until the last, repeatedly attempting to restore his authority while limiting the rising power of Suharto. There was little in Sukarno's actions that indicated his acceptance of a transfer of power or his willingness to give up his political life. However, the tide of events was against Sukarno and, with much of his power base destroyed or diminished, the remaining days of his period in office were numbered. In formal terms, the struggle for power between Sukarno and Suharto went on for another two years, but from 11 March 1966, and even since late 1965, power had been increasingly with Suharto.

Under the provisions of the letter of 11 March, Suharto used the establishment of the Operations Command to Restore Security and Order (Komando Operasi Pemulihan Keamanan dan Ketertiban, or 'Kopkamtib')[5] as his prime vehicle of control during this period. Kopkamtib not only had authority for tracking down remaining PKI members and sympathisers, but also soon took responsibility for quelling other signs of dissent, including the granting and withdrawal of licences to publish. A parallel body was Special Operations (Operasi Khusus, or 'Opsus'), which was built up by General Ali Murtopo and used for covert operations:

It was primarily a task-oriented covert political 'fix-it' agency with no set structure. First formed in 1962, as an executive agency of General Suharto's Mandala command for the Irian campaign, it also played a key role in the negotiations to end *Konfrontasi* [Sukarno's Confrontation with Malaysia], conducted political lobbying, manipulated elections within political organisations, arranged the outcome of the 'act of free choice' in Irian Jaya in 1969, was a key player in organising the first New Order elections in 1971, and was involved in the Timor dispute—among many other activities (Lowry 1996, p. 71).

---

5 Kopkamtib was formally dismantled in September 1988 in response to international criticism and to lower the profile of the army in internal security. It was replaced by the Body for Coordinating National Stability and Security (Badan Koordinasi Bantuan Pemantapan Stabilitas Nasional), known as Bakorstanas. Bakorstanas works under the same legislative provisions as Kopkamtib.

A more clandestine body, the State Intelligence Coordinating Body (Bakin), was also established in 1967. This was a type of military dominated secret police with responsibility for intelligence assessments and action aimed at the non-military population, such as political parties, dissidents, the Chinese community, and especially those thought to be planning a communist revival. After 1974, intelligence agencies were streamlined and concentrated under General Benny Murdani, then its nominal deputy head. From 1983, when Murdani was appointed commander-in-chief of ABRI, both domestic and military intelligence organisations were further concentrated under Murdani through Bakin. Like Opsus, Bakin was originally constructed as a pro-Suharto organisation and operated in that manner, until Murdani fell out with Suharto, and Bakin, still under Murdani's influence, was effectively dismantled and the intelligence organisations brought under tighter control in the early 1990s.

As an individual within the army, Suharto's initial grip on power was tenuous. While he had headed the army's response to Untung and the PKI, he was a junior member of the army's top echelon, and the few remaining senior officers believed that he should—and would—share power. There were many others who opposed him, but they had to wait for an opportune moment before they could challenge him. Such a moment never came. Although political tensions ran high during this period, no one, including both Sukarno and Suharto, wanted a show-down as the ensuing civil war would have produced no winners but many losers. There was also unease within the army-influenced Mejelis Permusyawaratan Rakyat (People's Consultative Assembly, or MPR) about Suharto's grab for power. But the choices were too stark, and while many had reservations about Suharto, there was no longer any question that Sukarno could return to his position as the country's leader. Within the army, officers and men who remained loyal to Sukarno were ousted or, where they were too well entrenched, were out-manœuvred or mollified until they could be dealt with, usually through retirements, non-military postings, and so on. The air force, a bastion of Sukarno support, was thoroughly purged, while the navy, which was largely loyal to Sukarno, was only slowly brought to heel. In the political manœuvring between late 1965 and March 1967, Suharto and his supporters in the army not only purged the armed forces, but also cleared the civil service of pro-

Sukarno elements. The process of bringing the bureaucracy to heel was partly brought about through the army's political organisation Golkar, originally the organisation of functional groups, which rapidly assumed the status of an institutionalised government party. A provisional session of the MPR, similarly purged of its old PKI and Leftist members, formally stripped Sukarno of the presidency in March 1967, from which time Sukarno was effectively placed under house arrest until his death in 1970. Riding a wave of anti-Sukarno sentiment (which was at least partly engineered) and his own growing authority, Suharto was named as acting president with the deposing of Sukarno, and was formally endorsed by the MPR as president in 1968.

Early opposition to Suharto

In the early years, there was much popular support for Suharto's initial commitment to law and order, which had been regarded as missing under Sukarno's Old Order government. But the legal system he inherited from Sukarno was developed by the Dutch, who:

simply created a dual system; one law for them, another for us. It was the Dutch who first recognised the principle of *adat*, the observance of regional cultural traditions among Indonesia's diverse societies. The legal system they created, with its emphasis on separateness, inequality and strong central control, passed more or less unchanged into the hands of the newly independent Indonesian government (Vatikiotis 1993, p. 55).

Not only did the legal system escape reform, but the promise of the rule of law in Indonesia was also dishonoured (Hadad 1989, p. 48). According to Michael Vatikiotis, 'The legal system itself is now considered the area most in need of urgent reform':

Under the New Order, attempts have been made to improve judicial procedure and the criminal code, but old attitudes and most of the old Dutch statutes on which the law is based, remain entrenched. The fact that the Dutch laws were designed by the colonial authorities to enhance administrative power and control has perpetuated their usefulness. Use of Dutch precedents has by all accounts increased under the New Order (Vatikiotis 1993, pp. 48–9).

This failure to address law-reform issues and to apply the rule of law in a consistent manner, as promised by Suharto (Vatikiotis 1993, p. 6; see also Hadad 1989; Schwartz 1994, pp. 247–63), fuelled discontent with the New Order government.

In seizing, maintaining, and building on power, Suharto demonstrated in this formative period the political wiliness for which he would later become famous. Suharto managed to stay one step ahead of his military colleagues and foes alike, and thus increased his grip on real political authority. From the outset there were those in the army who were concerned with Suharto's style, and in particular his personal domination of the political process. But Suharto quickly moved to marginalise or oust his opponents, both real and perceived, and increasingly consolidated his position as an exemplary, and in some senses more traditional, successor to Sukarno's 'traditional Javanese king'.

Indonesia's political elite plays a shadowy power game as a consequence of the suppression of open politics and the high stakes associated with change (Vatikiotis 1993, pp. 92–8, 103–5). Consequently, the New Order government, both institutionally and as individuals, tends to overstate the influence of tradition in the state's political composition (Vatikiotis 1993, p. 97), following Sukarno's grand reinvention of such tradition (Anderson 1990, p. 83). The reinvention of 'tradition'—effectively a precedence—helps to legitimise such 'palace politics,' which may in fact be motivated by contemporary considerations. This awareness of contemporary considerations, played out through sometimes Byzantine political manœuvrings against a back-drop of partly real and partly reconstructed traditional political history, has been the hallmark of the Indonesian government since Suharto came to power. Economic development and official corruption, public pronouncements and secrecy, and favour and repression have been dichotomies that have captured the attention of the country's elites as well as the broader population, particularly since the last years of the 1960s. These were overlaid by a commitment to 'consensus', in which the whole Indonesian 'family' would work together for mutual benefit and dissenters would be dealt with harshly.

Following the political showdown of 1965–66, the idea of consensus was given a new lease of political life. Yet it was, and remains, a polarised consensus. Indonesian (Javanese) politics is—or is held to be—an 'either–or' system; for example, it was posited that in 1965–66 the options were *either* Suharto *or* communism. This either–or political style, of course, has not allowed for a plurality of political views, and has maintained an official political monoculture, having captured 'the castle and the whole empire'.

With everything at stake, politics took on 'a kind of sacralized bitterness' (Geertz 1993, p. 167). Yet within a few years, despite the new 'consensus' and perhaps because of such 'sacralized bitterness', there were sporadic protests at the somewhat heavy handed and increasingly personalised New Order style of government. Tradition was being wheeled out to justify the New Order government's style:

Suharto's embodiment of Javanese culture, with its emphasis on respect for individuals who hold power, hindered the development of modern executive and bureaucratic branches of government answerable to elected representatives as broadly envisaged by the Constitution. The personalization of power Suharto achieved at the expense of institutionalized checks and balances, or any formal separation of powers, made the process of transferring that power to another individual an uncertain and risky prospect (Vatikiotis 1993, p. 147).

Suharto embodies everything that is known or understood about the contemporary Indonesian political system. So it had been with Sukarno, under whom the armed forces claimed to be the only institution with the organisational skill required to run the country. Once this was decided, any opposition to the idea was treated as fundamental opposition to the state and was thus classed as an 'enemy'. In this respect, Suharto followed the precedent established by Sukarno, continuing with Guided Democracy and a reinterpretation of Central Javanese political tradition, with all power being centred on the person of the king. To maintain Indonesia's new 'consensus', not only were the PKI and affiliated or suspected sympathetic organisations banned, but the New Order government also explicitly rejected liberalism and severely curtailed any aspirations for a participatory, representative democratic process. This was in large part based on the armed forces' view that 'anyone with a dissenting view became a suspect Communist or Muslim radical bent on the destruction of the state' (Vatikiotis 1993, p. 14).

According to Robert Lowry, who is a graduate of the Indonesian Army Command and Staff College at Bandung:

Because the regime is underpinned by force rather than by political consensus and compromise, the regular Army is at least twice as big as it needs to be given the regional security situation. At least 100 000 of the approximately 150 000 men employed in the territorial structure could be replaced by reserves or militiamen if the external threat were the only consideration. (Lowry 1996, p. 219)

As Suharto has consolidated his rule, he has increasingly appeared to adopt a putatively traditional Javanese kingly role. In some respects, this also follows his predecessor and, in this sense at least, can be seen to have a precedent, even though the precedent is very much a reinvention of a peculiarly Javanese tradition. To suggest a parallel with the style of Suharto's rule, it is as though the president of France had reconstructed a version of French royalty from the period before the revolution and had presumed to designate himself king.

The party system

In 1973, Suharto abolished the plethora of small political parties and created two new parties: the PPP, which comprises former Islamic parties, and the PDI, which comprises the two small Christian and other nationalist parties. Golkar, which is in effect the party of government, is not formally considered a party, although it operates as one.

In the 'elections' held since 1971, Golkar has won between 62 and 73 per cent of the vote. The PPP (or its predecessors in 1971) had achieved up to almost a third of votes, but its political strength was severely diminished when the NU pulled out in 1987 and its vote plummeted to 16 per cent. The PDI (or its predecessors in 1971) achieved a low of 8 per cent in 1982, but a high of 15 per cent in 1992, and looked to be gathering strength before its was split by government intervention in 1996, ahead of the 1997 election. An unofficial student group, known as the White Group (Golongan Putih, or 'Golput'), was established to encourage people not to vote or to lodge blank ballot papers. It has claimed support of between 8 and 10.5 per cent of the potential voting population since 1971.

Not surprisingly, there have also been numerous reports of voting irregularities, including more votes being cast than there are voters, a total vote strongly favouring Golkar being fully counted in Sulawesi even when counting in Jakarta had barely started, and ballot boxes being interfered with. Also, with some electorates broken down into voting stations of as few as 200 voters, officials are easily able to identify the general voting tendencies of those stations. With some stations located in factories or offices, senior officials can be pressured to ensure a strong vote in favour of Golkar.

Golkar has a number of advantages over its two 'rival' parties, in that all senior government employees must belong to Golkar and are, as a consequence, expected to vote for it. Further, a directive issued by the home affairs minister, Rudini, in 1992 explicitly stated that government employees must ask the permission of their superiors to vote for a party other than Golkar. At a local level, Golkar enjoys the support of regional administrators, village chiefs, and so on, who can be relied upon to ensure that voting favours Golkar. Close monitoring of political sympathies is standard practice.

As Golkar is not formally a party, it can conduct its affairs as it suits itself. However, as the PPP and PDI are formally political parties, they are restricted regarding when they can conduct meetings and may not campaign outside the election period. Further, the PPP and especially the PDI have been deeply influenced by government and ABRI agents, to the extent that the PDI 'pro-democracy' push of the early to mid-1990s in effect reflected the political aspirations of a significant faction of ABRI.[6] The ousting in 1996 of the PDI's leader, Megawati Sukarnoputri, by a government-supported rebel PDI congress reflected both the perception within sections of ABRI that she had gained too much popular support and Suharto's wish to see a potential competitor deposed.

As to the conduct of election campaigns, neither party is allowed to directly criticise the government or its policies; no campaigning is allowed in villages (where most people live), and government permission must be obtained for all rallies, among other restrictions. Anyone found to have violated election rules is liable to be charged with subversion, which potentially carries the death penalty. To further frustrate opposition efforts to effectively challenge Suharto, the electoral process, which is already heavily weighted in favour of the status quo, is not open to scrutiny. Just before the 1997 elections, the government announced that no group or individuals would be allowed to monitor the electoral process. And the day before the election, officials announced that representatives of the PPP and PDI would not be allowed to have

---

6   The 'pro-democracy movement' can be divided into a number of different groups and tendencies. At one end it genuinely strives for participatory democracy and, at the other, uses the term 'democracy' to mean other things, such as ending corruption, or as a means of asserting another, not necessarily democratic, political agenda.

access to the computerised election results database, 'fuelling speculation that the results might be manipulated. The United Development Party said it had evidence the Government plans to rig the polls' (Williams 1997a). Golkar came out of the elections with a record 74.3 per cent of the vote. The PPP scored 22.65 per cent, and the PDI was virtually wiped out with just over 3 per cent of the vote (*Kompas*, 1 June 1997, p. 1). This meant that, in the post-1997 DPR, Golkar held 322 seats, the PPP 82 seats, and the PDI just 10 seats. Amid allegations by PPP supporters of vote-rigging, for the first time ever the government agreed to recount votes at some polling stations on the island of Madura.

In structural terms, Indonesia has a political system in which the executive is independent of the legislature. The legislature itself also comprises half of the electoral assembly, which chooses the president and vice-president on a five-yearly basis. Indonesia's legislative assembly, the Dewan Perwakilan Rakyat (DPR, often incorrectly referred to in English as a 'parliament', despite its having no effective legislative function) has 500 members. It is divided into committees and oversees the work of government. Of the 500 positions, seventy-five (reduced from 100) positions are reserved for ABRI members, ranking from colonel to major-general. ABRI representatives are also appointed to 15 per cent of positions of all provincial and local governments. To counter this, members of ABRI are not allowed to participate in the voting process. However, the level of representation afforded them in the DPR (and other assemblies) far outweighs their actual numbers of about 300 000.[7] While the DPR is, in theory at least, the body that oversees the functioning of government, the 1945 Constitution ensures that 'All power and responsibility [is] in the hands of the president'. To this end, Suharto appoints his own Cabinet, makes his own decrees, and within the often flexible limits imposed by balancing factions and influences, runs Indonesia, if not singlehandedly then at least as the preserve of a patron-king.

Beyond the DPR, the political structure that formally supports Suharto and the New Order government relies for its legitimacy on the will of the MPR, which has 1000 members and is, in

---

7 The army comprised about 240 000 personnel in 1997, the air force about 20 000, and the navy about 44 000. These figures do not include about 185 000 police, who are technically also part of ABRI.

theory, Indonesia's highest sovereign body. It is the MPR that elects the president every five years and approves broad outlines of state policy, although it only acts as a rubber stamp. Members of the DPR have representation as members of the MPR. The president also directly appoints 100 members of the MPR (formerly one-third), while about half the assembly is comprised of members of the bureaucracy (and therefore Golkar members), ABRI, and other social organisations. Only 40 per cent of the MPR is actually openly elected. Even then—given the provisions of the Indonesian electoral system, in which Golkar is assured a majority of around two-thirds or more of the total vote, and the restrictions that apply even to MPR members who criticise the president or his government's policies—the president commands a very large and secure majority within the MPR. The MPR is, in effect, beholden to the president.

It is not surprising, then, that the MPR chose the president based on 'consensus' rather than an actual vote. Such consensus was usually reached well before the MPR actually met and was reflected in public calls for the reinstatement of Suharto by the various groups that comprise the MPR. These groups are either direct Suharto supporters or are manipulated into giving him their support well in advance of any meeting of the MPR.

However, despite Suharto's firm grip on the presidency and the process of presidential 'election', he faced challenges, most notably over the appointment of the vice-president. In the 1988 'election', ABRI opposed the election of Sudharmono as Suharto's vice-president. As State Secretary, Sudharmono had helped to engineer the decline of ABRI's influence over the bureaucracy, and in financial terms, he had ensured that all tenders and contracts valued at over Rp200 million were passed through his office. As Golkar chairperson between 1983 and 1988, Sudharmono also reduced ABRI's grip on power by cultivating civilian politicians. In 1988, the then ABRI commander-in-chief, General Benny Murdani, was sacked as a consequence of his suggestion that Suharto rein in his children's business interests and because of his pointed opposition to Sudharmono as vice-president. He was given the less powerful position of defence minister. Murdani continued to exercise considerable political power as defence minister, but his overall authority was diminished by the move. ABRI vehemently opposed Sudharmono's appointment in the

MPR, but lost the battle. Along with the gradual removal of senior ABRI officers from senior ministerial posts,[8] this had the effect of finally splitting Suharto's close links with ABRI. Suharto's diminishing links with ABRI could be ascribed to a 'generational' change, as older soldiers retired. However, they were not replaced by younger officers, and the role of ABRI in government was increasingly questioned from this time. In 1993 ABRI got its own back by having ABRI commander-in-chief Try Sutrisno elected as vice-president against Suharto's wishes, with Suharto then favouring Habibie (who was to become vice-president in 1998). In turn, Suharto moved to reduce ABRI's influence in Golkar. Although it had been started by ABRI, Golkar was increasingly seen as the president's personal political organisation, without the support of which he would have serious difficulty in maintaining the presidency. Suharto also moved to assuage the earlier concerns of Muslims about his leadership and to court their vote as a means of balancing the influence of ABRI.

Suharto's political strengths

In terms of the security of his position, Suharto's political strength lay in a number of related areas. He had effective control over Golkar, which in turn tightly controls the bureaucracy and is able to deliver a large and consistent number of votes. As supreme commander of ABRI, Suharto also appointed those officers he trusted most to senior positions, while shuffling off others to retirement or less influential posts. And he moved senior regional officers around, to ensure that they did not establish a strong base of loyalty among the troops, which could be later used to challenge him directly. Finally, an important element in any equation concerning Indonesia's politics is the issue of its economy. In simple terms, Suharto is personally so rich that he can direct or influence a significant proportion of Indonesia's economy, a position that is bolstered by the holdings of his children and other family members. The Suharto financial clique, which includes his close business associates, dominates the Indonesian economy, and through the funding of projects and businesses, this gave him enormous gravity in both the formal and informal political

---

8   No serving officer had been appointed to a senior ministerial post since 1980.

processes. As far as international capital is concerned, the fortunes of foreign investors, and even foreign banks and aid donors, have fluctuated depending on whether 'nationalists' or 'free marketeers' are at the helm of the economy, and that, in turn, usually depended on the prevailing health of the economy. Suharto sat at Indonesia's political and economic core, as did traditional Javanese kings.

The perception that Suharto increasingly saw himself in this light is born out by a number of his characteristics. These include the fact that, like Central Javanese sultans and maharajahs, he adopted a calm and inwardly reflective pose, rarely revealing his thoughts or feelings and always keeping his minions guessing. It is claimed that this represents the *halus* (smooth, refined) characteristics that both accompany power and are the mark of a noble Javanese. His apologists suggest that Suharto's accumulation of wealth was, in a related fashion, simply a by-product of his authority, and that, like the Javanese conception of power itself (*kasekten*), it neither has nor requires a moral basis. The granting of favours and patronage by Suharto was also in the traditional mould, as was the appointment of lackeys and sycophants rather than independently capable ministers to his Cabinet, most notably in early 1998. Suharto's children are like princes and princesses, each wielding considerable power as a consequence of their relationship to their father (with perhaps Tommy Suharto being the most conspicuous about it). Between them, they accrued economic benefit on a scale that would have made the late Philippines dictator Ferdinand Marcos blush.[9] The political process in Indonesia is also conducted in a manner reminiscent of the ancient *kratons*: Suharto's minions vied with each other for his favour, schemed and plotted against each other, and regarded him as, in effect, omnipotent. Those who opposed Suharto, or who even questioned some of his less acceptable financial practices within a modern economic context, soon found themselves out of favour. In the traditional balancing act of Javanese leaders, Suharto managed these competing tensions by playing off his juniors one against the other, giving contradictory and often discreet orders or advice, ensuring they were always divided.

---

9   If this analogy was valid when first used in the *Sydney Morning Herald* in 1986, it has only grown subsequently.

On a more personal level, Suharto was a village boy from Central Java who was passed between relatives and lived in considerable poverty (McIntyre 1996, pp. 8–10). This may have given rise to what has been regarded by some as an excessive desire for personal wealth, and to the closeness, tolerance, and indulgence with which he regards his children. Suharto is undoubtedly intelligent (McIntyre 1996, p. 16), even wily, and takes pride in his mental capabilities. As a child, he was also influenced by a local *dukun* (mystical practitioner) and came to value highly his knowledge of Javanese mysticism (Suharto 1989, pp. 441–2). Rising from such humble and traditional beginnings, Suharto is likely to have regarded himself as one marked for greatness, and to have concluded that assuming the leadership of his country was in keeping with an especially preordained state of affairs.

But the forces arrayed against Suharto were increasingly dangerous, from those who could potentially topple him or his successor through their control of large sections of the armed forces to those who simply do not accept the reconstruction of the allegedly traditional palace as a legitimate political concept. Even in traditional Javanese terms, the king is vulnerable to being toppled, his removal indicating his own loss of power in relation to his enemies. In order to lose power, the king must behave in a way that is wasteful, indulgent, or otherwise out of keeping with his *halus* form. Suharto was rarely given to outbursts, but increasingly his indulgence of his cronies, in particular non-*pribumi* (non-ethnic Indonesian) cronies, and his children is seen to have been his undoing. Had he indulged only himself, he might well have been allowed to get away with it and perhaps even to appoint his own successor with some certainty.

5

STATE-BUILDING, BLACK GOLD, AND ECONOMIC ACHIEVEMENT

If Suharto's new presidency and the New Order government were to survive in the long term, Suharto realised that he would have to placate the senior generals and, unlike his predecessor, provide an economic basis for Indonesia's future. Suharto's plan was twofold, although he later varied it depending on the prevailing circumstances. In the first instance, he would move to establish an economic environment that would be attractive to foreign capital, which in turn, it was hoped, would resuscitate Indonesia's collapsed economy. In the second instance, Suharto would ensure that his senior supporters were well looked after. But it was the unplanned and unexpected oil boom, which resulted from the rapid rise in world oil prices in the early 1970s, that cemented the success of Suharto's early years. While there were problems at home, the inflow of wealth from oil ensured that, by the time the boom ended, he would be firmly entrenched in power.

This chapter looks at the economic direction of the New Order government and considers the role of economic development in cementing the structures of state. In particular, it considers the competing influences of a more conventional free-market economic program and that of 'nationalism', which combines concern for national economic integrity with a marked tendency towards individual and institutional corruption. It is also intended to show how these issues are basic to Indonesia's political processes.

Buying support
From its first days, the New Order government instituted a number of policies to attract foreign investors, as well as to entice domestic investors to rejoin the market. The first move, in 1966,

was to invite the International Monetary Fund (IMF), banned by Sukarno, back into the country and to bring in a World Bank mission soon after. The end result was credits from donor countries amounting to US$300 million with which to help 'kick start' the country's ailing economy, and a further US$200 million the following year. Suharto had managed to reschedule old debts, tap into foreign supplies of rice and clothing—both of which were in short supply—and to obtain new pledges for credit. As foreign aid continued to flow into Indonesia over the next few years, foreign creditors pressed for more accountability and specific program aid and for less discretionary spending, such as for bureaucratic salaries.

In 1967 Suharto turned his attention directly towards private investors, sponsoring meetings and summits for both investors and the media in which representatives of the Indonesian government outlined new strategies to make Indonesia a more favourable place to invest, especially for long-term investments. Tax holidays were created and expanded, and licences and leases had their life span extended (with indications that they would become indefinite). And after the nationalisation of Dutch industries in 1957, which precipitated the worst phase of Indonesia's economic decline, there was a strong hint that no foreign-owned companies would ever be nationalised. However, official corruption, which had been a significant feature of Indonesia's economic landscape since the first days of the Republic, remained institutionalised. This institutionalised corruption was enhanced by a complicated bureaucracy, through which one could only navigate by the payment of bribes. It was not until 1978 that Indonesia offered foreign investors a 'one-stop' investment service, thereby limiting both the time-consuming bureaucratic procedure as well as the multiple points at which unofficial 'taxes' had to be paid. However, official bribery remained intact until the mid-1990s and was still common thereafter.

Suharto's own economic knowledge was limited, and the economic changes that were undertaken during this period were greatly influenced by a group of American-trained or influenced Indonesian economists who have been referred to as the 'Berkeley Group'. Only a handful of Indonesian economists at this time had graduated from that campus of the University of California,[1] but

---

1   The Indonesian economists who did graduate from Berkeley mostly did so in the late 1950s and 1960s.

the pro-business, technocratic economic development model that was prevalent at that time in the USA did directly shape their thinking. A primary policy goal of the Berkeley Group, headed by Professor Widjojo Nitisastro, who ran BAPPENAS (Baden Perencanaan Pembangunan Nasional, or the National Development Planning Board), was to attract foreign capital to Indonesia and, from 1969, to institute twenty-five orderly years of accelerated modernisation based on a series of five-year plans (Winters 1996, p. 75; Cribb & Brown 1995, p. 115).

The influence of the Berkeley Group was to last, in one form or another, until the late 1980s, when Johannes Sumarlin was finance minister.[2] However, as much as politics is driven by economics, it also reflects ideological considerations, and when it suited Suharto to switch his economic focus from conventional economic considerations to building his power base, he did so without hesitation.

At about the time that the New Order was consolidating itself, a number of senior ABRI officers began to see the potential for their own financial enhancement. Having operated in a semi-independent financial manner first during the revolution and then under Sukarno, through both private and army-run businesses, many generals saw no problem in seeking independent sources of income. However, when some senior officers started showing up in creditor countries seeking 'assistance' from which they could personally benefit, often by way of a percentage of the total aid package, creditors became increasingly wary. But the generals continued to expect a share of the profits, and they were soon to receive it from a different source.

In a political system in which patronage is not only widespread but expected, Suharto needed to be able to tap into a source of funds that was not directly tied to prying foreign donors or investors. In 1968, he turned to General Ibnu Sutowo, who was in charge of the state-owned oil company Pertamina. In 1958, in a campaign against corruption, General Nasution had suspended Sutowo (then a colonel) from the general staff. In the same campaign, a year later, Suharto (also then a colonel) was transferred

---

2   Sumarlin was named 'finance minister of the year' in 1989 by the magazine *Euromoney*, an honour that came after what was probably the high point of both his career and his influence.

from his post as Central Java commander.[3] The two had much in common, not the least of which was an interest in personal profit-taking. In order to finance projects ranging from education to industry development, which were thought necessary or expedient, and to ensure there was cash on hand to reward his supporters, Suharto received funding from Sutowo. In exchange, Sutowo was given almost entirely free reign over Pertamina, which was easily the country's largest source of foreign income and which operated in a manner that was effectively independent of official government policy.

Sutowo's primary method of raising funds was to borrow against the value of Pertamina, which was outside the existing government borrowing regime. This effectively raised the debt of the state well beyond levels regarded as acceptable by economists both in Indonesia and in aid-donor countries. But treating the company as his personal fiefdom, Sutowo limited the amount of information that was available about Pertamina's financial status, and creditors were left with an ambiguous, sometimes misleading, economic picture. The effect of this process of unofficial fund-raising was that Indonesia ended up running a 'two track' economic system. This dual economy deeply concerned Indonesia's economic ministers, but as the system suited his political and personal purposes, Suharto feigned ignorance and avoided action (Winters 1996, p. 84).

By 1972 the rogue economic policy of Pertamina was of such concern that, in support of IMF attempts to curtail the organisation's borrowings, the USA suspended eligibility for program loans. In 1973 the IMF urged Indonesia's other creditors to take steps to have Pertamina's borrowings limited. With this support, the economics ministers of the Indonesian government began to make some headway towards reining in Sutowo's borrowings through Pertamina. In May 1973 Suharto finally relented to pressure from the IMF, the USA, and his own economic ministers by agreeing to have Pertamina's borrowings limited to the short-term in order to cap overall borrowing, but to allow working capital to

---

3   Suharto had previously been divisional finance officer and chief supplier. The divisional finance officer at the time of Suharto's transfer was Sudjono Humardhani, who later rose to become a leading 'financial general' and one of Suharto's top 'fix-it' men during the early years of the New Order.

be made available (Winters 1996, p. 89). With long-term borrowing no longer available, Pertamina's debt became unsustainable.

Within three years, Pertamina's short-term debt escalated from US$140 million to over US$1000 million as Sutowo attempted to roll over debts from the long term into the short term. By May 1975 Pertamina's short- and long-term debt was US$3 billion, which was over twice the country's foreign currency reserves. The roll-over strategy came to an abrupt halt in early 1975 as Pertamina began to default on loan repayments. This flowed over into the conventional economy, with built-in cross-over provisions meaning that, should the Indonesian government not guarantee Pertamina's debts, it would default on its own borrowings and all debts would have to be repaid in full. Sutowo was effectively put out of business and formally sacked from his job by Suharto in 1976.[4] When Pertamina finally collapsed, it had over US$10 billion worth of debts (Mackie & MacIntyre 1994, p. 14; Hill 1994, p. 69). The political fallout was significant, but by then the unexpected income from the first surge in world oil prices, soon to quadruple the price of oil, had begun to come in. Indonesia's overall economy became buoyant, providing Suharto with yet another method of ensuring development and increasing his system of patronage. With the oil-price boom, a new phase in Indonesia's economy under the New Order government had begun. As an epilogue to this period, Sutowo was later made chairperson of the Indonesian Red Cross, by the 1990s owned a string of companies, including the Jakarta Hilton hotel and a family bank, and was said to still bring some influence to bear on his former patron, the president.

A shift in policy

With the new revenue from oil, many Indonesians, including Suharto, felt they could be less reliant on foreign investment and could afford to take a more nationalistic approach to economic development. Economic policies subsequently became more restrictive, opening the way for an elite group of business people, or

---

4   Sutowo's taste for corruption continued, however. In 1976 he was to have received a third of US$80 million to be withdrawn from two banks in Singapore by the widow of a senior Pertamina official. He had deposited the money, which came from bribes from two German firms awarded huge government contracts (Schwartz 1994, p. 138).

business people with close links to Suharto, to expand their business interests. As Suharto consolidated his political power, through reordering the economy and through his system of patronage, both resentment and concern began to grow among a number of his former supporters.

The early phase of this resentment first manifested itself in riots in Jakarta in 1974, which coincided with a visit by the Japanese prime minister, Kakuei Tanaka. The outward purpose of the riots was to oppose excessive Japanese investment, and they gave considerable impetus to what were becoming stricter foreign investment laws. The rioting soon developed an anti-Chinese sentiment, reflecting the long-standing concern of ethnically indigenous Indonesians (referred to as *pribumi*) about what was perceived to be an excessively firm ethnic Chinese grip on the domestic economy. In particular, a small group of ethnic Chinese financiers and other intermediaries had provided funds and supplies to ABRI in return for political favours, and corruption and profiteering were rampant. However, the so-called *Malari* (*Malapetaka Januri*, or January Disaster) riots also, more broadly, reflected growing political tensions within ABRI and a power struggle between senior officers. In particular, these officers included Kopkamtib commander General Sumitro and much of the hierarchy, led by Suharto, dominated by Ali Murtopo, and including military financier Sudjono Humardhani (Robison 1986, pp. 164–5). So what was, on the surface, a protest against a particular economic style, which seemed to include elements of an anti-corruption campaign, was perhaps also motivated by political manoeuvring among the country's elite. Complicated and often secret agendas are hidden behind what superficially appear to be economic or otherwise straightforward issues. Such agendas reflect 'palace politics' and have historically played a part in Indonesian politics from the first years of the state to the present time —and, no doubt, will continue to into the future.

The Pertamina scandal had rocked the government, and Suharto was said to be shaken by the turn of events. At another level, however, its impact was relatively limited, especially in so far as it did not significantly affect broader economic policy. At this time, the Berkeley Group of economists might have been able to use the example of the Pertamina fiasco to press their case for macro- and microeconomic reform, by scaling back Indonesia's less efficient industries and supporting more productive sectors, for example. However, government-backed enterprises in particular continued to receive official and often quite costly support. In large part, this support for less productive state enterprises was backed by a widely held view that they acted as a counterbalance, in favour of the *pribumi*, to ethnic Chinese economic power. This view reflected a tension between economic managers and nationalists (and self-aggrandising pseudo-nationalists) that dated back to the 1950s, and which still influences many of Indonesia's economic decisions. The other main feature of the oil price boom of the early 1970s was that Suharto believed that it freed him from having to follow a conventional economic line, and the influence of his economic ministers over state policy slid as a result. With wealth flowing in from oil receipts, Suharto was able to reorder aspects of the economy to suit his preferred system of patronage. Monopolies were granted to family and friends; lucrative government contracts were let on a non-commercial basis as favours, and government officials directed more enterprise.

One prominent example of such government-directed enterprise was the centralised government buying process conducted through the State Secretariat (Sekretariat Negara, or 'Sekneg'), which was controlled by Suharto's ally Sudharmono, rather than through the finance ministries. Sekneg had access to government revenue surpluses generated by oil wealth, as well as its own budget, and was the central agency for buying goods and equipment for the whole of the government. Within this structure, particularly through the freewheeling 'Team 10' group,[5] there was ample room for skimming off a very generous proportion of cream, as contracts were let to favoured companies and individuals, including Suharto's children (Winters 1996, pp. 123–39). A proportion of the funds made available through Team 10 ended up as the *Bantuan Presiden*, Suharto's personal slush fund. Unable to compete in such an unbalanced environment, many harder edged, more competitive enterprises were either forced into a marginal

---

5   Somewhat surprisingly, the idea for Team 10 (an agency within the agency) came from Berkeley-trained Professor Widjoyo Nitisastro, who was head of the National Development Planning Board (Bappenas) from 1967 until 1983, and Minister of State Coordinating Economics, Finance, Industry, and Development from 1973 to 1983. As such, Widjoyo was perhaps the most senior technocrat in the Suharto government at this time.

existence or put out of business altogether. To ensure that companies or individuals that were a part of the patronage system did not feel too slighted if they did not win a contract, a margin was built in to this system of letting tenders in order to pay off losing bidders, so that everyone was 'looked after'. It was not until 1988 that Team 10 was finally wound up and government procurement was shifted away from Sekneg. The generally accepted reason for its late demise was that it was so closely (and profitably) connected directly to the president himself (Winters 1996, pp. 157–60).

While this was going on, the debt accumulated by Pertamina remained in the background. One effect of the US$10 billion Pertamina debt was to tilt the structure of the economy off balance. Between having to meet debt repayments for the Pertamina fiasco and having to pay for new satellite communications, by 1975 Indonesia's foreign reserves had shrunk to dangerously low levels. Added to this was an international recession in 1974–75, inspired by the sudden jump in oil prices, which meant that foreign demand for Indonesia's non-oil exports slumped. Indonesia's finance ministers regained some influence over economic development, in what was shaping up to be a roller coaster ride of influence and economic policy direction. By 1978 Indonesia's economy was dominated by a system of patronage and discretion that exceeded the heights of the Sutowo era. But it was not to last, with the first move towards a shake-out coming with criticism from the World Bank in 1980.

The World Bank drafted a large report on Indonesia's economy, which was the subject of bitter debate between the bank and Indonesian government officials. It was not that the officials disagreed with the report's contents, but that they did not want the report to be seen at all. The report was most unflattering in terms of its analysis of Indonesia's political and economic processes, and the Javanese-influenced government officials regarded this as being most *kasar* (coarse). It was also a genuine embarrassment to the government, and for more practical and less culturally precious reasons the government viewed the report with some dismay and considerable alarm. A draft version of the report was eventually leaked to the *Far Eastern Economic Review*, which described Indonesia as a 'bureaucratic mess', maintaining that its procedures and regulations for business activities were 'counterproductive and lead to corruption' (*Far East Economic Review*, no. 112, 29 May

1981, p. 46). The Indonesian government continued to refuse to accept the report and, with oil revenues still coming in, could effectively afford to do so. Not until the oil price collapses of 1982–83 and 1985–86, and the 'investment crisis' of 1984,[6] did Indonesia's New Order government begin seriously to rethink its economic policy direction and, along with it, the relationships that had developed between members of the country's political, military, and economic elites.

The roller coaster heads down

In some senses, 1986 was a more difficult year than most for Suharto. With the price of oil having dropped to real pre-1973 prices, Indonesia's main source of income had all but dried up, its non-oil economy was a shambles, and the funds for the 'patronage' through which Suharto continued to derive support were becoming increasingly difficult to come by. Suharto's personal 'business methods' were well known among Indonesia's elites and increasingly well known among foreign bankers. However, the publication, on 10 April, of an article by David Jenkins entitled 'After Marcos, Now for the Soeharto Billions' in the *Sydney Morning Herald* gave the issue of Suharto's corruption an international audience. The actual readership of the *Sydney Morning Herald* and the Australian response to the article were limited, but what raised the issue to the international level was Indonesia's strident reactions to the article. The possible reasons for these responses—which came from different quarters and varied in tone, intensity, and effect—reflected, at least in some respects, Indonesia's internal politicking. But the outcome was that the issue was raised in Indonesia during a visit by the then United States vice-president, George Bush, who was there to discuss the slump in world oil prices. And the issue resurfaced again later among the media entourage of the then United States president, Ronald Reagan, as a consequence of two Washington-based Australian journalists being banned from entering Indonesia with

---

6   The term 'investment crisis' reflects the plunge in foreign investment in 1984. However, this followed an unusually high spike in foreign investment the previous year, much of which was not forthcoming when the Indonesian government decided to withdraw offers of 'tax holidays' to foreign investors. In reality, foreign investment levels remained relatively steady, based on early investment patterns, but it did cause concern at the time.

Reagan. Instead of being good publicity for Indonesia, Reagan's visit became a public relations 'disaster' (Branigan 1986) and led to other journalists from some of the world's leading news organisations picking up and running the story. Corruption at the highest levels had become an issue for both foreign creditors and foreign investors, and this aspect of Indonesia's economy increasingly dogged Suharto, both at home and abroad.

As a consequence of the collapse in oil prices from 1983 until 1989, Indonesia's Berkeley Group was able to reassert its influence over economic policy, and the New Order government implemented a number of initiatives aimed at restoring the country's economic health. The most significant aspects of this economic reordering included: the phased but substantial deregulation of the banking industry to increase capital availability for business investment and efficiencies through competition; streamlined tax collection and reduced taxation rates for investors; a tariff rebate on imports intended for export; a significant, phased loosening of trade and investment reform, including lowered import duties and the establishment of a private stock exchange.

Perhaps the most significant changes during this period concerned taxation. Income tax in Indonesia was not levied on the limited earnings of ordinary people, and in particular farmers, which meant that the government did not have access to this otherwise conventional source of revenue. This lack of access to tax-based funds was primarily addressed with the introduction of a value-added tax on goods. The other main area of tax reform was that the roles of tax assessor and collector were separated, so that assessors could no longer come to cosy deals with businesses, by which businesses had saved on some tax by paying graft to the assessors. This new arrangement was enhanced by simplifying what had been extraordinarily complex tax laws, by which assessors could trap tax-payers who were unwilling to pay them a per centum. The other main method of straightening out the economy was by reducing the independence of Pertamina so that it paid tax on something resembling its real income. Nevertheless, while Pertamina might not have been the discretionary slush fund it was in the early 1970s, it still managed to avoid the close scrutiny of Indonesia's Department of Finance, and its affairs continued to be clouded by a high degree of secrecy.

. . . and then up again

By the late 1980s—despite the after-taste of the Pertamina scandal, high and growing levels of corruption, and economic policy that zigzagged between a type of free-market rationalism and crony-oriented profit-taking—foreign investors were looking at Indonesia very closely. The New Order government looked to be securely in control, and foreign investors have always regarded such political stability as desirable. Suharto and the New Order government were also considered to be 'friendly' to the West, which further enhanced Indonesia's foreign financial appeal. Indonesia's appeal as a place to invest was even further improved by the fact that foreign investors could establish businesses in Indonesia—at different times with varying degrees of ease, palm-greasing, and rent-taking through joint ventures—and could, to a large extent, take advantage of the country's natural wealth and large, poor pool of workers. Some businesses did baulk at investing in Indonesia, seeing the country's lack of business rectitude as leading to too many potential problems. But many took a more adventurous approach, especially in light of the cheap labour that was not only available but that, under the country's formalised low-wage structure and regressive labour laws, also appeared secure for the indefinite future.

And finally, Indonesia profited immensely because of its geography. Being located in South-East Asia, Indonesia was almost inevitably in line for at least some of the flow-on effect of the boom in the East Asian economies in the 1980s and 1990s. Japan's economic 'miracle' was not so much a miracle as a rebuilding of its pre-war economic might. It combined the boost afforded by the nearby Korean War with technological knowledge and application, along with an inflow of primarily United States funds and an outflow to a strong, primarily United States market. As Japan moved higher up the technological and price scale, the lower technology industries with which it launched its economic re-birth either moved offshore or were adopted, in the first instance by the former Japanese colonies of South Korea and Taiwan. The British (or formerly British) entrepôt centres of Hong Kong and Singapore also mopped up much of the spillage from Japan's economic growth, as well as benefiting through on-passing trade. Then Thailand and Malaysia moved into the next phase of economic 'take-off', becoming Asia's new 'tiger' economies, while the Philippines struggled to sort itself out both economically and politically in the wake of twenty years of rule and robbery by Ferdinand Marcos. For Indonesia to have missed the flow-on benefits of this type of regional economic development would have taken a wilfully anti-investment oriented government. Because the New Order government was pro-investment, especially from the later 1980s, such investment did begin to flow in, the wealth from which most obviously manifested itself in the high-rise developments that had begun to transform central Jakarta's skyline. The slums at the feet of these skyscrapers, however, indicated that the inflow of investment was being less than evenly spread.

Issues in analysing economic performance

Although economic growth in Indonesia has been inconsistent, the country has, since the first Five Year Development Plan was implemented in 1969, managed to record an average growth rate of about 5 per cent up until 1997 (including the negative growth of 1982) (Hill 1994, pp. 61–2). Average growth rates have been around or just above 7 per cent from 1990 until 1996, rising to 8 per cent by 1996–97, but slumping to near zero in 1997–98 following a collapse of the currency.[7] Inflation had also significantly reduced, until 1998, and the more broad social indicators showed that standards of living had improved since the late 1960s (though they could hardly have failed to rise above what was then such widespread and absolute poverty). Serious inflation of about 20 per cent per month set in from early 1998, hinting at future hyperinflation. Notably, there had been the marked development of a 'middle class', which was primarily identified as the part of the population that could afford to buy motorbikes and own a television set. Depending on definitions, this class could have arguably comprised up to 15 per cent of the population. The middle class was made up mainly of middle-level government bureaucrats, medium-level employees in larger enterprises, and

---

7   The rupiah fell by almost 80 per cent from July to early 1998, following falls in the value of the Thai bhat and other regional currencies and from the effects of drought, widespread forest fires, doubts about Suharto's health, the issue of presidential succession, and Suharto's seeming unwillingness to straighten out the economy.

small business owners. Education levels of this group ranged from the last years of primary school through to university education, with high educational qualifications being achieved especially among the younger ones, who benefited from the expansion of education under the New Order government. As a political group, the 'middle class' was the largest sector of public support for the PDI and was influential in the PPP. However, many, perhaps most, were still encouraged or obliged to support Golkar (especially government workers). The middle class had its income slashed in the economic collapse that started in late 1997.

Nevertheless, while a middle class was emerging in Indonesia, there remained serious questions about income distribution and, in particular, the increasing gap between rich and poor. Before the late 1990s, Indonesia's economy moved ahead at a steady if not spectacular pace (and notably off a low base, which makes gains somewhat easier). But by the Indonesian government's own accounts, there remained at least 20 per cent of the population who lived in absolute poverty (probably more) even before the economic collapse, and even this depends on what criteria are employed to determine 'absolute poverty' and on who does the measuring. For example, is 'absolute poverty' a level at which families cannot afford to have their children attend school through lack of money? Or does it imply a diet that engenders malnutrition? Or is it characterised by death or permanent disability through lack of access to adequate health care? Definitions of absolute poverty vary, and those employed by non-government aid organisations are often very different from the definition employed by the Indonesian government.

Unemployment and underemployment are also chronic. Between them, in mid-1997, they directly affected more than 40 per cent of the population. From late 1997 this rate has been growing rapidly. Where Indonesia's developing secondary industries might have provided the basis of a further political grouping—urban workers—unofficial industrial and political organisation is severely curtailed, with most workers not far from being out of a formal job. This large pool of unemployed and underemployed people waiting for work has also acted as a brake on labour unrest. While some sort of political mobilisation of urban workers could take place, it would most likely only occur if the existing political structure came close to a complete breakdown.

Even more disturbing than the admittedly high levels of unemployment, underemployment, and poverty, the figures provided by the Indonesian government or its representatives on wealth, average income, and income distribution appear to be seriously flawed by internal contradictions. In short, Indonesia's economy progressed until 1997, but perhaps not to the extent claimed by its representatives or those who champion the Indonesian economic (or political) cause. The political riots of 1997 and 1998, which focused on income inequality, corruption, food shortages, and the inability to change or influence the government to redress these problems, gave the lie to the comfortable belief that Indonesia's progress as a 'tiger' economy was proceeding in a manner acceptable to all, even before the economic collapse.

Income inequality, corruption, and an inability to change or influence the government were perhaps most keenly felt with regard to what was perceived to be the gap between Java and the other islands. There was also a question mark over the reliability of many of the statistics offered by the Indonesian government to support its claims of 'development'. Hal Hill noted that, despite what appeared to be strong evidence that there had been a sharp decline in poverty rates, 'Indonesia's equity and poverty record continues to be the subject of vigorous domestic debate' (Hill 1994, p. 106). Hill noted five qualifications to what otherwise appeared to be the conclusion that Indonesia's economic development was being shared. The results, Hill noted, depended on increasingly politicised data, in which there were discrepancies between expenditure and per capita personal consumption. Rural researchers and particularly anthropologists also reported mixed economic results, and there was a concurring divergence of macro and micro data, which in part reflected difficulty in obtaining quantitative time series information. Further, there was no hard data on wealth distribution. The incidence of poverty was also 'sensitive to the measure used. There is no consensus concerning the appropriate definition in Indonesia and elsewhere . . . The most commonly used poverty lines in Indonesia are lower than many other countries'. Finally, Hill said, analysis focused primarily on monetary measures of poverty and inequality, and failed to incorporate other 'quality of life' indicators (Hill 1994, pp. 106–7). This disinclination to include quality of life indicators could raise standards above those indicated by simple per capita gross

domestic product (GDP). However, given poor income distribution and a lack of access to basic facilities in some regions, per
capita GDP could also overstate quality of life.

Having noted the unreliability of official statistics and the potential for questioning their outcomes, Hill claimed with some justification that overall standards of living had increased since the
beginning of the New Order government. Clearly this was correct. However, Hill and others tend to compare the achievements
of the New Order government with the failures of the Sukarno
period of government, in which absolute poverty was widespread
and the economy in a shambles. They fail to note what an
abysmally low standard of living many Indonesians were forced to
endure under Sukarno (especially during the early 1960s), the
extent to which Indonesians have been able specifically to
improve their lot under the New Order government, and how
much this improvement in living conditions reflects overall economic growth. That is, measured against what, with a longer term
perspective, could only be regarded as a period of catastrophic
decline in living standards, there remains a serious question over
the rate of economic growth and the median increase in standards
of living. A qualitative assessment suggests very strongly that
median standards of living have fallen a long way behind total
growth, reflecting very poor income distribution. And this does
not begin to factor in what economic growth could have been
like had Indonesia not had to endure such economic debacles as
the Pertamina collapse or continuing and widespread high level
corruption. According to Mackie: 'The extremes of wealth you
see today have really only developed since about 1970. There was
nothing like the obscenely extravagant housing you now see in
Jakarta. The social ethos was all about egalitarianism and the *jiwa
revolusi* (revolutionary spirit)' (Mackie 1996).

But even taking into account the sometimes overstated appearance of Indonesia's economic performance, it was until 1998 a far
from totally bleak picture and there is no doubt that the country
had improved markedly since the last days of the Sukarno era.
Economic growth over the period from 1960 to 1967 was at less
than 2 per cent per year, while inflation was rampant. Based on 100
units in 1957, by 1966 the cost of living had risen to 150 000 (Winters 1996, p. 48). The inflation rate for 1966 was just under 1500
per cent. After having fluctuated (inflation in 1973 hit 40 per cent)

and during the early to middle 1980s, by the middle 1990s GDP appeared stable at around 7 per cent growth, while inflation had declined to 7.5 per cent by 1996.[8] In 1998 inflation was expected to jump to over 100 per cent, following the collapse of the value of the rupiah from 2300 per US dollar in June 1997 to more than 12 500 (spiking to 16 000) per US dollar by early 1998. The currency collapse was based to a significant extent on panic selling by international money speculators. However, it also pointed to underlying economic problems, which had largely been ignored until attention was drawn to them in a more broad examination of South-East Asian economies by money dealers in the international financial markets. Paramount among those economic problems was high–level corruption and nepotism, and inadequate banking controls and unsupervised (usually foreign-denominated) lending regimes and capital flights. This was compounded by a totally unrealistic initial budget forecast in January 1998, an inability to meet IMF agreements, and widespread concern about the issue of the presidential succession.

To look at the change to Indonesia's economy in another, perhaps more concrete way, in 1966 Indonesia was poorer than India or East Pakistan (Bangladesh), which were themselves bitterly poor. At least 60 per cent of Indonesia's population was believed to be living in absolute poverty and in some areas, including the usually fertile Java, malnutrition and starvation were serious problems. By the early 1990s, officially determined levels of poverty had declined to less than 20 per cent of the population, while until 1998, starvation existed only in isolated incidents.

Other economic indicators present a mixed picture. Foreign debt levels remained worryingly high, at around $US115 billion, or more than 60 per cent of GDP (in June 1997, before the currency collapse), while the increasingly loud concerns being expressed about the distribution of income in Indonesia's growing economy had taken on a sharp political edge. In short (and with considerable justification), the rich were believed to be getting significantly richer while the poor, in real terms, were barely surviving. Fewer may have been living in absolute poverty, but poverty was still widespread—an income of US$1 per day (or

---

8   At the time of writing, Indonesia was undergoing an economic convulsion (see note
     6), with growth rates reduced to zero, or less.

less)[9] was common, particularly for women, who comprise about 40 per cent of the labour market. Even the new 'middle classes' were still often only earning around US$6–10 per day before the currency collapse. Unemployment remained at around 25 per cent of the employable population, while under-employment or employment at below the legal minimum of Rp3000 (US$1.30) a day was rife. As noted in chapter 7, workers in Indonesia have little recourse to redressing such matters. The only legal trade union organisation is controlled by the government, striking is effectively banned and union activists are threatened, beaten, arrested and sometimes 'disappear'.

One major difficulty in assessing the status of Indonesia's economy in terms of what it means for Indonesian people, as noted by Hill, was that not only were some of the figures supplied by the government potentially or actually unreliable (or unavailable) but they were not necessarily applicable across the archipelago. As Christine Drake notes (1989, pp. 145–84), there was considerable scope for regional variation. Apart from the types of economies that tend to dominate each of the major island centres and the extent to which they have contributed, or continue to contribute, to the country's exports or imports, cost structures throughout Indonesia are uneven, meaning that money has a variable real value. In the cities, especially Jakarta, and in the outlying islands, where incomes are generally lower than on Java, living costs are relatively high, reducing even the purchasing power of what might otherwise be considered a moderate income. This means that, while one might look at per capita income as a ratio of GDP (despite it being almost meaningless in a country with such disparities of income) or even average purchasing power, this is not a consistent measure of standards of living throughout the archipelago. What might be a livable income in rural Java might not be a livable income in Jakarta or a more remote part of the country.

A black art?

At least a part of the problem, both in assessing the state of Indonesia's economy and in constructing policies for its future development, goes to the core of economics as a discipline.

---

9   This was based on late 1997 exchange rates.

Economics is presented to the public as a science, in which formulations can be made, models constructed, and outcomes identified or predicted. Perhaps if, like physics or chemistry, economic realities could be replicated in exact models, its claim to being a science would be on firmer ground. However, economic theorising and modelling cannot possibly take into account the multiplicity of uncontrollable variables (natural, personal, cultural, institutional) that beset any given real, living environment, especially one as large and complex as that of Indonesia. An economic model has serious difficulty in incorporating fluctuating public responses to high level corruption, for instance, or the economic consequences of political change. Markets might do this, but they tend to respond to short-term stimuli rather than some over-arching or long-term assessment of projected economic (and consequently social and political) health. Even centralised economic planning has not proven a success in this respect, running counter to personal economic gain, which appears to drive economic growth (and certainly drives capitalism). In this sense, economics is not a science; it is educated guesswork; it is an art. And in some cases, when economists get it very wrong, it is a decidedly black art. The economic policies that Indonesia has adopted under the New Order government have reflected particular ideological perspectives. On one hand they have promoted free markets, foreign investment, and private enterprise, and on the other the desire and ability of political and economic elites to manufacture economic circumstances to suit themselves. Neither approach appears to be designed to offer the greatest benefit to the greatest number of people (although this observation too reflects a particular ideological bias, one that doubts the economic egalitarianism of the 'trickle down effect' or the necessity of high levels of capital accumulation in few hands as opposed to an increase in more general disposable income). Capital accumulation can be used for investment, but it can also be squandered on imported luxuries or located offshore.[10] More general disposable income can reduce the capital available for major investment, but as it is almost always quickly disposed of, it can also provide economic stimulus.

---

10 About US$85 billion is believed to have been located off-shore by Indonesian business people.

If one were to look for an answer, then, regarding the state of Indonesia's economy and perhaps what policies could or should be pursued, one would need to undertake a qualitative assessment. Yet even a sample survey among more than 200 million people over 13 000 islands, to be useful, would require resources that even the Indonesian government would be unlikely to effectively muster. A quantitative survey is not a viable option, and nor is quantitative analysis especially useful in determining just how it is that people lead their material lives, as a comparison of the existing data with real, lived experiences demonstrates. One can find approximate correlations between quantitative analysis and life as it is lived, but not always, not always accurately, and not always without them being distorted, interfered with, or otherwise manipulated to show one set of circumstances in a different light. The answers received are in large part determined by the questions asked. Qualitative analysis, too, is problematic, at the very least because qualitative methodology rarely has the scope of quantitative methods—that is, its sample size is suspect—and it is in many cases little more than the ground over which competing theories and ideological positions do battle. Similarly, the sort of anecdotal evidence used by anthropologists, as noted by Hill, might offer useful insights into specific conditions, times, and places. But, even more than statistics, anecdotes can be used to add weight to a pre-existing view rather than to illuminate something that was not previously known.

Regardless of methodology, by mid to late 1997, Indonesia's 'economic miracle' had veered badly off the rails. At the forefront of Indonesia's economic problems was its debt of US$115 billion (PERC 1997), in large part in unhedged US dollars and in many cases privately borrowed in excess of borrowing limits. This debt began to fall due at a faster rate than many banks could repay it. It was widely acknowledged that there was already a problem with debt, but with the Indonesian currency devaluing by around 40 per cent against the US dollar over the space of a few weeks and then losing half that value, the unhedged debts became unmanageable. That the country was allowed to accumulate such a debt reflected the profligate lending of Indonesia's many private banks, the skewing of the economy through institutionalised corruption, and the fact that the owners of many of the major, often corrupt, businesses were also the owners of the banks.

In response, the IMF and a group of other countries in the region agreed in principle to a rescue package for Indonesia totalling US$43 billion (the second biggest such package ever, after Mexico in 1994–95). It was assumed that the conditions for the package would include a significant restructuring of the Indonesian economy, to reduce subsidies and price-setting, but more specifically the dismantling of the corrupt links between government and business. The closure of a bank—Bank Andromeda, partly owned by President Suharto's middle son, Bambang Trihatmodjo (or Bambang 'Tri')—and the resignation of Suharto's youngest son, Hutomo Mandala Putra (Tommy Suharto), as head of Indonesia's Timor 'national' car project, could have been interpreted as steps towards constructing a more conventional economy. But Tommy Suharto's resignation still left him not only with his existing 70 per cent ownership of the project, but also, and importantly, initially with the existing, highly controversial tax concessions still in place. He simply no longer had to bother himself with the day-to-day affairs of this particular source of income. An agreement to phase out the tax concessions after two years if the World Trade Organisation so requests is redundant, as such a phase-out was planned in any case, or could have been reversed had Suharto still been in power. Further, Tommy's clove monopoly was initially left effectively untouched, despite its poor performance, its debilitating effect on clove producers, its political unpopularity, and the public façade of its having been dismantled.

With Bambang Tri, the fact that his own father should preside over a government that reduced a small part of his considerable interests reflects perhaps more on the poor relationship between the two. Bambang Tri has been at odds with his father since at least 1996 over a number of issues, not least of which was Tommy's Timor car project. (Bambang Tri has his own car company, which does not receive tax breaks.) Bambang Tri has also been forging alliances with military figures who have been manoeuvring to replace Suharto. Bambang Tri's loss of a small section of his business would not cause Suharto to lose any sleep in any case. In November 1997, soon after the closure of Bank Andromeda, Bambang Tri bought another bank, Bank Alfa.

To illustrate the 'smoke and mirrors' method of economic reform instigated as a consequence of the proposed IMF bail-out, a large number of the projects that were 'cancelled', worth almost

US$10 billion, had not actually then been financed (PERC 1997):

It was a similar story in the case of toll roads, with most projects associated with PT Citra Marga, the listed toll-road company run by the president's daughter, reportedly unaffected on the grounds that the finance had already been obtained. Tellingly, several large projects by well-connected companies funded with high interest debts were given the green light, while other projects financed by low interest loans under the umbrella of the Consultative Group on Indonesia (creditor consortium) were rescheduled (PERC 1997).

While the currency crisis did ruffle political and economic feathers, and attracted a lot of public attention, it was probably not the main issue and proved, if anything, that little was likely to change while Suharto remained in office. Despite Suharto's apparent reluctance to make significant changes, the economic crisis could have been expected to swing influence back in favour of the finance ministries and the descendants of the 'Berkeley mafia'. However, depending on how the political forces of the day are arranged, this will probably be a short- to medium-term policy shift, as it has been in the past. As for the rest of the IMF package, some monopolies (such as wheat, flour, soybeans, and garlic) and controls or subsidies on prices for fuel and cement were cut. Politically more importantly, though, the government was required to implement an austerity campaign. Such campaigns rarely affect the people who have creamed off corrupt profits in the good times though; rather, the already struggling workers—and the increasing numbers of unemployed—will be expected to bear the burden.

With the IMF-sponsored closure of faltering banks (some sixteen in all), there seemed to be an echo of the Pertamina fiasco of the early 1970s, as the short-term debts caught up with an unsustainable longer-term debt position. The primary difference appeared to be that the focus of the debt was more widely distributed, but it is unlikely to be known for some time just to what extent the private banks were allowed to debilitate Indonesia's economy.

Clearly there has been, in Indonesia, a tendency towards a sometimes crippling level of corruption, which could perhaps be more kindly interpreted as gross mismanagement. Similarly, there has been substantial, if uneven, economic growth in absolute terms, although it would have required an even more fundamentally inept form of national management not to have at least built some sort of economic edifice on the smoking ruins of the Indonesian economy in 1966. But what really brought the precarious state of Indonesia's economy home to analysts most forcefully, even before the economic collapse, was the fact that ordinary Indonesians themselves believed that something was fundamentally amiss in their own country. They have complained of poverty, of inadequate distribution of the country's wealth, and of corruption. Economics is fundamental to politics. Political policy usually addresses economic issues or incorporates economic considerations, and such policy is fundamental to the material conditions of people's lives. Economics, then, reflects political considerations. Yet there is a marked lack of public access to the political process in Indonesia, and if there is something essentially amiss within the Indonesian political structure, the Indonesian public cannot, within the established framework, do anything about it. Virtually every report and every private comment that came out of Indonesia in the lead-up to the 1997 elections cited economics, in its various guises, as being the primary political issue. Those who believed things were so economically rosy in Indonesia needed to ask themselves, with economics as the main issue, why in 1997 and 1998 the country had experienced the worst, most consistent, and most widespread rioting since the dark days of 1966. And what were the causes and, more importantly, the longer term consequences of the economy's collapse in late 1997 and 1998?

6
SIGNS OF DIVISION IN INDONESIAN DOMESTIC POLITICS

The rigid 'stability' that had been the hallmark of Indonesia's New Order government, and which underlined Indonesia's economic growth particularly from the late 1980s, had begun to show signs of serious cracking by the early 1990s. To the outside world, Indonesia's New Order government has long presented a united front, with general (and not entirely incorrect) perceptions being that Suharto retained his presidency with the direct support of, and control over, ABRI. According to this perception, whatever ABRI did reflected Suharto's wishes, from the 1975 invasion of East Timor to the quelling of the 1996 PDI-linked riots. Yet Suharto's grip on power, while firm, was challenged at various times by groups and individuals who might otherwise have been thought to be a part of the New Order government's united front.

Opposition to Suharto mounts
The divisions that have beset the New Order government have surfaced on a number of occasions in relation to a varied group of interests or concerns. However, towards the end of Suharto's reign, his scattered opponents, once or still within the New Order's framework, had begun to unite in a common cause. This did not mean that Suharto's opponents could be expected to provide a united front after Suharto left office. Indeed much of Indonesia's political future was expected to be predicated on the successes and failures of the respective groups and individuals in staking their claims to influencing or controlling Indonesia's future political leadership. But what it did show was that, in so far as there was a viable opposition to Suharto's presidency, it came not from without but, according with the traditional format of Javanese palace

politics, from those who had privileged access to the corridors of power.

The cracks in the surface of the ostensibly *halus* Indonesian political life are long and deep. But by the end of 1993, the increasingly obvious signs emanating both publicly and privately from the media, academia, the military, and the Indonesian body politic were that the succession of the ageing Suharto was the country's paramount political issue. Effectively all the observations made by all commentators, both within and outside Indonesia, from around 1993 onwards were that, in so many respects, Indonesia needed to begin to change and that change was virtually impossible while Suharto remained president. The inevitable logical conclusion was that Suharto's time was up. In some quarters this conclusion was accepted reluctantly; in others it was accepted enthusiastically. But the sum total was that, of those people who thought about politics at all, there were very few left, apart from direct beneficiaries, who did not see Indonesia's political process under Suharto as just marking time. Frustrations began to build, especially among critics in the 'red and white' (secular, nationalist) faction of the armed forces, but also among many of the New Order's other supporters.

The implications of this were that policy-making and the administration of the state were predicated not on a single position or a secure government, but in response to pressures that had existed for several years. In particular, the political ethos informing the New Order government and, to a considerable extent, the divisions within it determined its responses to a range of issues. These issues included the rise of Islam and the factionalism therein, the rise and fall of the PDI, internal security issues, economic direction at both macro and micro levels, and foreign relations (reflecting internal considerations). In regard to this last issue particularly, Indonesia presented, or tried to present, one face to the world while preserving another for its domestic constituencies. While the foreign minister, Ali Alatas, now strutted, now stumbled across the world stage in the role of public-relations flack- and damage-control expert for the New Order government, little at home had actually changed, and this lack of change increasingly concerned the international community. Alatas did bring back to Jakarta a very real sense that the rest of the world was quickly tiring of Indonesia's various political and economic games. However, he was ignored by almost everyone except the president and a few of the president's flunkeys, such as the former industry and technology minister and former vice-president Habibie, and former information minister and Golkar chairperson Harmoko. Having the president's ear should have itself guaranteed Alatas some say in Indonesia's affairs, but increasingly it seemed that even Suharto only kept Alatas as foreign minister because he was a suitable means of keeping the annoying world at a comfortable distance. With its inward focus and overriding domestic preoccupation (greater in some ways than most states within the international community), Indonesia has been little concerned with the views of the world. It has played a role in regional affairs, primarily through the Association of South East Asian Nations, which in practical terms it dominates, and it has sometimes been concerned about international responses to its economic progress. But Indonesia, both under Sukarno and Suharto, has been less than gracious in responding to expressions of concern about issues such as long-term economic planning, corruption, democratisation, and human rights. At one level this appears to reflect the traditional Javanese conception of power being concentrated at the exemplary centre, leading to a rejection of the concerns of the outside world. But it can also be seen to reflect the practical power politics of a regime style that is in very large part about preserving and expanding its position, in both a political and economic sense. Yet not all was *halus* in Indonesian politics, with divisions not only between those outside the New Order government and those within it, but as earlier noted, between the major actors or factions within the government itself.

The origins of division

The divisions within the New Order government dated from its earliest days and, in the case of the armed forces, stemmed from the earliest days of the Republic. Needing to finance themselves independently of the government in the period from 1945 to 1949, many army units engaged in their own business activities and were effectively self-supporting. This situation continued into the 1950s as the fledgling Republic struggled to meet its various spending commitments. However, as private army business became a lucrative source of unaccountable income, often supplementing income from the government, many generals were not only reluctant to give it up, but also saw it as a golden opportunity to keep more of the profits. Hence a core of 'corrupt generals' became established within ABRI. Even Suharto was acknowledged as being one of the 'corrupt generals' by the head of the army, General Nasution (Crouch 1988a, p. 40), and later by the Sultan of Yogyakarta, with whom he had close contact during his period as a regional commander. The problem with corrupt generals, which dates back to at least the early 1950s, can be traced through to the present time.

Despite the blot of corruption on his record, Suharto managed to sufficiently redeem himself at staff school to be appointed by Sukarno as commander of Operation Mandala, which was the planned military invasion of West Papua in 1963.[1] Suharto was viewed at this time as a Sukarno loyalist and, after his run-in with the armed forces chief of staff General Nasution, was appointed as Kostrad commander, which as later became apparent, was a crucial position to hold and would have only been entrusted to a loyalist. As a consequence of this perceived loyalty, Suharto was apparently not targeted along with the other generals for whatever fate had in store for them on the night of 30 September 1965. While the remaining senior officers backed his obvious grip on power in the events after 1 October 1965, many thought he had assumed too much personal authority. This marked the beginning of Suharto's delicate dismantling of the armed forces' 'old guard'. In the tense and uncertain days after 1 October, Suharto needed all the support he could get if he was to prevail in toppling Sukarno. But as he became more assured in his authority, Suharto began marginalising and neutralising those officers he believed did not offer him total support.

Regardless of the extent to which Suharto planned his role in the unfolding events, from the very outset he seized the military, and hence political, initiative and kept it. With the deaths of most of Indonesia's top military command on 30 September 1965, Suharto took upon himself the role of Indonesia's political saviour.

---

1   The formal invasion did not take place, as Irian Barat, or Irian Jaya as it was later called, was ceded by the Netherlands to Indonesia in August 1962 and formally occupied on 1 May 1963.

Having quickly put down the military aspect of the 30 September affair, Suharto then turned on the real political opponents to the armed forces and his own consolidation of power: the PKI. Although there was some hesitancy, those who were sympathetic to the PKI or who believed that the armed forces actions were unwarranted were removed from their posts. As Suharto consolidated his position, particularly after Sukarno was obliged to hand over his authority to secure and stabilise Indonesia's political environment on 11 March 1966,[2] there were many within the armed forces who supported Suharto's general thrust but who believed that he was acquiring too much personal authority. The government that was evolving was not an ABRI or New Order government so much as a Suharto government.

Sumitro and the *Malari* riots

By the early 1970s, the New Order government began to split more forcefully within itself. Having established himself, Suharto moved to silence dissenters, posting potential rivals to overseas posts where they could watch but do little, or moving more senior officers into retirement. From around this time Suharto began to employ financial patronage extensively as a means of achieving loyalty. This caused divisions between those generals who were happy to benefit financially from their association with, or support for, Suharto and those who either were not included in his largesse or opposed it on the grounds that it compromised ABRI's professionalism. Already having alienated some of the more senior figures within ABRI, as well as some of his more idealistic younger supporters, Suharto had to contend with a growing general concern about corruption, particularly from the early 1970s. Internal divisions began to manifest themselves more clearly, especially between the so-called 'financial' (business-oriented or corrupt) and 'non-financial' (purely professional) generals, marking the beginning of an open split between Suharto and many of his earlier supporters. By 1973 issues of corruption, patronage, and the benefits perceived to be accruing to Indonesia's Chinese

---

2 Sukarno's Surat Perintah Sebelas Maret (Letter of Instruction of 11 March) was abbreviated as 'Supersemar', which was a play on the name of probably the most affectionately regarded figure in the *wayang* pantheon, a humble clown figure who became the most powerful and wise of the gods (see Anderson 1965, pp. 22–3).

minority spilled over, and there were anti-Chinese riots in Bandung. In particular there was concern revolving around the government's failure to eliminate corruption, including corruption among the 'financial generals' and a small group of ethnic Chinese business people, which was the trigger for the *Malari* riots of 1974.

Like so much in Indonesian political life, the reasons for the riots remain at least partly obscured. But it is now widely accepted that the riots—ostensibly against the Japanese prime minister, Kakuei Tanaka, and excessive foreign ownership, and less directly against corrupt senior officials—were the result of this power struggle within Indonesia's top military ranks. The prevailing view, in part encouraged by Sumitro himself, is that in 1973 Sumitro and a number of other generals believed that Suharto should step down from the presidency, and it was assumed that Sumitro envisaged himself in that role.

Among the generals who believed Suharto should step down was Lt General Sarwo Edhie Wibowo, who was highly influential in persuading Sukarno to hand over effective control of Indonesia to Suharto on 11 March 1966. Sarwo Edhie, as commander of the RPKAD (Resimen Para Komando Angkatan, or Army Para-commando Regiment), had been given the task by Suharto of restoring order in Jakarta after the 30 September and 1 October 1965 incidents, including at the Halim air base. He later crushed opposition in Central Java. Hartono Rekso Dharsono and Kemal Idris were also influential in helping bring Suharto to power by forcing Sukarno's hand in 1966. Sarwo Edhie was given the un-influential job of North Sumatra regional commander in 1968, was later posted to the army academy at Magelang, and following the *Malari* riots, was sent as ambassador to South Korea, which was a standard shunting move. Of the four officers who played a leading role in helping to bring Suharto to power, only Amir Machmud remained loyal to Suharto.

The affair started in 1973 with public discontent over favouritism shown to Chinese business people and foreign corporations at the expense of indigenous businesses, a position that gained considerable sympathy within sections of the army. Muslims were also concerned about proposed uniform marriage and divorce laws, which were proposed by the head of the intelligence network Opsus (Operasi Khusus, or Special Operations) and former

Suharto aide from his Central Java days, Ali Murtopo. As head of Kopkamtib, Sumitro not only refrained from taking action against protesters, but also visited university campuses throughout Java. He also approached Muslim leaders and offered to help work out new marriage laws, which were eventually passed with Muslim support in December 1973 (Crouch 1988a, p. 313). Sumitro was clearly working against Murtopo and, by extension, against Suharto. It has been suggested that Sumitro initially asked for Suharto to step down, but Suharto declined and instead reprimanded Sumitro, in two meetings on 1 and 2 January 1974. Sumitro's position was increasingly untenable, and it was apparent that Suharto was about to sack him.

In a last-ditch bid to save his own position, topple Murtopo, and by extension, challenge Suharto (Vatikiotis 1993, pp. 75–6), Sumitro did not oppose student protests when Tanaka visited on 14 January and is believed by many to have encouraged them. The protests, while specifically against Tanaka, were in fact also against the 'financial generals', who, in effect, included Suharto. After two days, the riots were quelled, and Sumitro was sacked as Kopkamtib head and forced to resign as deputy head of the army (Crouch 1988a, pp. 304–17). Sumitro was offered an appointment as ambassador to Washington but turned it down and went into private business. Sarwo Edhie was also removed, his posting as ambassador to South Korea being fulfilled, and appointment as ambassador being a move traditionally used to dispose of unwanted senior officers. Sumitro, however, remained influential within the armed forces and continued to be a vocal critic of Suharto. It is to this time that the recent dissent within ABRI towards Suharto can be most clearly traced.

The *Malari* riots of 1974 marked the end of the last direct challenge by other generals for authority within the new government. It was not until the mid to late 1980s that such a strong source of opposition would again emerge, this time with the aim not so much of displacing Suharto but of determining his eventual replacement. Interestingly, the next round of overt anti-Suharto feeling within ABRI arose in 1988 over the appointment of Sudharmono as vice-president. Sarwo Edhie, then a member of the DPR, resigned in protest. It was from this time that Murdani, previously a public Suharto supporter, also fell out with the president, indicating a link between those ABRI officers who opposed Suharto from the early 1970s and the group that has worked against Suharto since the late 1980s.

Murtopo and Murdani: the hard men

After the *Malari* riots, perhaps the next indication that not all was right was when Murtopo and the rising military star Benny Murdani began planning for the invasion of East Timor. Suharto was nervous about following the plans of these hard-liners too closely, accurately noting that any annexation of what was then Portuguese Timor would invite a negative international response. Yet the plan developed, initially through more covert means, by influencing or supporting the newly emerging political groupings within the colony. However, as the political and military situation in East Timor deteriorated by August 1975, which was at least partly a result of Murtopo's scheming, the argument for decisive action became stronger and Suharto's hand was forced. Murtopo and Murdani might have remained Suharto loyalists, but Murdani's harder line on this issue marked the first time he was known to differ with Suharto.

One aspect of Jakarta's political schism relates to the role of Murtopo. In Suharto's earlier years as president, Murtopo was Suharto's fixer and was viewed by some as the person who actually made the decisions. Indeed, Murtopo was viewed as a *dalang* (puppet master), manipulating his minions like so many shadow puppets. Even Suharto was seen by some to be under Murtopo's influence, which Suharto later went out of his way to deny (Schwartz 1994, p. 45). Javanese frequently describe Indonesian politics in terms of who is seen to act and who pulls the strings, in line with the traditional art form of *wayang kulit*. Hence, the *dalang* was seen by some to be the power behind the throne. While Murtopo worked for Suharto, his favourite was General Leonardus Benyamin 'Benny' Murdani. Murdani was a rising young officer in the army during Sukarno's period of Guided Democracy, and according to Murdani, Sukarno viewed him so favourably, as a 'man of ideals' and as a 'hero', that he even proposed that his daughter Megawati should marry him (McIntyre 1996, pp. 3, 6). Murdani was already about to marry Hartini (whose family was also known to Sukarno), but both Murdani and Megawati were later to become Suharto's nemeses. In any case, although Murdani was under Suharto's command during the West Papua Mandala campaign,

Suharto sent Murdani as defence attaché to the Indonesian embassy in Kuala Lumpur,[3] followed by a posting to Seoul, the latter move often reserved for officers who had become troublesome. Murdani returned to Jakarta in 1974, although then as Murtopo's protégé. Murdani was appointed as chief of the Intelligence Task Forces (Kesatuan Tugas Intel, or 'Satgas Intel'), which were responsible for much of the direct intimidation of and violence against dissenters. It was from this time that he became widely regarded as a hard-liner on suppressing opposition and dissent.

From the time of Murdani's return to Jakarta, he appeared to form a close alliance with his mentor, Murtopo. This was particularly noticeable from around the time of the 1975 invasion of East Timor, which Murtopo planned, Murdani played a significant role in, and Suharto only reluctantly endorsed. Suharto was well aware of the international furore that could follow such an invasion and was keen to try more subtle methods first. Murtopo was given authority to support a pro-integrationist group within East Timor, but when this strategy failed, he helped intensify divisions between the Leftist Fretilin (Revolutionary Front for an Independent East Timor) and the Rightist UDT (Uniao Democratica Timorese, or Timorese Democratic Union), sparking the brief civil war of August 1975, after which UDT, Apodeti (Timorese Popular Democratic Association), and others fled across the border into West Timor. Murdani was thereafter in charge of incursions across the border—ostensibly under the banner of UDT–Apodeti, but in fact using Indonesian commandos—and later the more formal invasion. It is believed that Suharto had not been happy about how the whole affair had been handled, and although this slowed the careers of neither Murtopo nor Murdani, it did leave some lingering doubts about Suharto's commitment to ABRI among senior and rising officers.

Dissidence and the Petition of Fifty
In 1977, following years of poor rice harvests and the closure of a dozen newspapers as a consequence of the *Malari* riots, public concern about officially condoned corruption again came to the forefront with student demonstrations in the Javanese cities of Surabaya and Yogyakarta, and in the Sumatran cities of Medan

---

3   Murdani worked for Murtopo in Kuala Lumpur in 1965 as an intelligence agent.

and Palembang. Although these demonstrations did not explicitly reflect tensions within the New Order government, those within the government who believed that corruption was economically debilitating and ethically unacceptable felt their cause was bolstered. As the presidential elections of 1978 approached, the governor of Jakarta, Lt General Ali Sadikin, was nominated by the students as an alternative president. Another major figure identified with the student protests of 1977–78 was former Suharto supporter and then secretary general of ASEAN, Lt General Dharsono. Other former New Order military figures were involved in a 'Study and Communications Forum' (Forum Studi dan Komminikasi, or 'Fosko') and in the Institute of Constitutional Awareness (LKB), in which former ABRI chief General Nasution (retired) as well as Sadikin were prominent. LKB also attracted the support of former vice-president Mohammad Hatta. Sympathisers included the army's chief of staff, General Widodo, and the defence minister, General Jusuf.

In 1979 and early 1980, the PPP and the PDI called for an overhaul of the electoral system, which prevented them from campaigning openly and ensured that they would be subordinate in the DPR to both ABRI and Golkar. When in 1980 a bill was passed that further restricted the activities of political parties in the lead-up to the 1982 elections, fifty PPP members walked out in protest. The tensions that existed between Suharto and ABRI, particularly over the financial generals and over ABRI's inability to settle the East Timor question once and for all, were heightened in March 1980, when in a speech at Pekanbaru, Suharto 'succeeded in insulting virtually everybody in an off-the-cuff speech to regional Military commanders' (Coman 1987, p. 55). Then on 27 March 1980, at an annual meeting of regional army commanders at Palembang, Suharto responded to criticisms over the dominance of ABRI and Golkar by saying that ABRI would continue its high-profile role in government and by questioning the loyalty of Muslim organisations. Notably, for the first time, Suharto acknowledged that his wife, Tien Suharto, had been accused of taking commissions on business deals.[4] These speeches indicated that Suharto was campaigning for the 1982 DPR elec-

---

4   Tien was widely known as 'Madame Tien Per Cen' as a result of her alleged graft. She was later referred to by some as 'Madame Twenty Per Cen'.

tions and for his own re-election in 1983, implicitly acknowledging opposition to his tenure within ABRI.

On 13 May 1980, arising out of the views expressed by Fosko and LKB, a petition by fifty prominent Indonesians, including retired generals, former politicians, lawyers, intellectuals, and students, expressed concern about Suharto's speeches. This petition, known as the *Petisi Limapuluh* (Petition of Fifty), and one soon after by General Jasin, led to a domestic news blackout. Jasin's petition, which alleged corruption on the part of Suharto and his wife, was widely circulated by photocopy. This was the first public expression of concern about the types of issues, particularly corruption, that were later canvassed by Jenkins in his 'Soeharto Billions' article (1986), and that were more thoroughly and formally explored in Richard Robison's book *Indonesia: The Rise of Capital* (1986), which drew international attention to high-level corruption in Indonesia. From about this time, Suharto began to formally distance himself from ABRI, moving to appoint civilian rather than military personnel to Cabinet positions. It was also from about this time that the outside world began to perceive a split in the New Order government (Crouch 1988).

The Petition of Fifty marked a very public rift with the government and demonstrated that even among Indonesia's elites there was growing disquiet about the country's political direction under Suharto. In particular, there was increasing concern about the domination of the political process by ABRI and the reduction of democratic rights as guaranteed under the 1945 constitution. The Petition of Fifty was an extraordinary statement in light of the covert manner in which dissent within the New Order's ranks had been conducted, although in many cases the petitioners traced their political roots to the Old Order government of Sukarno. But coming from the political elite, the petition stung, and it attracted widespread attention.

Entitled a 'Statement of Concern', the petition listed six main grievances: a polarisation of the Five Principles (*Pancasila*) of government, which could lead to communal violence; the use of the *Pancasila* to threaten political opponents; the systematic paralysis of the 1945 Constitution; the taking of political sides by ABRI; the attempted personification of the *Pancasila* in the person of the president; and allegations of preparations for subversion or armed uprising ahead of the elections.

Among the signatories to the petition were four generals who played a significant role in establishing the legitimacy of the New Order government: former ABRI chief Nasution, and Mokoginta, Jasin, and Hoegeng. There were also Muslims, non-Muslims, and representatives of Java and other regions. There was, in fact, no specific cultural or ideological basis to the petition. Although the petition's broad focus was on its opposition to the dominance of ABRI in government, and the increasingly authoritarian and exclusive role of the president, there was also concern about issues of corruption and the style of Indonesian development, the rule of law, and human rights. During this period at least, dissent within ABRI was muted, although this was primarily because ABRI's more open dissenters had been removed. Not surprisingly, from 1980 the signatories were threatened and intimidated, were assaulted, had their offices and homes raided, and were placed under close surveillance (Bourchier 1987).

The challenge was suppressed, but discontent with Suharto's increasingly imperious style remained. As David Jenkins noted, 'In the fifteen years since he had come to power Suharto has changed quite considerably. He had become more rigid, more authoritarian, more feudalistic, more mystical, more cynical, more corrupt, very much less inclined to listen to criticism' (Jenkins 1984, p. 159). In this sense, Suharto was beginning to replicate aspects of his predecessor, Sukarno. While Sukarno and Suharto were in many respects similar, particularly in their use and appreciation of Javanese symbolism, the two men came out of very different cultural moulds. Sukarno was of Jakarta's intellectual elite; Suharto was a soldier from the provinces. Following the generation of Dutch-educated liberals:

their roughly educated, less travelled military successors were more imbued with traditional notions of social order. In their world—primarily the rigidly structured feudal culture of Central Java—the people have always to be guided from above. Wisdom is the monopoly of the rulers, ignorance is a burden the people must bear relieved only by the generosity and charity of the wise and powerful. Corruption is regarded as a prerogative of the elite (Vatikiotis 1993, p. 54).

Suharto's style and his accumulation of wealth, both while in the army and later in office, well fits this mould. However, according to many in Jakarta, there were genuine and widespread ethical concerns, even among his former army colleagues, about

Suharto's behaviour, as well as the implications of his business dealings for the wider economy.

The early 1980s were difficult for Suharto. Not only was there a distance growing between himself and ABRI (Schwartz 1994, pp. 283–4), but the promise of economic development upon which he based his rule was also under threat as a result of a collapse in world oil prices. Partly by way of diverting attention from domestic issues, and no doubt partly as a response to his own developing sense of importance, Suharto began to assert Indonesia as a leading player within the South East Asian region: 'Incidents such as these indicate[d] Indonesia's desire to stand on its own feet as much as possible in relations with its near neighbours' (McMichael 1987, p. 23). As part of Indonesia's regional reassessment of its role, it cut its limited defence links with Australia, allegedly as a result of the fall-out over Jenkins's and Robison's publications. It pushed for a new defence arrangement with Malaysia and Singapore to replace the Five Power Defence Arrangement between Australia, New Zealand, the United Kingdom, Malaysia, and Singapore. Initial responses from Malaysia and Singapore to Indonesia's proposal were 'lukewarm', but the move did indicate that Indonesia intended to take a more prominent role in regional security arrangements (Selochan 1992, pp. 9–16).

Corruption, poverty, and Islam: the Tanjung Priok incident

One of the most controversial events of the mid-1980s was the Tanjung Priok incident. On 12 September 1984, at least sixty local people were shot dead—with some suggesting that up to 200 died (Vatikiotis 1993, p. 128)—and a further 100 or so were wounded when soldiers opened fire on a demonstration in Jakarta's impoverished port district. The protest was sparked when officials entered a local mosque to remove a poster inviting people to the mosque's Islamic youth teaching. It was believed that this meeting would address the issue of the hard and declining economic conditions in the area, which were a product of local poverty exacerbated by Indonesia's foreign income collapse. People from the mosque complained but were arrested, sparking a protest by about 1500 locals, who marched to the local police station to demand their release. The locals were confronted by soldiers, who then opened fire. The issuing of a *White Paper of Tanjung Priok* in 1984 led to two of the Petition of Fifty group, Haji A. M. Fatwa and H. M. Sanusi, being convicted of stimulating 'extremist and terrorist activities' and being sentenced to gaol until the year 2003.

In 1985, following Suharto's reinstatement as president for a fourth five-year term, the New Order government imposed its final constraints on free political organisation. Under the Law on Mass Organisation, those parties that were officially allowed to exist (other than Golkar)—that is, the PDI and the PPP—had to subscribe to the state ideology of the *Pancasila*, their executive boards and members had to be registered with the government, and they could not organise between elections. Under the legislation, the government could restrict or close down any mass organisation if it disturbed public order or received aid from foreign parties without government approval. It also deprived parties of the right to promote Islam as the central platform of their manifesto: 'Anyone who publicly preached against the law was tried for subversion' (Vatikiotis 1993, p. 104). Further, the MPR, which is theoretically capable of changing the Constitution by a two-thirds majority vote, was hamstrung with between a half and two-thirds of its members being effectively appointed by the government (Vatikiotis 1993, p. 104).

From the 1980s, to help ensure that Golkar remained under his control, Suharto began to take a more direct interest in the appointment of Golkar representatives. As two members of his extended family were promoted to senior positions within ABRI, so too were members of his family proposed for positions within Golkar's representation in the DPR. Of the 829 candidates listed by Golkar, four include Suharto's children and a daughter-in-law, as well as the wives of two of the country's most senior military officers. While this is a small proportion of the total number, the influence they were able to bring to bear far outweighed their numbers.

When Murdani rose to the position of commander-in-chief of ABRI in 1983, he was at perhaps his most powerful, yet there were already signs of tensions between him and Suharto, with Suharto regarding him as too much of a 'hawk'. For his own part, Murdani was not fond of having Suharto increasingly discuss matters with him in a patronising manner. Murdani was never one to be patronised, by anyone. Issues also began to surface between the two over the role of ABRI in government, the tensions between 'professional' and 'political' officers in ABRI, high-level corruption, and particularly the issue of succession, as later demonstrated by Sudharmono's appointment as vice-president. When the falling out between the two men became public in 1988, majority support within ABRI for Suharto began to slip away. A significant group within ABRI had long been disenchanted with Suharto, but had comprised a minority. By the late 1980s the tide was turning, and the proportion who privately questioned Suharto's leadership was in the majority, the core of what was to become the 'red and white' faction of ABRI. Suharto recognised this and moved to downgrade or remove ABRI's influence, primarily within Cabinet.

One who questioned the direction of the New Order government, and who suffered the consequences, was Lt General Hartono Rekso Dharsono. Dharsono was one of the 'generation of '45', who had fought against the Dutch and participated in the suppression of the PKI's Madiun revolt in 1948 and the PRRI–Permesta rebellion in 1958. In 1965 he rose to become chief of staff of the crack Siliwangi Division and was among the most vehemently opposed to Sukarno's continuing tenure as president after the killing of six generals in 1965. Suharto promoted Dharsono to commander of the Siliwangi Division, and from that position he was, along with Kemal Idris and Sarwo Edhie, among the strongest supporters of Suharto's move to oust Sukarno from office, often taking a harder line than Suharto himself.

Dharsono began to run foul of Suharto by opposing Indonesia's corrupt 'financial' generals, in particular Pertamina head Ibnu Sutowo, who was crucial to Suharto's building of patronage. Along with a plan to bring all political parties into two groupings, which he attempted to instigate in West Java, Suharto decided Dharsono's excessive 'enthusiasm' was better placed out of domestic politics and sent him as ambassador to Bangkok and then Phnom Penh. Returning to Indonesia in 1976, Dharsono was appointed as secretary-general of ASEAN. By 1978, however, Dharsono stated that he believed the New Order government had deviated from its original ideas and, refusing to back down, was dismissed from his post in ASEAN. Dharsono continued to move away from Suharto, calling for greater democracy as a cure to what he saw as the country's ills. Dharsono did not sign the Petition of Fifty, but was close to some who did, and in 1984 he did sign the 'White Paper' on the Tanjung Priok riots. At a meeting of radical Muslims soon after, he opposed a violent response to the Tanjung Priok killings. Nevertheless he was arrested and charged under the anti-subversion law. Being called a 'threat to the dignity of the government' (Dharsono 1986), Dharsono was duly convicted in 1986 and gaoled for ten years, but was released from prison in 1990. If nothing else, the 'Dharsono affair' clarified once and for all the lengths to which the New Order government would go to repress even implied criticism.

Two conspiracy theories

In the arcane and sometimes even Byzantine world of Indonesian 'palace politics', conspiracy theories are standard fare, and almost every move or manoeuvre is understood as having at least one ulterior motive. Many outside sceptics try to write off these conspiracy theories as a product of over-active imaginations, choosing instead to adopt the less confrontational view that political life is 95 per cent accident and 5 per cent clever planning. But Indonesia is not like many other places, and many of these conspiracy theories have subsequently been borne out, validating what appeared to be incredible interpretations of events.[5] Two of the most important and controversial conspiracy theories, revolving around the tussle between Suharto and Murdani for ultimate control of Indonesia, concerned a diplomatic dispute with Australia in 1986 over the publication of an article outlining Suharto's corruption, and in 1991 the most internationally recognised event in recent Indonesian history, the Dili massacre.

Murdani displayed a penchant for embarrassing Suharto in front of an international audience in 1986 when he pushed along Indonesia's dispute with Australia over a newspaper report outlining Suharto's corruption (Jenkins 1986). In that incident, Murdani overrode Indonesia's Department of Foreign Affairs, which wanted to settle the dispute, and was seen to be behind ensuring that the report and the diplomatic fallout it engendered

---

5   Some observers who have worked in both cities have likened the intrigues of Jakarta
    to those of the Kremlin in the days of the USSR.

remained firmly on the national and international agenda. The initial Indonesian response to the article included scathing commentaries in the army newspaper *Harian Umum Angkatan Bersenjata* (or AB).

When the initial, relatively low-key phase of the Jenkins affair began to die down, an order was given to cancel the visa-free entry of Australian tourists to Indonesia, resulting in an aeroplane load of tourists being sent back to Australia upon arrival at Denpasar Airport, Bali. The turning back of the flight was primarily orchestrated by Murdani, although the order for the cancellation of visa-free travel for Australians to Indonesia was given, at least nominally, by the then Indonesian justice minister, Ismail Saleh. This development in the dispute drew considerable attention in Indonesia to a newspaper article that was read by 200 000 Australians. As the dispute escalated, photocopies of the article became widely available in Jakarta. Indeed, not only were copies of the article available, but there was even a case in which a newspaper vendor in Jakarta's Chinese district, Glodok, was seen throwing copies of a translation of the article into passing cars: 'He said he'd been paid to do so' (*Asiaweek*, 18 May 1986, p. 46). Further, a document by Bakin (the State Intelligence Coordinating Body) on reprisals against Australia over the 'Soeharto Billions' story was widely leaked in Jakarta from mid-May 1986: 'the mystery surrounding [the Bakin documents'] appearance has prompted speculation that their intended result was to favour the interests of those factions in the Indonesian Government which initially escalated the dispute with Australia' (Byrnes 1986a). The leaked document noted that 'The measures [taken in reaction to the 'Soeharto Billions' story] could also develop into becoming not just against reporters but for example the possibility of free visas for Australian[s] being reviewed or cancelled altogether, could occur [*sic*]' (Appendix 2, in Byrnes 1994, p. 258). In this dispute Australia was used, at least to some extent, as a cat's paw for Murdani's factional gain. In terms of cost in bilateral relations, Murdani claimed that Indonesia could live without Australia, but that Australia could not live without Indonesia. Murdani also noted that the dispute could escalate further (Byrnes 1994, p. 258). The following September, a similar dispute arose over the publication of Robison's *Indonesia: The Rise of Capital*, which expanded on the issues raised in the 'Soeharto Billions' article (Jenkins 1986).

Indonesia's initial response was to withdraw landing rights for Royal Australian Air Force aircraft: 'Attempts to have the order rescinded or at least explained have since "drawn a comprehensive blank", according to Foreign Affairs sources' (*Adelaide Advertiser*, 5 September 1986, p. 1). This action was not instigated by an over-zealous junior Indonesian official, but by someone at almost the highest level of the Indonesian government. Rather than suppress discussion, the military response, directed by Murdani, served primarily to highlight the issue of Suharto's corruption (Byrnes 1992). John Stackhouse notes the internal rivalries that led to the 'institutionalisation' of the official Indonesian response to the 'Soeharto Billions' article:

Local analysts have since explained the phenomenon by noting that the capital's power bases are exhibiting rivalry in the political climate induced firstly by the coming Indonesian election but also by the fact that Suharto has had a good innings, is not immortal and probably there will be planning for a phased succession during the next few years . . . The Australian press was the lightning rod (Stackhouse 1986, p. 28).

Stackhouse also notes that Suharto personally intervened and 'forced a row-back' after the Australian tourists were turned back from Denpasar, following Saleh's order. Saleh was a very senior official—not a junior official, as initially claimed by the Indonesian government (*Far Eastern Economic Review*, 8 May 1986, p. 45). It was also extremely unusual for Suharto to become personally involved in such a matter, as this was the sort of task he would usually require his subordinates to perform. It also reflects the possibility that he could not trust all his senior colleagues to act on his behalf. Interestingly, just when the matter was beginning to settle, ABRI's newspaper *AB* again went on the attack:

A major article carried on the paper's main editorial and feature page yesterday not only resurrected the inflammatory line pushed at the height of the flare-up in relations with Indonesia in April—that Australia is aiming guns at Indonesia's back—but went further and listed five reasons why Australia cannot be trusted . . . In AB's view, Australia presents Indonesia with a threat because of communists in the ALP, because of subversive freedom of the Australian press, because of Australia's relations with Britain, the US and Japan, because of Australia's presence in the South Pacific, even because of Australian academic studies in Indonesian culture and affairs (Byrnes 1986b).

It is also worth noting that the controversy over the Jenkins article coincided with a visit to Indonesia by the then United States vice-president, George Bush. Bush's visit to Indonesia came just before a visit by then United States president Ronald Reagan, from which the accompanying Australian news media were barred. Bush visited Indonesia as a part of a tour of oil-producing nations to discuss the slump in world oil prices, which that month had dropped to US$9 a barrel. At the beginning of April, before leaving for Saudi Arabia, Bush expressed anxiety over the 'free fall' in oil prices. This was interpreted as support for some sort of price-fixing mechanism for oil, and the price of oil immediately jumped US$3.45 a barrel. However, this contradicted Reagan's oil-pricing policy, which viewed market forces as the only appropriate means of determining prices.

Suharto was effectively asking for support for an economic policy that had already put Bush in a difficult political position, and the allegations that Suharto was engaged in corruption on a grand scale would have further complicated that position. It was difficult for Indonesia to sustain its own position—that oil-reliant governments depended on a certain level of oil-based revenue—when it was alleged that large volumes of public money had been siphoned off by a corrupt political leader. As a consequence, such a public disclosure could have indirectly damaged the Indonesian economic cause. But probably more to the point, the disclosure and its attendant complications would have caused Suharto considerable embarrassment—causing him to 'lose face' in the eyes of the United States vice-president. Further, the furore over the article and the details of the allegations of corruption were made available to Reagan's party, including its media entourage, when it visited Indonesia some weeks later.

The Reagan visit did not proceed as Suharto had hoped, especially after two Washington-based journalists from the Australian Broadcasting Corporation and a *New York Times* journalist, Barbara Crossett, were expelled from Indonesia upon landing with the official party. The English newspaper the *Guardian* ran the headline 'Reagan Visit Turns into a Disaster for Suharto', and *Washington Post* journalist William Branigan called the visit a 'public relations disaster': 'the government's mishandling of the foreign press has shifted the focus of the Reagan visit from Indonesia's considerable achievements in development to its sensitivities about dissent, press censorship, human-rights issues, *the role of the military in society and factionalism within the Suharto administration*' (Branigan 1986, my emphasis).

By highlighting Suharto's corruption, the Jenkins article led to similar reports by American journalists, which adversely affected the international reputation of Indonesia. Articles similar to that written by Jenkins were subsequently published in the *New York Times*, the *Washington Post*, the *Asian Wall Street Journal*, the *Guardian*, the *Far Eastern Economic Review*, the *International Herald Tribune*, and the *Australian Financial Review*. If it had been Murdani's intention to embarrass Suharto and to bring public pressure to bear on him at home, the plan could not have worked better.

The more conventional explanation is that Murdani attacked Australia in an effort to show his loyalty to Suharto. Yet at this time his loyalty was not publicly questioned, and even though it was embarrassing Suharto, Murdani continued to draw attention to the issue. If this version of events is to be believed, it shows Murdani as an extraordinarily inept, unaware, and ham-fisted political player, which are not characteristics for which he is known.

In the late 1980s, Suharto increasingly consolidated power in his own hands, allocating as much power as he felt necessary to those he trusted and who depended on his direct support for their own political survival. This was partly a response to a growing perception that ABRI was not absolutely committed to Suharto's presidency, and in part the result of Suharto's 'traditional anxiety about a dispersion of power' (Crouch 1994, p. 11) inspired by that lack of commitment. With power being taken away, even Suharto loyalists were left with no option but to join a quickly coalescing opposition camp. The move that most alienated ABRI officers was the 'election' of Lt General Sudharmono to the position of vice-president, technically only a heart-beat away from the presidency itself. Sudharmono had been instrumental in reducing ABRI's access to funds through private business activities and helped limit senior officers' scope for corruption. He also oversaw the reduction of ABRI's involvement in Golkar and the DPR, which paralleled the decline of traditional ABRI personnel in senior ministerial posts. In ensuring that Sudharmono was appointed to the vice-presidency, Suharto knew he was on a collision course with a very large part of ABRI. It was most likely a collision that Suharto knew would eventually come in any case, and which he engineered to give himself the greatest strategic advantage. At the same time that Sudharmono was made vice-president, ABRI commander Benny Murdani was 'kicked upstairs' to the less influential position of defence minister. ABRI thereafter campaigned vigorously against Sudharmono, spending large sums trying to dislodge him as chairperson of Golkar at the party's congress in November 1988. To do this, many serving ABRI officers had to retire from their posts and stand as regional Golkar chairmen, which 120 did, securing about two-thirds of all regional delegates to the congress (Vatikiotis 1993, p. 87). Sudharmono was dumped from the Golkar chair at the congress, but that position was no longer really suitable for a person who was now vice-president. Sudharmono's dumping also suited Suharto, who regarded his dual position as affording just a little more personalised power than he was comfortable with.

Though so much of Indonesian politics comprises intricate manœuvrings, much is also very blunt. After 1988, the contest between a large proportion of ABRI and Suharto's camp increasingly looked less like shadow boxing and more like a match in which the gloves had well and truly been taken off. In 1991, Murdani was half way through his term as defence minister, and was no doubt aware that he had few remaining opportunities to push his case against Suharto from within the government. According to one version of events, Murdani encouraged army units in East Timor to step up pressure on anti-government activists at a time when he knew there would be representatives of the international media visiting the disputed territory. Suharto was about to go on a world tour, and his son-in-law, Prabowo, was stationed in East Timor at that time. The army knew, through its informers, that pro-independence supporters would demonstrate before the foreign journalists accompanying a Portuguese parliamentary delegation to Dili, and so it was decided to achieve two results with one action. A strong military response to the protesters would reassert ABRI's authority in East Timor, and it would also show up Suharto as the supreme commander of an army over which he had little control. Finally, it would also put then Lt Colonel Prabowo in a difficult position with Suharto, hampering Suharto's options for succession. Thus, the lives of over 100 civilians in East Timor were written off as dispensable in the power play between

Murdani and Suharto. (See Schwartz 1994, pp. 215–16, 345, note 56, for a similar version of events, based on the second-hand comments of Prabowo.)

Not to be outdone, Suharto used international public outrage to round on the pro-Murdani group within ABRI, removing from active duty East Timor commander Brigadier General Rudolph Warouw and Warouw's regional superior in Bali, Major General Sintong Panjaitan. Both men were considered to be pro-tégés of Murdani. Prabowo was not held accountable for any aspect of the incident. Nor was any responsibility attributed to Suharto's brother-in-law Wismoyo, who was commander of the Kostrad troops involved in the killings, or Try Sutrisno, who was ABRI commander at that time (Wismoyo and Try were still then regarded as Suharto loyalists). Panjaitan had been considered one of Wismoyo's main rivals for the position of army chief of staff.

Again, there is also a more conventional view of events. According to this, the military response was simply an attempt to reassert the army's authority in East Timor and had no other motivation. Yet to act in this way when it was known that journalists were present (IRIP 1991, p. 6) seems bizarre—especially since this was Indonesia's most sensitive international issue. Another 'conventional' theory was that, in a bid to disperse them, ill-disciplined soldiers simply opened fire on the unarmed demonstrators, who had been organised by Fretilin.[6] However, this does not accord with eye-witness accounts of the event, according to which the protest was noisy but peaceful, while the attack by the soldiers was highly organised (IRIP 1991, p. 4).

ABRI reasserts itself

In 1993, having been frustrated by Suharto's continual sidelining of ABRI in national affairs, a significant faction within ABRI moved to reassert its authority. One way in which it did so was through expanding its representation in the MPR and regional political forums. Apart from the seats automatically allocated to ABRI officers, many officers also retired early from ABRI and officially stood for national, provincial, and regency seats and

---

6   According to later discussion with a Fretilin representative, the protest was in fact organised by Fretilin.

senior party positions as Golkar members. By the early 1990s, it was estimated that about 40 per cent of Golkar's seats in the DPR were held by ex–ABRI members (Soejipto 1992). There was a belief at this time, and particularly from around 1993, that the move by a significant number of ABRI officers towards forming a political base from which to challenge Suharto was linked to a reform agenda. The 'reform agenda' attributed to these officers included greater democratisation and openness. However, since that time, the move by ABRI to reassert itself in the political process has featured less democratisation and openness, and more authoritarianism and control. Populist causes were useful for mobilising support, but in the final analysis it appeared that they were a means to an end rather than an end in themselves.

In 1993 ABRI played the hard political game with Suharto, nominating just retired armed forces commander-in-chief General Try Sutrisno for the vice-presidency. Try had been an adjutant to Suharto and, as a notable Muslim, had accompanied Suharto to Mecca on the hajj, which was a part of Suharto's strategy to shore up the Muslim vote. However, as ABRI commander, Try increasingly came under the influence of Murdani. Most notably, Try was commander of ABRI at the time of the Dili massacre. Suharto roundly castigated ABRI over the incident and took advantage of the issue to dispose of senior officers who were arrayed against him. Although supporting the military action against the protesters in Dili and making demonstrably false public claims about the extent of the killings, Try survived Suharto's wrath and retained his position. However, if Try was not firmly within the anti-Suharto camp before this, the political fallout from the Dili massacre appears to have confirmed him in this position.

In early 1993, Try allowed himself to be nominated by ABRI for the vice-presidency before Suharto had publicly named his deputy. This was unheard of in Indonesian politics, as the president has traditionally had the right of appointing his own deputy, who is then endorsed by consensus within the MPR. However, with ABRI taking the public step of nominating one of their own before Suharto could choose, a decision that was openly supported by the PPP, and then engineering the vote in the MPR, Suharto had little choice but accept him. It has been said by some insiders that Suharto might well have appointed Try in any case, or that he was not seriously opposed to having Try as vice-president. However, even this view acknowledges that Suharto was furious at least with the method of Try's appointment, if not with its fact, and it is now generally believed that he had favoured Habibie for the position. It was foisted upon him as a deliberate gesture of defiance by ABRI, one that would have begged a more broad and debilitating fallout had Suharto not accepted it. By having Try appointed vice-president, ABRI was in effect saying that, although Suharto was still president, it would be ABRI that determined his successor. Suharto's response to Try's appointment was to sack Murdani, the person most strongly associated with Try's appointment, from his position as defence minister. Murdani lost a public position as a consequence of ABRI's tussle with Suharto, but he did not lose his influence within ABRI, or on Try.[7]

The year 1993 was a watershed for the anti-Suharto faction of ABRI in two other areas as well. The first was the banning of the state lottery, a decision that was foisted upon Suharto by militant Muslims who were believed to have been encouraged, or at least given free rein, by ABRI. Suharto was overseas when this issue blew up, and it seems to have been timed so that Suharto would be unable to react in any meaningful way before it was too late. As Suharto financially benefited from the lottery, through a family-controlled *yayasan* (charitable foundation), the issue was a particularly personal snub. Then, in December 1993, a number of senior ABRI officers publicly supported the campaign by Megawati Sukarnoputri to become chair of the PDI, despite Suharto's best efforts to have her appointment derailed. As a daughter of Suharto's predecessor, ABRI's support for Megawati's appointment was a highly symbolic gesture of defiance of Suharto's leadership.

Yet within ABRI, there was clearly no single formal position on these or other matters. While a significant group within ABRI appeared to support moves against Suharto, there were divisions over other issues, and it was not simply a case of ABRI being divided into one majority and one minority camp. Further, while Benny Murdani was seen very much as the symbolic leader of the anti-Suharto camp, there has been considerable debate about the degree to which he has orchestrated events to conspire against

---

7 Greg Sheridan recounts an anecdote that Try so highly regarded Murdani that he had to fight back an urge to salute when he saw the former defence minister (1993).

Suharto, and the degree to which his supporters are united on a range of other issues.

Factions or fractions: ABRI divides

Some analysts have talked about ABRI as comprising 'factions' or, as the consensus-conscious Javanese called them, *fraksi* (fractions) —factions being oppositional and fractions being a part of a whole. To this end, the *fraksi* have been identified as being anti- or pro-Suharto, or more recently as 'red and white' or 'green'. The 'red and white' *fraksi* is generally anti–Suharto, secular, nationalist, and was briefly pro–PDI (at least as a vehicle for destabilising Suharto). It is not aligned with the rise of political Islam and is generally opposed to the influence wielded by ICMI. The 'green' *fraksi* is generally pro–Suharto, pro–Islam, supported by or linked with ICMI, and at least until late 1996 and early 1997, with some tendency towards supporting the PPP, or groups within it. On balance, the 'red and white' *fraksi* has been identified with Murdani, while the 'green' *fraksi* has been identified with former ABRI commander General Feisal Tanjung.[8]

This discussion of 'red and white' and 'green' failed to acknowledge that there were more than two groups within ABRI. The view that there were just two opposing groups, by definition, meant there was some sort of genuine, internal opposition to Suharto. However, there were, in fact, a number of groups, or 'clusters', located around key generals within ABRI and varying between themselves over a range of issues. It is tempting here to use the Javanese term *aliran* (streams), which have traditionally designated the influence and patronage exercised by key individuals within Java's, and more recently Indonesia's, religious and political systems. Perhaps Abdurrahman Wahid could have been said to have an *aliran* in the traditional sense, through his personal domination of the NU and the Forum Demokrasi, a political discussion group. However, some observers believe that this term should be restricted to its religious usage and regard clear patronage as being a key feature.

The types of issues that determine the 'clustering' within ABRI are: whether the senior officers are pro- or anti-Suharto, *santri*, *abangan*, or even non-Muslim; their view of ABRI's dual

---

8 Feisal left the position to become, briefly, the defence minister in 1998.

function of protecting the state and being a political player; levels of funding for ABRI in relation to other national projects; issues concerning political and economic centralisation (including whether Indonesia should revert to a form of federation rather than remain as a unitary state); whether they are pro- or anti-democratisation; their responses to (and benefits from) corruption; their links with various members of the civilian elites, and so on.

Crouch termed it thus:

These assumptions have long been accepted by many observers of the Indonesian military who have therefore been trying for many years to detect lines of cleavage within ABRI—whether hard-liners versus soft-liners, Javanese versus non-Javanese, Diponogoro versus the other divisions, 'centrists' versus 'militants', Angkatan 45 versus Angkatan Magelang [a generational divide], 'professional' versus 'political' and 'financial' officers, 'pragmatic' versus 'principled' officers or whatever (Crouch 1994, p. 20).

Some senior officers have been seen to be developing power bases, and to counter this, Suharto has had many officers shifted around, to discourage them from building personal loyalty among regional troops. Yet such power bases have been established nevertheless, in much the same way that they were in the late 1950s, and it is from such power bases that a challenge to Suharto or his successor could come. 'Today there is no such thing as a military position', according to one senior, but unnamed officer: 'There are only the opinions of certain officers' (Berfield & Loveard 1997).

Beyond the 'clusters' of which ABRI appeared to be comprised, a small group of younger officers, each of whom had their own 'cluster', but who formed a sort of alliance, appeared to be readying themselves for the post-Suharto period. These officers represented some of ABRI's core commands, as well as having links to the more politically important parts of the outer islands. A number of senior officers also have links with key members of Indonesia's economic elite, which provides those in the economic elite with some military security while providing some potential revenue to the officers should central sources of funds dry up. To suggest that these officers are, or could become, 'warlords'—in the way that a number of the senior officers of ABRI in the 1950s were 'warlords'—is an overstatement. However, they had increased, and could have been expected to increase, their very considerable power, in both military and political terms. These officers, identified in the last chapter, were certainly arranged in opposition to Suharto, or were at least determined to influence the issue of his succession. Rather than mount a *coup d'état* (which was kept on the back-burner as an option of last resort), they thought it preferable for Indonesia's economic standing and for the legitimacy of the next government that they exercise their power only *after* Suharto had died or retired. The idea was that the real opposition to Suharto should not try to displace him. Rather, if it was not forced to act sooner, it should ensure that its own candidates were appointed to the positions of president and vice-president after Suharto, even if in the middle term such positions were far less influential than they had been when occupied by, or under, Suharto and even Sukarno.

Opposition to Suharto, then, began almost as soon as he moved to take power and, with brief lulls, has continued in a number of guises since then, albeit sponsored by different groups and individuals with somewhat different agendas. Much of Suharto's reign has been committed to out-manœuvring such opposition and continuing to shore up his support base by turning to different individuals and groups for support. What had begun to unite opposition to Suharto, though, and what gave it such force in his final years, were the combined issues of his personalisation of power and the economic benefits that he, his family, and his associates had derived from it. Beyond that, the troubles that had brought Suharto to power more than three decades earlier had very much become a part of history. As a consequence, so had the real reason for his attainment of power.

Murdani remained in the background. The younger, up-and-coming officers, who could be expected to play a significant role in Indonesia's political future, all acknowledged Murdani as their greatest influence. Many informed insiders and other commentators claimed that Murdani was ABRI's *dalang*, controlling the puppets. Others, however, who even acknowledged the rise of the younger officers, doubted Murdani's continuing influence, and one senior observer was given to describing Murdani as 'just another bitter old general who lost his job'. Murdani was certainly not happy about losing his position as commander of ABRI or being dumped as defence minister. But he is definitely not 'just another' displaced general.

Perhaps in real terms it matters little what Murdani's actual contribution was to the internal opposition to Suharto, apart from giving Jakarta's legion of rumour-mongers a continuous supply of subject material. There is no doubt that, as this is being written, Murdani still has the respect and loyalty of very many in ABRI. Many of the generation of senior officers who trained in the 1960s and particularly in the early 1970s still see him as something of a father figure. In this sense, Murdani was a rallying point for the 'clusters' that might more broadly be identified as making up the 'red and white' faction. In a country where symbolism is often thought to be more important than reality, the fact that so many people *believed* Murdani to be the head of the anti-Suharto faction, and that he did little to dispel that belief, was enough to announce that Suharto could no longer rely on the majority of ABRI to be his loyal supporters.

7

POLITICAL
OPPOSITION WITHIN
INDONESIA

Publicly, the New Order government liked to present Indonesia's political milieu as satisfying the people's needs and desires, and therefore as essentially uncontested. However, it is readily apparent to even the most casual observer that the Indonesian political field is both overtly and covertly contested, very often in the strongest possible ways. Broadly, the main sources of contestation within Indonesia have been from within the official political structure itself, as noted in the chapter 6, and from regional dissidence, to be discussed in chapter 9. The third and most troubling source of discontent and opposition is from domestic public opposition.

Domestic opposition to the New Order government

The official non-government parties are the most obvious source of opposition to the New Order government, although they are not formally allowed to act as an official Opposition *per se*. They are official in the sense that the parties were formed under the auspices of the New Order government and are officially sanctioned. In addition to the official parties, a range of tolerated and banned political, legal, union, and development organisations act as an informal opposition to the New Order government. These groups are the most troubling source of discontent because, in the final analysis, they are the groups most likely to act as a catalyst for both internal oppositions and for regional dissent. They have the greatest (perhaps the only) chance to bring about genuine political change, such as to a pluralist or democratic political system. This is because dissenters *within* the system, such as those within ABRI and Golkar, do not hold out genuine hope for significant change, while regional dissidence alone has not shown itself capable of successfully challenging the central government. In the period from the beginning of 1997 until after the MPR elections in March 1998, contestation spilled over into frequent, overtly political rioting in one part of the archipelago or another. Whatever shallow facade of consensus Indonesia's government had tried to present had been left in tattered shreds by these events.

Disputes within Golkar and ABRI, particularly over the issue of succession, contributed to Suharto's effective resignation, but such a split is unlikely to alter fundamentally Indonesia's political structure or its orientation towards authoritarian rule; indeed, through the reimposing of 'order', such an outcome could eventually reinforce authoritarian rule. Opposition from this source can be characterised more accurately as opposition to Suharto and the excesses related to him than as opposition to the idea of military dominated authoritarian rule as such. Rebellion in the outlying provinces has been troublesome for Indonesia's government. But while these rebellions and especially the human rights issues they raise create diplomatic difficulties for Indonesia abroad, they do not genuinely threaten Indonesia's existing power structures. At best, the rebellious provinces could hope to receive special administrative status—as Aceh Province (Daerah Istemewa Aceh, or Aceh Special Region) already has, albeit only nominally. They are unlikely to be allowed genuine autonomy or to break away under any circumstances, short of the dissolution of the state. These political, legal, union, and development groups, then, are the most troubling source of discontent for the government. Although disunited, they represent the potential for opposition to coalesce around core ideas (such as participatory democratic pluralism and a separation of executive and judicial powers) or around an emerging political structure (such as was briefly illustrated by the PDI under Megawati). In this way, they could potentially emerge as a genuine[1] and potentially viable opposition.

The two legal 'opposition' parties that are allowed to contest Indonesia's 'festivals of democracy' are, as already noted, the PPP

---

1   An opposition to Suharto but not, in principle, to the system through which he rules is not, I think, a 'genuine' opposition.

and the PDI. Both parties were created by the New Order government in 1973 by bringing together the remaining legal parties into two groups. Both parties have been subject to government interference in their affairs. Their policies, which until the early 1990s were tightly controlled by the government and were obliged to conform to government stipulated principles, were pale reflections of government policy. Beyond that, the candidates for both parties have to be approved by the government, which can reorder their standing on candidature lists and hence exclude candidates who are regarded as potentially troublesome. In some respects, both parties can be said to reflect the interests of factions within the New Order government and have been used at various times as front organisations for those New Order factions. If either the PPP or the PDI is to represent a base around which an opposition can coalesce, then, they will require significant impetus and probably permission from one of the major internal factions, most probably the influential dissident wing of ABRI.

As a part of the process by which the PDI and PPP are allowed to exist, they are banned from engaging in campaigning outside strictly limited election periods, unlike Golkar. The idea behind this is that the general population should be politically inactive in between election periods, so as to be able to get on with the government-defined task of development without troubling distractions. In between elections, the general population is regarded as an apolitical, but in reality depoliticised, 'floating mass'. Like so much of New Order rhetoric, this term is intended to disguise what amounts to the effective emasculation of public politics. What it means is that the *wong cilik* (little people) are—in a part-patronising and part-oppressive manner—excluded from conventional political discussion, association, or activity, other than during the circumscribed windows of opportunity that are the 'festivals of democracy' (elections).

PPP: an Islamic party

To an observer of Indonesian politics in 1998, the PPP is the strongest source of potential opposition to the New Order government, almost entirely as a consequence of the collapse of the PDI. However, the PPP has its own series of tensions and agendas, not all of which are comfortably accommodated within, or controlled by, the party (as demonstrated by extensive pro-PPP rioting in Indonesia in the lead-up to the 1997 DPR elections). These internal divisions reflect the PPP's heterogeneous origins as a composite of separate political parties that, to a greater or lesser degree, had the establishment of Indonesia as an Islamic state as their covert, unifying policy.

The PPP was established by the New Order government in 1973, and the then existing Muslim parties were 'encouraged' to join it. Those that took up this offer included NU, which was the strongest non-government political grouping at that time, Partai Muslimin Indonesia (or 'Parmusi', a government created successor to Masyumi), the Sumatran-based social welfare group Perti, and Partai Sarekat Islam Indonesia. Comprising the four Muslim parties, the PPP was the more prominent of the two 'opposition' parties until the NU made the tactical move of 'withdrawing from politics' in 1984. The withdrawal of the NU dealt a significant blow to the PPP, depriving it of a solid core of voters and freeing up erstwhile PPP voters to vote for Golkar or, more probably, the PDI.

As a creation of the government, the PPP has traditionally had difficulty in justifying its existence to its supporters and even to itself. Comprised of distinct factions with competing agendas, the PPP has historically lacked a sense of cohesion or legal purpose, as the idea of creating an Islamic state is strictly forbidden from the official political agenda. This lack of cohesion and purpose has been manifested in the PPP's political platform, which, already tightly constrained by government policy requirements, has been unable to articulate a clear goal. As representatives of Islamic organisations, the *raison d'être* of the constituent parts of the PPP was the creation of an Islamic state or the imposition of Islamic law within the secular state (as applies to the indigenous Malays of Malaysia). However, the Old Order government of Sukarno was at pains to suppress this tendency, particularly because of its potential to incite regional rebellion, such as the *Dar'ul Islam* rebellion and the Masyumi-backed PRRI–Permesta rebellion. Islam was accepted as a part of Sukarno's syncretic ideological trilogy of *Nasakom*, a composite word incorporating *nasionalisme* (nationalism), *agama* (religion), and *komunisme* (communism). But he could not allow Islam to dominate lest it challenge the nationalist element of government (including ABRI) or the strongly developing PKI, which is not to mention his own *abangan* (nominally Islamic) sympathies.

The New Order government under Suharto further restricted the political rise of Islam, for the same reasons as Sukarno (although by this time the PKI was no longer part of the equation), and by the late 1970s had identified Islamic extremism as a threat to national security. Beyond wanting to control the potentially explosive force of a highly politicised Islam, especially at a time when Islamic fundamentalism was radicalising politics from north Africa to Malaysia, Suharto recognised that the emergence of a politically dominant Islam would cleave Indonesian political society along religious lines. To this end, the *Pancasila* principle of belief in one god does not apply to a specific god. It is a sop to Muslim fundamentalists, who insist that the only god is Allah but who are prepared to accept, as lesser religions, the observance of a single deity. As a consequence, Indonesia's five recognised religions (dividing Christianity in two) incorporate some greatly differing systems of belief in a rationalisation of this monotheism. The one clear advantage for the New Order government in this, apart from partly pacifying Islamic demands for religious observance, is that all Indonesians must subscribe to one of these religions, which has the effect of limiting alternative belief systems, as communism has been argued to be. The other main reason for wanting to control the political rise of Islam is that it has the potential to create tensions between both Muslim and non-Muslim communities, especially with the Chinese and outer islanders, as well as between *santri* and *abangan* Muslims, the latter traditionally having quite different religious perspectives and non-religiously oriented political aspirations. Nevertheless, since the later 1980s, Suharto has been keen to be seen as an observant Muslim and has promoted a number of Islamic causes, including the building of mosques (which is largely paid for by a Suharto-controlled *yayasan*, which is funded by an official levy on Indonesia's public servants). He was also involved in establishing the Islamic intellectuals' organisation ICMI and its constituent think-tank CIDES (Centre for Information and Development Studies), which was established largely to counter the Murdani-influenced (if not controlled) think-tank CSIS (Centre for Strategic and International Studies).

If there has been one unifying role for the PPP since the effective, almost ritual disembowelling[2] of the PDI, it has been as the predominant remaining legal voice of opposition to Suharto and Golkar. For over two years Megawati Sukarnoputri and the PDI acted as a rallying point for opposition to Suharto and as an ostensible push towards democracy, but as a consequence of the effective destruction of the PDI, the PPP has assumed that role, to the point where members of the PDI's Megawati faction joined the PPP for street marches and other protests. Megawati announced that she would not vote in the 1997 DPR elections, which gave a signal to her followers not to do so either; to ask them explicitly not to vote is illegal. But too many of her supporters were still angry about the destruction of the PDI the previous year, and they took the opportunity of PPP rallies to display their anger.

Many members of the PPP also took strength from both the new, unofficial PDI support and what was seen as a rising tide of opposition to Suharto.[3] In March 1997, just ahead of the DPR election in May and in a move that was almost unheard of for its audacity (at least for an organisation that hoped to survive), seven branches of the PPP announced their objection to the continuing structure of the lower house. They argued that, because of government manipulation of the electoral process, it was impossible for the PPP (or the PDI) ever to achieve a majority. Other, similar, protestations in the past have been strongly dealt with. Picking up on Megawati's call and the university-based *golput* (blank electoral card) movement, in which voters were encouraged not to fill in their electoral cards as a sign of protest against a fundamentally compromised political system, the branches proposed a boycott of the elections. But these comments invited the predictable government response that encouraging citizens not to vote, even though they may legally choose not to, would be regarded as subversion and would be punished. The 'crime' of 'subversion', as it is regarded in Indonesia, can be punished by the death penalty. Although this penalty has not been enforced since 1988, the law still allows for lengthy prison sentences and acts as a considerable deterrent to potential 'subversives'. Nevertheless,

---

2 I am thinking here of the old English punishment for treason, rather than the Japanese *hara kiri*.

3 If this opposition to Suharto was not reflected in the final DPR vote, it was because of the tight grip that Golkar had over the electoral process.

support for the 'boycott' option was beginning to emerge as a practical expression of dissatisfaction with the existing political system.

With so few outlets for expression of dissent, however, any organisation that was able to organise mass gatherings legally could have been expected to act as a rallying point for anti-government forces. And in the period leading up to the election, if public protests could be interpreted as a reflection of a wider prevailing view, the PPP rallies indicated a high and increasing level of opposition to the government, as did continuing student protest after the 1998 presidential 'election'. The underlying fact, though, was that the PPP, as it stood, did not have a credible policy alternative to Golkar, apart from a greater commitment to ending corruption. Too much of its vote was clearly gained from drawing disillusioned PDI voters across in a protest against the government, but the total PPP–PDI vote in 1997 actually represented an overall decline in voting opposition to Golkar, based on the percentage of the population that decided to vote. As a force within Indonesian politics, the PPP could have been expected to decline once the 1997–98 election period was over and it was no longer allowed to organise public rallies. Further, by making so small a dent in Golkar's standing in the polls as a consequence of institutionalised vote management, the PPP's true weakness would mean that it could not expect to hold on to even the putative support it received during the 1997 DPR elections campaign. The dissident groups that had rallied to the PPP as a source of opposition to Suharto were more interested in pursuing their own agendas and policies, none of which included the promotion of pro-Islamic ideals. Having recognised the real-world ineffectualness of the PPP, its lack of policy development, and its internal divisions, they were expected to seek other outlets for expressing their frustrations, just as the NU had earlier done.

The reawakened Islamic scholars

In 1984 the leader of the NU, the charismatic Abdurrahman Wahid—more commonly referred to as Gus Dur after his inherited title *gusti* (lord)—argued that the NU's involvement in politics limited its acceptance to the government and to ABRI, and that it could better pursue the interests of its members as a non-government and theoretically non-political organisation

(Vatikiotis 1993, p. 124). He later admitted that there was no longer any point in the NU remaining within the PPP, as the latter was structurally ineffectual and the NU could wield more political clout outside the formal political system.

The NU is a formal Islamic organisation and, originally based on a rural constituency, was once the most politically conservative of the major Islamic groups. However, under Gus Dur's leadership, the NU has moved towards taking a more liberal stance on a range of issues, although his commitment to such liberalism is tainted by a sense of what is achievable under the New Order government and what is likely to further his personal political cause. It could also be suggested that Gus Dur's liberalism is based on populism and, not being grounded in principle, is at least flexible and is perhaps changing. Gus Dur moved from being openly against Suharto until late 1996 to openly backing him from early 1997, although he again distanced himself in early 1998. Certainly this indicated a shift in position that, at one level, was difficult to justify, especially given that, as Indonesian politics was becoming more polarised, others had become more firmly entrenched in their opposition to Suharto. Such a shift on Gus Dur's part could be ascribed to the playing of a waiting game, or even to a Javanese sense of syncretism in which opposites can be combined while retaining an outwardly calm and reconciled appearance. There is little doubt that Gus Dur would also have been greatly concerned about the future of the NU, with that future perhaps coming under a darker cloud the longer and more fervently it opposed Suharto.

But the shift also reflected the very real challenge that was thrown up to Gus Dur personally, which came from within the NU and which was backed by Suharto loyalists. Gus Dur's somewhat flamboyant leadership style was destined to find opposition within the traditionally conservative NU, and campaigning as strongly against Suharto as he did, there was considerable impetus from outside for him to be removed from the position of NU leadership. At the NU's congress in December 1994, opposition to Gus Dur's continued leadership of the NU was backed by Suharto's daughter Tutut, the Golkar chairperson and then information minister Harmoko, then research and technology minister Habibie, and ABRI's then head of social and political affairs (later interior minister), retired Lt General Raden Hartono, who openly dispensed funds to Gus Dur's opponents (Grant 1996, p. 92). Added to the pressure applied by then ABRI head General Feisal Tanjung, ten ministers, and the then vice-president, Try Sutrisno, the anti-Gus Dur faction almost toppled him from the NU's top job, failing by 142 votes to 174. This failure made Suharto furious, but Gus Dur no doubt received the message that he was not invulnerable to the president's displeasure. Whatever it was that motivated Gus Dur to shift fundamentally his public position to one in favour of Suharto and *against* political change, there are decreasingly few in Indonesian politics who take seriously the ability to reconcile polar opposites and still retain any sense of credibility.

One of the main losers from Gus Dur's defection from the anti-Suharto camp was the Forum Demokrasi, which brought together some members from the liberal wing of the NU with smaller Christian and non-government, pro-democracy organisations and individuals. The Forum Demokrasi was technically not a political organisation, but was said to be, in effect, a significantly smaller but more embracing version of the 'non-political' NU. However, observers have seen the Forum as being very much a political vehicle, arguably for democratically minded groups and people outside the PDI, but more transparently for Gus Dur himself. With Gus Dur's shift closer to Suharto in 1997, the Forum Demokrasi was left adrift like a ship whose captain had opted to sail on another vessel in what looked like smoother waters.

A democratic challenge

As a consequence of the diminution of the PPP after the withdrawal of the NU in 1984, the PDI became Indonesia's most viable opposition party to the New Order government until being effectively destroyed by the government in 1996. Like the PPP, the PDI was formed in 1973, and nationalist and Christian-based parties were 'encouraged' to join it. The PDI comprises the old PNI, which was the party originally associated with Indonesia's first president, Sukarno, the Parti Katolik, the (Protestant) Partai Kristen Indonesia (or 'Parkindo'), the Leftist but anti-PKI Partai Murba (which included former foreign minister Adam Malik), and the formerly army-sponsored League of Upholders of Indonesian Independence (IPKI), which General Nasution was instrumental in forming in the early 1950s.

Looking at the origins of the PDI, it is hardly surprising that it became (for a few years at least) the vehicle through which many ordinary Indonesians expressed opposition, or that it received support from individuals who were once central to the establishment and maintenance of the New Order government but who had become disenchanted with Suharto. Indeed, it could be suggested that remnants of disaffection within ABRI towards Suharto, especially by those opposed to the PKI but still in favour of Sukarno, were able to later find allies within the PDI through its PNI and IPKI links. Or, perhaps more plausibly, formerly staunch supporters of Golkar found within the PDI a not entirely unacceptable vehicle through which to pursue their own, ulterior ambitions. In any case, the ousting of Megawati in June 1996 destroyed the PDI as a focus of opposition to the New Order government, although it did potentially show that a coalescence of anti-New Order groups was possible.

As previously noted, ABRI has always taken an active interest in the affairs of the two smaller parties, but has been particularly involved in the affairs of the PDI since 1993, with a number of senior officers being closely linked to the rise of Megawati Sukarnoputri to the chair of the party. In the past, senior ABRI figures worked to help discredit opposing figures, to provide or ensure the provision of financing for campaigns (or to withdraw it from others), and to boost numbers at rallies by encouraging associated youth groups and others to attend. In this last respect, Java's traditional streams of patronage can be seen at work, where particular individuals are able to cultivate other groups and individuals as a support base. The fact that Megawati was able to demonstrate that she had support from at least some senior officers added to her credibility as a genuine figure of opposition to Suharto. Hence, she was seen as a real political leader rather than as a mere cat's paw, as her successor, Suryadi, was so widely viewed. It is worth noting that Suryadi had himself been removed as chairperson of the PDI as a consequence of Suharto-inspired ABRI manipulation. Following the PDI's reasonable electoral showing in 1987, leading PDI figures had called on Suryadi to demand changes to the electoral system, including an open vote for the president, and an end to corruption, injustice, and other abuses of power. Golkar and ABRI pressured Suryadi to back down, which he and other senior PDI figures did in January 1993. But this damaged the credibility of the PDI with the public and left Suryadi with little support within the party. However, Suharto had decided he wanted Suryadi out anyway, as a result of his earlier critical statements. At its national congress in July, the PDI held an election for a new chairperson, but procedural irregularities caused a revote. Megawati was nominated, and a significant faction within ABRI saw an opportunity to embarrass Suharto and pushed Megawati's candidature. Despite the Suharto camp's best and most intimidating efforts, in December 1993 Megawati was elected as leader of the PDI. For a while she actually looked like establishing a genuine base of opposition to Suharto, but because of this, Megawati was dumped as PDI leader in a government-orchestrated congress in Medan in June 1996.

Perhaps forgetting that, as a political leader, she was in part a creation of a faction of ABRI (although she also had considerable personal appeal), Megawati refused to accept the outcome of the 'rebel congress' in Medan and continued to occupy the PDI headquarters in Jakarta. As government pressure for her to vacate the PDI headquarters mounted, Megawati's supporters barricaded themselves in the building. After weeks of government criticism of Megawati for not accepting the results of the Medan congress and agreeing to step down, anti-Megawati PDI members and soldiers wearing the PDI's red T-shirts with a bull's head logo stormed the building on 27 July. In the ensuing mayhem, it is believed that a number of PDI members in the headquarters were killed, many disappeared, and others were arrested. Various estimates suggest that dozens, perhaps more than a hundred, were killed in the violence.[4] The attack on the PDI headquarters enraged Megawati's supporters and others sympathetic to the PDI cause, as a consequence of which there were two days of rioting in Jakarta. It was the worst rioting seen in Jakarta since 1974, with shops, banks, and cars being looted and burned. The government responded by sending soldiers into the streets, although such was the fervour of the outburst that they could not immediately restore order.

In the wash-up of the riots, New Order officials started to look for culprits on whom to pin responsibility. It was not long before they identified the student-led, left-wing PRD and accused it of being a front for a revival of the old PKI. Although an official platform of the PRD has not been published, the organisation has a

---

4 Abdurrahman Wahid said that about 100 were killed, while Megawati said that 158 of her supporters were still missing.

democratic socialist outlook and is (or was) associated with social-ist organisations overseas.[5] The official view was that the PRD had infiltrated the PDI and was attempting to use the otherwise com-pliant party for its own revolutionary purposes. Megawati denied that the PRD was involved with the PDI, while PRD members denied orchestrating the July riots. However, PRD activists were present at the PDI headquarters before the raid, and PRD leaders did address pro-Megawati groups there. The PRD is affiliated with a number of organisations, including the group Student Soli-darity for Indonesian Democracy (students being a common base for radical politics) and the Indonesian Centre for Workers' Struggle (inadequately represented workers being another prime source of political discontent). These groups have also been targeted by the government for their political activities. The chairperson of the PRD, Budiman Sujatmiko, and its Secretary General, Petrus Hary-anto, as well as the President of the Indonesian Centre for Labour Struggle, Dita Indahsari, were gaoled on charges of subversion. Charges were also laid against eleven other PRD members. Fur-thermore, among leading activists arrested was the independent trade union leader Mochtar Pakpahan. The PRD is now a banned organisation in Indonesia and membership of it is illegal. Its members have gone underground, although government security agencies have continued to track and, where possible, arrest them.

Beyond the PRD, there is the small, unofficial Muslim United Development Party, headed by Sri Bintang Pamungkas, a DPR member and outspoken critic of the New Order government. Sri Bintang was charged before the 1997 DPR elections with inciting citizens not to vote, which is regarded as subversion, and for de-faming the president. While Sri Bintang regards himself as an independent, those within the political system see him more as a renegade PPP member, reflecting the types of factionalism that underlie much of the party's structure. Sri Bintang is hardly a con-ventional representative of the PPP, as no one else has been as outspoken about what they perceive as Indonesia's political short-comings. But his background is in the PPP, and like Gus Dur and NU, Sri Bintang has split off primarily because he does not regard the PPP as constituting a viable opposition.

---

5   This is based on discussions with PRD members and an organisation with which it
     is associated in Australia.

'Non-political' Islam

Beyond political parties, other politically active organisations include the three Islamic groups—ICMI, Muhammadiyah, and the NU—and the influential human rights advocacy group the Indonesian Legal Aid Foundation (LBHI), as well as a number of small 'underground' organisations. Apart from the mosques, the two main Islamic organisations, NU and Muhammadiyah, are the only major organisations in Indonesia to exist outside formal government control.

As an independent force, the NU was slow in developing a 'non-political' profile, but in the 1990s began to assert itself as one of the main players in the political game. As NU chairperson, Gus Dur became one of Indonesia's leading advocates for democratic reform and used the conservative, rural-based, 135 million-strong NU as a platform for asserting the democratic principles implied in Islam. Until 1997 Gus Dur counted Megawati Sukarnoputri, and retired ABRI chief and former defence minister Benny Murdani among his close peers. Both Megawati and Murdani have positioned themselves as opponents of Suharto, one overtly and the other covertly, and Gus Dur's association with them and his later switch to Suharto clearly identified him and the NU as being politically active, perhaps more so than had the NU remained in the PPP.

In the lead-up to the May 1997 DPR elections, Gus Dur was critical of at least some members of the government by blaming a spate of riots, in particular religious riots, on a lack of respect for the government. 'I see that our government's respectability is declining because there are too many confusing policies and improper acts by top government officials', he said:

Violence reflects a government's respectability. If a government is respected, it will win people's trust. If people trust the government, they will leave all the problems they are facing to the government. Thus no-one will take the law into their own hands nor take their dissatisfaction to the street. Violence will automatically come to the fore when the government loses its respectability (*Jakarta Post*, 11 April 1997).

Gus Dur's criticism came after he and President Suharto appeared to have resolved, at least in public, their outstanding differences, and was sharply at odds with his support for the continued tenure of Suharto. Gus Dur had even appeared at rallies before the May elections with Suharto's daughter, Siti Hardiyanti

Rukmana ('Tutut'), who was then deputy chairperson of Golkar. But this criticism indicated that Gus Dur continued to hold deep reservations about at least some members of the government, especially in his veiled reference to 'confusing policies and improper acts by top government officials'. This could be construed as a comment on the conflict between the government's anti-corruption policy and the involvement of Suharto's family in favourable, perhaps corrupt, business dealings. Or it could have been an attack on ministers who were about to fall from grace with Suharto and who were popular neither with ABRI nor the wider population. In this sense, Gus Dur could have been referring to Habibie, whose role in Indonesia's purchase of East German warships and its proposed nuclear energy policy were both highly controversial, the warships being unrealistically expensive to refit and the nuclear energy policy unwise in an area prone to volcanic activity. Further, Habibie's leadership in drawing significant levels of government funding into high-technology industries had failed to show a profit, or look like they would do so within a politically acceptable period. Gus Dur could also have included in the reference the former Golkar chairperson and information minister Harmoko, whose pre-election comments in 1997 about the size of Golkar's impending victory were widely regarded as injudicious. Harmoko was removed from the Ministry of Information a few weeks after the elections, being given the position of Minister of State for Special Affairs.

If Gus Dur's public pronouncements were occasionally confusing, and if his shift from an anti- to a pro- and back to an anti-Suharto position in 1997–98 only further underlined the unsettled state of his political position, this reflected at least in part the prevailing ambiguity of Indonesia's elites (particularly those from Java) regarding their own positions and conventional democratic principles more generally. Even while opposing Suharto and openly promoting democracy, Gus Dur continued to use his inherited title '*gusti*' and was known to run the NU as something of a personal fiefdom. Further, Gus Dur's notion of respect for authority sits more comfortably with traditional—and dominant —central Javanese values of piety, respect, and deference than it does with conceptions of democracy. A similar criticism has been levelled against Gus Dur's former political ally Megawati, who espoused democratic principles but shared a similar sense of *noblesse oblige* rather than encouraging an openly participatory political framework.

There have been several attempts by government agents to depose Gus Dur as leader of the NU, and he was marked as a public opponent of the New Order government. However, Suharto has found their late-blooming alliance to be tactically useful in helping to appease at least one section of the Islamic community and in giving the last period of the New Order government a type of respectability, which it was quickly losing, or at least wider acceptance. The NU has survived as an organisation primarily by being able to bend with the prevailing winds, and at least at its top level, it has clearly been prepared to do this in the late 1990s. Having said this, Suharto is understood to have very little trust in Gus Dur, regarding him as a person whose allegiances are fickle. Many within Golkar viewed Gus Dur's move towards Suharto with a mild form of horror. In late January 1998, Gus Dur suffered a stroke, which curtailed his career in politics.

Muhammadiyah

The Muhammadiyah (or Followers of Muhammad) is one of Indonesia's oldest organisations, having been founded in 1912 and having survived largely intact to present times. The Muhammadiyah is no longer an overtly political organisation, being formed originally for social and educational purposes, primarily in urban areas, to present a less syncretic form of Islam to Java's Islamic community. Being an urban-based organisation, the Muhammadiyah has tended towards a modernist view of the role of Islam, seeing it as a force for evolutionary change towards a more liberal society (see Barton 1994 for further discussion of the liberal aspects of Indonesian Islam).

The Muhammadiyah was most involved in the political process after being incorporated, along with the NU and other Islamic organisations, into Masyumi by Japan in 1943. The Muhammadiyah remained in Masyumi throughout the 1950s and, as such, was a significant player in Indonesian politics. However, leading Masyumi figures were involved in the PRRI–Permesta rebellion in 1947–48, and in 1960 Sukarno banned the organisation. The Muhammadiyah separated itself from the politically dead Masyumi and continued its activities, albeit as an ostensibly non-political organisation.

As well as its social and educational functions, the Muhammadiyah has, as a *santri* organisation, a long history of intolerance towards ethnic Chinese and Christians, particularly where they are seen to be trying to convert others or have erected temples or churches in Muhammadiyah strongholds. Muhammadiyah leaders have also been critical of any Chinese business presence in rural areas, and they remain openly critical of large ethnic Chinese business interests in Indonesia. However, as a leading Islamic organisation, with a claimed membership base of some 28 million, the Muhammadiyah was openly courted by Suharto as a part of his campaign to win over Indonesia's Muslims. The leader of the Muhammadiyah, Amien Rais, was invited to join ICMI, where he played an influential role. However, in February 1997—in a split that highlighted the divisions that were developing in Indonesian politics between Suharto's group and large sections of the Islamic community—Rais was forced to resign his membership of an ICMI committee (and effectively of ICMI) because he had attacked the New Order government's policy on mining. Rais had said that foreign investors received too large a share of Indonesia's natural resources.

The government was particularly sensitive to his criticism following a series of what appeared to be religious riots in the preceding weeks, and although ICMI had been distancing itself from the government up to that time, it still retained a number of influential supporters of its head, Habibie, and Suharto. In 1990, under Suharto's auspices, ICMI was created from scratch as a society for Islamic intellectuals. The move was largely designed to bolster Suharto's standing with the Islamic community and to provide a base of intellectual support that was an alternative to what he perceived to be the pro-Murdani, putatively Christian-led CSIS. Suharto appointed his trusted research and technology minister, Habibie, as the head of this new organisation, ensuring that ICMI would not escape his influence as the CSIS appeared to have done.

However, as the PPP and some other Muslims distanced themselves from the New Order government, and as Suharto's courting of the 'Muslim vote' increasingly appeared to be a cynical exercise in bolstering his support base, some members of ICMI began increasingly to question government policies. Rais's criticisms of the government's mining policy constituted a broad, though diffuse, attack on Suharto himself. They could be seen as a veiled reference not just to foreign-owned businesses, but also (reflecting a kind of chauvinistic nationalism and religious intolerance) to Indonesia's Chinese community, the leading members of which were closely connected with Suharto. As tensions between Suharto and the PPP increased in late 1996 and early 1997, members of ICMI found themselves increasingly compromised. Habibie stepped in and resolved the issue of Rais's criticisms by forcing him to resign, but this move signalled that the period of courtship between Suharto and Islamic organisations was drawing to a close, and that Suharto might no longer be able to count on Islamic support to counter the influence of the more secular factions of ABRI.

Other Islam

Ever since the *Dar'ul Islam* rebellion of the 1950s and early 1960s, there has been discomfort within ABRI with the more militant wing of Indonesian Islam. There has been similar discomfort among Indonesia's more nominal, *abangan* Muslims, who are concerned that their *santri* brothers and sisters might force them to live in a Muslim state under strict Islamic law. Indonesia's small but influential Chinese community was also fearful of a politically dominant Islamic movement, which would probably not be well disposed towards either their economic power in relation to *pribumi* business people or their religious affiliations, which tend to be Buddhist or Christian. The fears of the Chinese community were increased when, in 1984 during the Tanjung Priok riots in Jakarta, nine Chinese were killed by an avowedly Islamic mob. These fears have not been allayed, given that small and sometimes even large Chinese businesses, homes, and temples have consistently been the targets of rioting, particularly in Java and Sumatra in the lead-up to the 1997 DPR elections and in the period before and after the 1998 presidential 'election'. Such Islamic extremism has a long although localised history in Indonesia, resulting in the *Dar'ul Islam* rebellion and partly fuelling the PRRI–Permesta rebellion, the sporadic but continuing rebellion in Acch, and a number of smaller outbreaks of violence. In large part, this violence has been a product of often firmly held religious and moral views fuelled by genuine economic concerns within the context of an unresponsive political system.

In the early 1980s, as a consequence of the ineffectiveness of the parliamentary process (as indicated soon after by the withdrawal of the NU from the PPP) and because of the international revival of militant Islam, some Indonesian Muslims decided that the only way to achieve real change was through an armed revolt, thus justifying ABRI's fears. There were a number of groups with such aims, and they launched attacks against symbolic targets including churches, banks, the ancient Buddhist temple of Borobudur in Central Java, the headquarters of the national radio and television, and a police station. One such group hijacked a Garuda aircraft to Bangkok in 1981. While most of these attacks and the resentment against Indonesia's inflexible political structure were very real, the revival of a militant Islam also gave ABRI a new enemy with which to justify its tight control. ABRI even linked Muslim extremists to the old PKI, more to highlight its alleged extremism than because of any ideological sympathy between the two groups. Indeed, it was *santri* Muslims who were the main perpetrators of violence against real and suspected PKI members in 1965–66. There have also been persistent rumours that at least some of the acts of Islamic terrorism in Indonesia during the late 1970s and early 1980s were performed either by government agents or by *agents provocateurs*, perhaps revealing something about the methods of ABRI and the New Order government. These provocations are said to have been organised by Suharto's chief fixer and dirty tricks man, Opsus chief General Ali Murtopo. In any case, the threat of an organised *Kommando Jihad* was used to arrest hundreds of political dissenters.

Often, a situation that is explained in terms of one set of circumstances has actually been motivated by another. The most common scenario is that protest and dissent will be linked to ideological or religious beliefs when they really reflect more basic concerns, such as living conditions or loss of work or land. For example, in 1989, in the province of Lampung in southern Sumatra, a young army captain was murdered by what were said to be Islamic extremists. It is likely that Muslims carried out the murder and used religion as a rallying point for their grievances. Over the next three days, as a consequence of the murder, soldiers killed many local people accused of being Muslim fundamentalists. The official death toll was forty-one, although unofficially the figure could have been 200 or more. The Lampung incident turned out to have less to do with Islam than to do with local people believing they were losing their land to Javanese transmigrants.

Non-government organisations

Beyond these formal political organisations (although in some cases they are linked to them), a number of non-government organisations (NGOs) also play an implicit oppositional role within Indonesian politics. Although technically they are non-partisan, and some are more explicitly in favour of government policies than others, NGOs are concerned with the welfare of ordinary people and claim, with considerable justification, to have closer contact with them than government agencies. This 'grass roots' orientation of many NGOs almost by definition puts many of them at odds with the New Order government, although the NGOs did receive considerable impetus from the government in 1980 as a part of its wider development program. Perhaps being concerned with the welfare of ordinary Indonesians, the NGOs tend to champion causes that pit them against government policies and projects, or the businesses of those with close connections to the government. In particular NGOs run into conflict with the government over human rights issues, with NGOs tending to take a fairly conventional, internationalist approach to definitions of human rights, while the government, so far, has not.

Some NGOs that are potentially opposed to the government or its policies include the Centre for the Study of Democracy, the Dewan Nasional Indonesia Untuk Kesejahteraan Social (Indonesian National Council for Social Welfare), the Kelompok Pembela Kebesan Pers (Group for the Defence of Press Freedom), the Kelompok Solidaritas Korban Pembangunan Kedung Ombo (Solidarity Group for Kedung Ombo Development Dam Victims), the Lembaga Bantuan Hukum (Legal Aid Institute), the Lembaga Pembela Hukum (Legal Defence Institute), the Lembaga Pembela Hak-Hak Asasi Manusia (Institute for the Defence of Human Rights), the Sekretariat Pelestarian Hutan Indonesia (Secretariat of Indonesian Forest Preservation), and the Yayasan Pusat Studi Hak-Hak Asasi Manusia (Foundation of the Centre for the Study of Human Rights). These NGOs do not include the numerous foreign NGOs that work in Indonesia, which are viewed by the government with anything from affection, inattention, or tolerance to outright hostility.

145

A divided opposition

On balance, it would seem that among Indonesia's informed political community there is considerable opposition to the New Order government, which, in a more genuinely pluralist framework, might offer scope for change. Depending on how ordinary Indonesians are viewed, it would seem that the majority of their interests, from (grass roots) participation to economic policy, find representation somewhere within the range of opposition groups. But there is no effective cohesion between the opposition groups —between the PPP and the PDI in real terms, between activists of one stripe or another, or among the NGOs, which have been concerned not to allow one of their number to dominate the others. In part, this inability to find a common cause has stemmed from the different motivations of the opposition groups, from their varying degrees of acceptance or rejection of the *Pancasila* ideology and 1945 Constitution, and, indeed, from the role and person of Suharto when he was president. Beyond that, the New Order government does dominate the political process, through Golkar, which has left the opposition in disarray. And, of course, in Indonesia there is no such thing as (and nor is there allowed to be) a loyal Opposition, which can genuinely question government policies, and this further fragments opposition.

Even though the opposition groups have organised themselves to some extent, if only for the purpose of forming an anti-Suharto coalition, they still face three virtually insurmountable challenges. The first challenge is the political system, which disallows political organisation between elections, scrutinises and vetoes electoral platforms, and ensures a majority for Golkar. The second challenge is the voting process, which coerces a significant bloc of voters to support Golkar on pain of losing their jobs or not receiving funding for important local projects. The third challenge is that genuine opposition, which opposes fundamental aspects of the government's program or style, is not regarded as an expression of democratic plurality but as subversion, which, as noted above, is a crime punishable by a range of sentences including the death penalty. In this 'either/or' political climate, in which everything is up for grabs or in which everything is lost, the government makes little room for a genuine, public opposition to its rule.

8

THE ROLE AND
REQUIREMENTS OF
THE MEDIA

As the primary means of mass communication in Indonesia, the media are a special case in Indonesian politics, being theoretically free but in practice being required to act as an arm of government. Where they fail to do so, it has not been uncommon for publications to be closed and offending journalists have been banned, gaoled, or worse. Censorship remains a fact of life in Indonesia, and even occasional moves towards freeing up restrictions do not last long. Many Indonesian journalists do test the limits of government control and find ways to circumvent government restrictions, but the reality is that their courage stands in opposition to an environment marked by the generally successful repression of information. The tension between the government and the Indonesian media continues unabated, except where the increasing ownership or control of media outlets by the Suharto family or Golkar members has brought the media under direct control.

Pancasila journalism
The Indonesian government exercises tight control over the media through a variety of methods and requires the provision of information to promote the state and the government under the guise of '*Pancasila* journalism'. According to this version of journalism, media reports should be positive and promote state welfare, or at the very least they should not be negative. A part of the common interpretation of the state ideology of the *Pancasila* is that criticism of state leaders, the role of ABRI, or the *Pancasila* itself should not be tolerated because it is against the national interest (Milne 1989). Indeed, articles 134, 154, 155, and 160 of the Indonesian Criminal Code ban 'the public expression of feelings of hostility,

hatred or contempt toward the government', disobedience of a government order, or insults directed at the president. It is worth noting that the Dutch colonial government introduced these articles in the early twentieth century as a part of the process of social and political control (Amnesty International 1994, pp. 38–40). Ostensibly, the Indonesian government uses various methods of media regulation to assist in national development and to preserve national unity and harmony. However, given the style of Indonesia's political system, 'national interest' is also conflated with the interests of government, most notably vested in the person of the president, even though freedom of the news media is guaranteed under Indonesia's 1945 Constitution. As a consequence, the Indonesian government has never been particularly reluctant to take direct action to curtail adventurous media. According to Vatikiotis:

The state prefers to exercise its control over the press more indirectly—by employing patronage and co-options. An amendment to the 1966 Press Law in 1982 stipulated that the press should conduct itself in a 'free and responsible' manner. The US-based human rights organisation, Asia Watch, interpreted this to mean that the press 'is very much a partner of the government, and not an independent or autonomous institution'. If this is the case, the partnership works. Rather than face interminable closure, the press has adapted to the restrictions largely by censoring itself. A style of writing has developed which accommodates the establishment's rejections of direct criticism of its policies and practices. Thus a report on the problems of development in a certain province is more likely to lead off with the line '. . . has yet to realize its full potential', rather than state bluntly the shortcomings of local officials or a lack of funds . . . In a startling reification of Javanese cultural values of respect and politeness towards those in authority, the New Order insists on the positive being stressed and the negative being suppressed. Editors receive regular briefings or telephone calls with 'advice' on how to report sensitive issues. Styled 'telephone culture', the system can suggest a story idea as well as suppress them. More often than not something can be said, but the real story is buried in an oblique and, to the untrained eye, meaningless stream of stodgy prose (Vatikiotis 1993, pp. 107–8).

In so far as notions of freedom of expression exist within Indonesia, the Indonesian government's requirements of the domestic Indonesian media and its position on the foreign media are fairly consistent. In both cases they are required to refrain from openly challenging the government or its policies; nor are they to engage in activities that could cause agitation against the government or its policies. The Indonesian government has had considerable success in achieving this aim, although a method of 'writing between the lines' in the Indonesian media ensures that newspaper and magazine audiences, perhaps less than two million people within a population of around 200 million, potentially have access to sources of critical information. Literacy is a determining factor in news consumption; so too is cost and, perhaps more importantly, the journalistic use of a linguistically restrictive and esoteric bureaucratic vernacular (Dhakidae 1992, p. 6). Those Indonesians who have regular access to the news media, and who are sufficiently informed to be able to interpret it, in most cases also have access to critical information through informal channels.

Control of the media

Government control of the media is primarily exercised in two ways, the first being through licensing and legal codes, and the second an informal system of requests, advice, and orders. A third and growing method of regulating the media is through ownership of media outlets by family members of elite officials.

The formal system of media control is through the Press Act, which in part (article 11) prohibits publication of material contrary to the five tenets of the *Pancasila*, which is variously interpreted by the government depending on the circumstances. According to Indonesian journalist Daniel Dhakidae, the Indonesian government polices the use of language and maintains 'a sort of "law and order" for linguistic behaviour' (Dhakidae 1992, p. 2).

Further, all media must be registered and hold a *Surat Izin Usaha Penerbitan Pers* (SIUPP, or Press Publication Business Licence). Withdrawal or non-renewal of the licence, at the discretion of the information minister, means suspension of permission to publish (or broadcast). Penalties for offences under these two acts vary, but according to a number of my informants, as the judiciary is open to influence by the government, so penalties usually equate with how the government views the particular offence (see also Alamsjah 1989, p. 48).

The SIUPP was preceded by the *Surat Izin Terbit* (Publishing Permit), introduced as a 'transitional' measure under the transfer of power from Sukarno to Suharto in 1966, which operated in a similar manner to the SIUPP and was regarded by Indonesian journalists as highly restrictive. It was replaced by the SIUPP in 1982. When the editor of *Indonesia Raya*, Mochtar Lubis, was asked what he would do if, hypothetically, he was made information minister, he answered, 'My first decision would be to abolish the *Surat Izin Terbit*': 'This reflects a widely held opinion among Indonesian media persons. The publishing permit issue was accepted grudgingly as a reality. However the permit itself contravenes Press Law No. 11' (Hidayat 1987, p. 39).

The most common informal system of government control was by telephone call, where a journalist or editor was advised not to write or publish a particular article, to not continue with a particular line of inquiry, or less commonly to pursue a particular angle on a story. This *budaya telepon* (telephone culture) was, until the early 1990s, by far the most pervasive method of government control of the media. Such was the cumulative effect of these limitations that the Indonesian media actively engaged in self-censorship, and this 'wisdom of cowardice' has itself become a part of the local media culture (Aristides Katoppo, as quoted in Hill 1991, p. 47). The closeness and frequency of interaction between the Indonesian media and the government, particularly from 1966 until the 1970s, meant that where conflict was avoided, a mutually supporting relationship based on solidarity and an exchange of favours had developed between the two institutions. (Nono 1978, p. 271). Up until this time, the Indonesian news media, particularly the print media, were primarily a media for the educated elite rather than the masses (Nono 1978, p. 262). The exception to this tendency was the influence of the relatively inexpensive and increasingly available transistor radio, which required neither constant financial outlay nor literacy.

Up until the early 1990s, perhaps the single biggest radio broadcaster in the Indonesian language (at least outside a few major metropolitan centres), was Radio Australia, which had an often difficult and at times openly confrontational relationship with the Indonesian government. This difficulty arose over Radio Australia's policy of reporting Indonesian affairs 'warts and all' or, from the Indonesian government's perspective, 'interfering in Indonesia's internal affairs'. The tension that arose over Radio Australia's broadcasts and, more generally, the frequently critical tone of the domestic Australian news media with regard to Indonesian affairs was so great that it was officially regarded by both governments as the primary cause of what were often very difficult bilateral relations. In the mid-1980s, relations between Indonesia and Australia were so bad, ostensibly over the issue of the Australian news media's reports on Indonesia, that the Australian Department of Foreign Affairs feared that diplomatic relations could be severed. What this highlighted was how important the issue of information control was to the Indonesian government and how quick it was to anger when it found a media outlet that it could not control.[1]

Government involvement in the media business

Apart from formal and informal methods of control, the Indonesian government has increasingly exercised control over the media through ownership by government members or people closely associated with the government. For example, during his time in office, the former information minister Harmoko owned 40 per cent of ten publications in the Pos Kota publishing group, 20 per cent of three publications, 50 per cent of another two, 5 per cent of one in the Kompas–Gramedia Group, and between 5 and 100 per cent of fourteen further media outlets (*Inside Indonesia*, no. 42, March 1995, pp. 2–4). Suharto family members also owned media outlets. All three of the commercial television stations, and a major publishing group, Media Indonesia, were controlled by family members. Suharto's eldest daughter, Hardiyanti Siti Rukmana ('Tutut'), was also chairperson of the Association of Private Radio Stations (Vatikiotis 1993, p. 108). In television, Suharto's son, Bambang Trihatmojo, owned RCTI, which in 1987 received the first commercial television licence. His foster brother, Sudwikatmono, gained the second commercial licence in 1990, heading Surya Citra Televisi, while in 1990 daughter Hardiyanti gained the third licence and controlled Televisi Pendidikan Indonesia through her holding company Cipta Lamtoro Gung Persada (Hill 1994, p. 99). In 1985, ten Golkar leaders bought 60 per cent of *Pelita*, which replaced the modernist Islamic publication *Abadi*, which was banned in 1974. In 1988 the then

---

1   As I have noted elsewhere (Kingsbury 1997a, ch. 9), it is highly likely that there was a lot more to the falling out between Australia and Indonesia than just the role of the Australian news media. But both governments gave this as the officially stated reason for the falling out, a position they both maintained until at least 1993.

vice-president, Sudharmono, became an official 'adviser' to *Pelita*'s editorial board (Hill 1994, p. 45).

From 1991 Sudwikatmono also headed a foundation publishing the entertainment tabloid *Bintang Indonesia* and in 1993 founded the 'development newsweekly' *Sinar*, which by 1994 was in financial trouble (Hill 1994, p. 100). However, *Sinar* was well placed to take advantage of the banning of Indonesia's most respected and influential news magazine, *Tempo*, in 1993. Tutut was also publisher of the women's publication *Wanita Indonesia*. And Bambang was also reported to have developed an interest in the holding company of *Media Indonesia* (Hill 1994, p. 102).

As if this did not secure a large enough section of the news media, supplies of newsprint in Indonesia are limited to three suppliers, the major one of which is run by the government, while the Pos Kota Group's P. T. Gede Karang only produces newsprint for its own print needs. Of the remaining 12 000 tonnes of newsprint required each month, Kertas Leces produces 1500 tonnes, leaving the rest to the government-owned company Aspex. Many Indonesian publishers believe the government's effective monopoly on newsprint artificially inflated prices, thus forcing newspapers to reduce their number of pages, as Suharto recommended they do (*Jakarta Post*, 21 June 1995, p. 1).

Indonesia's domestic radio programming has had an insignificant impact on Indonesia's political process, primarily because, like domestic television broadcasting, it is required to rebroadcast government-supplied news programs. These news programs promote an uncritical acceptance of government policy and are very careful not to find fault with the president, his family, government ministers (at least while they remain in favour), or government policy. There has been some limited scope in the electronic media for genuine journalism through current affairs and talk-back programming, but even in this area journalists and presenters have been very careful not to offend government sensibilities, especially as 'independent' television broadcasting is under the control of Suharto family members.

Some precedents for control

While there was the precedent of an unfettered news media in Indonesia during the early and mid-1950s (Tickell 1992, p. 6), the period of Guided Democracy from the late 1950s saw the imposition of increasingly tight controls over the free flow of information. Sukarno suppressed large sections of the news media for both 'national' and personal political reasons and was, until late in his reign, backed in doing so by ABRI (Hill 1994, p. 30). As Indonesian politics grew increasingly volatile and polarised, such suppression increased and set the stage for the early years of the New Order government's own suppression of politically unfavourable media. Yet the military used the media to its own advantage in the lead-up to the change of government, with a number of media outlets either taking advantage of the political disarray to oppose Sukarno or being actively encouraged by ABRI to do so. Yet this brief flourishing of what seemed to be media freedom was not to last: 'The Press, which had been nurtured by the military to rail so effectively against Sukarno in the 1960s, became the subject in the 1970s of progressively severe censorship' (Vatikiotis 1993, p. 107).

As a part of the process of the change of government in 1965–66, and under his newly acquired powers, Suharto began by cutting 'a swathe through the country's newspapers' (Hill 1994, p. 11). In that period, nearly a third of all Indonesian newspapers were closed down, and journalists suspected of having communist or Left-leaning sympathies were persecuted, losing their jobs, being gaoled, or worse (Hill 1994, p. 35; see also Schwartz 1994, pp. 238–47):

In promoting this adherence to a common Pancasila ideology, the Suharto Government sought to eliminate party organs or critical papers, domesticate the vociferous press, and ensure that press workers and management were answerable ultimately to the government. By 1969, savage bans by the in-coming regime cut the number of newspapers and magazines, and their total circulation, to less than half the 1964 level (Hill 1994, p. 15).

Difficult relations between the news media and the Indonesian government persisted through the early 1970s, with brief bans or suspension of licences being employed to curtail active, independent reporting. This limited control, however, was replaced by a 'slash and burn' approach to media control employed in 1974 and again in 1978 (Hill 1994, p. 38).

In 1974, in response to reporting of the *Malari* riots in Jakarta, the government closed several newspapers. Included in the closures were six Jakarta dailies (*Harian KAMI*, *Indonesia Raya*, *Nusanatara*, *Abadi*, *Pedonan*, and the *Jakarta Times*), along with two regional dailies (*Suluh Berita* in Surabaya and *Indonesia Pos* in Ujung Pandang) and four weeklies (*Mahasiswa Indonesia*, *Mingguan Wenag*, *Pemuda Indonesia*, and *Ekspres*). Ten of these twelve newspapers were closed permanently, with two reappearing with changed mastheads and diminished staff (*Pelita* replaced *Abadi*, and the *Indonesian Times* replaced the *Jakarta Times*) (Hill 1994, p. 37). Many journalists were also held without trial, or were blacklisted, requiring clearance from the director general of Press and Graphics before being allowed to work again.

In response to mounting criticism of government development policies, the role of foreign investors, Chinese financiers, and government officials, including direct criticism of Suharto by university students in 1977–78, the government closed a further seven Jakarta-based newspapers, including *Sinar Harapan* and *Kompas*, for two weeks. A further seven student newspapers were also closed; more than 200 students were arrested, and university campuses were occupied by the military. While the daily newspapers were allowed to resume publishing soon after, their closure was enough to modify their future reporting (Hill 1994, p. 39).

Bans and closures continued into the 1980s, with *Tempo* being banned for two months in 1982 for its 'incisive' reporting of the general elections, and the *Jurnal Ekuin* being banned in 1983. *Expo* lost its publishing licence in 1984 after it published the first two parts of a series on the 100 wealthiest men in Indonesia. Thirty-nine of the first forty-four were ethnic Chinese, and several were business associates of the Suharto family. In the case of *Expo*, 'Harmoko reintroduced provisions—through ministerial fiat—for the revocation of a newspaper's licence after it had been issued a series of warnings for repeated offences' (Aznam 1992). Six weeks later, the news magazine *Topik* was banned after it published information on poverty in Indonesia, and three months after that another news magazine, *Fokus*, was closed after it published a list of 200 Indonesian millionaires, about a third of whom were ethnic Chinese. *Topik* was again closed in 1984 (Jenkins 1986, p. 154; Hill 1994, pp. 39, 44–5).

Two years later, in 1986, the long-running *Sinar Harapan* was closed over commentaries on government economic policies, in particular those related to Suharto family business monopolies

(Lane 1986). Given that it had skated close to the edge of being banned on many previous occasions, the ban was perhaps as much for cumulative reasons as for the single 'offence'. However, after considerable negotiating and a substantial restructuring, the publication was allowed to reappear the following February under the title *Suara Pembaruan*, although under much tighter government rein, its chairperson being a Golkar MPR member (Hill 1994, pp. 40, 86–7). That year, the recently established economic daily *Prioritas* was closed for devoting too much space to political news, when its permit required it to publish at least 75 per cent economic news. In an assessment of the Indonesian media situation in 1988, the Asia Watch human rights report noted that:

The Indonesian press is governed by an extensive regime of legal restraints, the press organs operate under the pervasive threat of closure. Formal and informal pressures are regularly brought to bear to prevent the media from reporting news that the government would prefer to ignore and journalists, enveloped by the 'culture of fear' censor themselves. Positive inducements in the form of bribes are also used to ensure that journalists write articles favorable to the government. Foreign publications are censored, and foreign correspondents can only enter—and remain—in Indonesia at the government's unbridled discretion (as quoted in Rickard 1988, p. 12).

Two years later, Asia Watch noted that censorship prevailed in Indonesia and that 'Freedom of expression . . . remains severely curtailed' (Asia Watch Committee 1990, p. 51).

The brief period of 'openness'
Protestations by the government that there is legislated media freedom have little meaning in the day-to-day operations of Indonesia's media. However, from 1991, there was a lessening of government control over, or interference in, the media. In particular, according to a number of Indonesian journalists, from about 1991 the 'telephone culture' was reduced. In part, this was because the Indonesian news media were operating within the safe 'limits' imposed by the government, and also because of a greater sense of freedom following Suharto's *keterbukaan* (openness) speech on 17 August 1991. In this speech he formally noted that Indonesia was moving towards a period of greater openness, including a freeing of the media. Some seven months later, a Committee to Protect Journalists report indicated that such openness was not deeply rooted (Clancy 1992). The move towards

greater openness later came to be viewed as a part of the manœuvring between Suharto and the 'red and white' faction of ABRI, reflecting little real belief in the idea of a free media. Indeed, during 1991 fourteen books, a calendar, and one other publication were banned, extending the bans that characterised government control of expression in 1990 and 1991 (Indonesian Human Rights Forum 1991, pp. 5–11).

Further, as noted in the *Far Eastern Economic Review*:

The press acknowledges a number of topics as strictly taboo. These include Suharto's family, questions of ethnicity, race and religion and the activities of separatist movements—such as those in Aceh, Irian Jaya and East Timor. In addition, individual arms of the government or the military sometimes object to the coverage of specific 'sensitive' subjects. Examples have included differences between Asean [*sic.*] neighbors, a military aircrash and speculation over the rupiah's devaluation (Aznam 1992).

For example, a challenge to a five-year-old order closing the publication *Prioritas* also indicates a more relaxed attitude towards free flow of information. But:

This is not to say that real press freedom is yet in sight . . . 'We are a developing nation,' said Aminullah Ibrahim, deputy chairman of the parliamentary committee on press freedoms. 'Obviously we still need laws to control the press because there are those who break the rules. The press has begun to mature, but not enough in terms of knowing its limitations' (Aznam 1992).

This limited sense of openness applied equally, or possibly even more, to the foreign media than it does to the domestic media. If there is a bias towards the foreign media, this probably reflects the Indonesian government's preoccupation with attracting foreign investment, which, since about 1990, has been substantial.

According to the editors of two influential Indonesian magazines, Suharto used the trend towards 'openness' as a way of courting general popularity in the face of a looming challenge from the armed forces faction of government identified with Murdani. However, such moves towards greater 'openness' were constrained by the political realities of an authoritarian state. Three journalists from the weekly magazine *Jakarta Jakarta* were sacked after publishing an article, on 4 January 1992, that quoted sixteen witnesses of the shooting of unarmed civilians at the Santa Cruz Cemetery at Dili on the previous 12 November (*Age*,

18 January 1992, p. 6). It is understood that the journalists were sacked after pressure was applied by the government, including from then ABRI commander General Try Sutrisno. Mark Baker noted that 'those who spoke to the reporters from *Jakarta Jakarta* gave new weight to earlier, unofficial evidence of systematic and unrestrained atrocities by the military' (Baker 1992). The Dili massacre was an extraordinarily sensitive issue for Indonesia in international terms and caused considerable disquiet at home. Regardless of any claimed moves towards media freedom, the government did not want journalists providing information that contradicted its clearly fabricated official line.

The process of 'openness', such as it was, abruptly ended in mid-1994 in response to raised tensions between Suharto and the Murdani faction in ABRI. The Director General of Indonesia's Department of Information, Subrata, acknowledged the move away from a freer media when he told me in December 1993 that: 'I think everybody must know that it is very hard now to make more openness—now it becomes very difficult' (Subrata 1993). The government's response was to 'remind' Indonesia's leading editors of their responsibilities under the principles of '*Pancasila* journalism'. The editor of one influential news magazine, speaking anonymously, referred to '*Pancasila*, whatever that means'. Another senior journalist, interviewed off the record, said that the term '*Pancasila* means whatever the government wants it to mean'. A third senior journalist said the result of the government's interference in the domestic news media did not so much require 'reading between the lines, but reading between the lies'.

'Openness' ends

The event that formally reversed Indonesia's move towards 'openness' came on 22 June 1994, when Indonesia's brittle politics snapped and the influential publications *Tempo*, *De Tik*, and *Editor* had their publishing licences suspended by the information minister, Harmoko. This move followed their publication of articles outlining a dispute between a large section of ABRI and the finance minister, Mar'ie Mohammad, on one hand, and the then research and technology minister, Bucharuddin Habibie, on the other, over the purchase of thirty-nine former East German warships for the Indonesian navy. Within a week of the suspension of the publishing licences, it was clear that the publications had been closed permanently. *Tempo*'s co-editor, Fikri Jufri, told Patrick Walters, Jakarta correspondent for the *Australian*, 'There is no political openness nor press freedom any more. After things have been opening up for so long this is a totally contradictory move' (*Australian* 22 June 1994, p. 1). Within days of the closure, there were public protests in Jakarta, and one protest in Jakarta's main thoroughfare, Jalan Thamrin, was broken up by 400 club-wielding police. The 'police riot' directed at the peaceful protesters was reportedly a brutal one (Serril 1994).

Habibie was a close confidant of Suharto and was his longest serving minister before becoming vice-president in March 1998. ABRI's attack on Habibie could have been construed as an attack on Suharto himself, especially after Suharto announced that he had personally authorised the purchase of the ships. The dispute between ABR and Habibie–Suharto was ostensibly over the purchase price of the ships (US$12.9 million) and the cost of refitting them (US$1.2 billion). Interestingly, the defence minister, General Edi Sudrajat, also criticised the purchase and refitting of the ships. That he supported the attack on Habibie and, by extension, Suharto indicated that the purchase of the ships was indeed a very poor decision, for he no doubt alienated Suharto by criticising the purchase. Habibie was extraordinarily unpopular with ABRI, however, and Edi's comments may have been an attack on Habibie alone. Both the *Age*'s Mark Baker and an editorial leading article in the *Australian* noted that ABRI's criticism of the purchase probably also reflected ABRI's continued campaign to destabilise Suharto. Australia's then foreign minister, Senator Gareth Evans, also admitted that the dispute reflected divisions within the Indonesian political elite. Notably, ABRI did not leap to the president's defence or support him after the three publications were banned. In fact, they kept silent on the issue, which itself spoke volumes given ABRI's former outspoken defence of Suharto in other circumstances. Looked at in this light, the three publications were just another set of victims in the continuing struggle between Suharto and ABRI.

The role of the *Press Act of Indonesia*

Any analysis of Indonesia's response to the news media necessarily falls within the framework of both the *Press Act of Indonesia 1966* (revised in 1982) and the 1945 Constitution, which, according to

Subrata, provide the main guidance for the news media's required participation in national development (Subrata 1993). The reasons for the news media being required to conform to the Press Act and the 1945 Constitution were outlined by Subrata in five points:

The first is we have to make social understanding, where we are going to and what kind of aspects we are going to do and such . . . Of course, [number two is so that] we have social confidence, to convince our people that they do understand where we are going to about our developmental structure. Then number three is the social responsibility, the sense of belonging to our nation's spirit. Again . . . that sense of belonging means that social responsibility is the most important thing for our nation, for our people here. Number four, of course, is social control, must be there. *This is one of the main parts of the press, to make social control. This social control must be constructive and must be responsible to the kinds of examples I just mentioned, of unity, of all of our main tasks.* And then number five, of course, social participation. So all the media, including the press, have to be aware of this and have to motivate our people how to make participation in the developmental project (Subrata 1993, my emphasis).

In particular, participation in the 'developmental project' cannot be hampered by 'non-constructive' criticism. To this end:

In Indonesia, according to our law, it's still not to allow for criticism—it's under the law, to criticise the president, et cetera. But I don't know in your country. So we have to respect each other according to the law. Because if we broke the law, then it is different. So we have the law here about that, the same maybe with our colleagues in Singapore. What they call it? The Internal Security Act. So they have the law, so we have to respect each other. So in this case we always welcome the criticism, but please understand about the basic law and the regulations and the way to criticise here is very important for all the journalists (Subrata 1993).

The Press Act of Indonesia is the main repository of 'the basic law and the regulations' concerning the news media and governs its codes of behaviour. It is a detailed document, allowing considerable scope for government interpretation and control of the news media. While the Act provides for considerable control over domestic news media, it imposes further conditions on foreign news media. Chapter VII, article 17.3 of the Act reads, 'The Government prohibits the entry and circulation of publications of Foreign Press which harm or endanger the Society, State and the Indonesian Revolution'. Disregarding the Sukarnoist rhetoric about the 'Revolution' (which in other legislation has been deleted), this point has been as widely interpreted as applying to a range of other legal provisions concerning harm to the 'the Society, [or] State', and in some cases beyond. That is, if the government determines that reports by foreign news media are not in its interest, it can ban them, legally, on that basis. In the first instance, foreign journalists must first obtain permission to work in Indonesia. Furthermore, article 17.4 reads, 'Further provisions concerning the Foreign Press in Indonesia are to be regulated jointly by the Government and the Press Council'. This phrase provides a broad net for any matters that might fall outside article 17.3 but that still require legal but unilateral government action. The inclusion of the Press Council could be interpreted as a safeguard against abuse of this provision, except that according to Chapter III, article 6 of the Indonesian Press Act:

(3) Requirements for Press Organisations which may send their representatives to the Press Council dealing with the number of members and the requirements for membership shall be fixed by Government Regulation.

(4) The appointment of expert members in the field of the Press and additional membership are to be decided by the Government together with the members representing Press Organisations.

(5) The membership of the Press Council shall be legalised by a Government Regulation.

Article 7

(1) The Chairman of the Press Council is the Minister for Information.

That is, the Press Council is established by the government; the terms of sending representatives are set by the government; membership of the Press Council is ultimately determined by the government (including the power of veto); and the Press Council is overseen by the information minister, who is appointed by the president. Further, the vice-chairman of the Press Council is the Director General of Press and Graphics, who recommends to the information minister who should be issued with publishing permits.

There are a range of further controls and restrictions in the Press Act of Indonesia that are placed on journalists and that refer to 'high morals and responsibility' (chapter VI, article 16), not 'disturbing public order' (elucidation on Act 4 of 1967), not 'betraying the National Struggle' (Act 21 of 1982, article 1A), heightening 'responsibility feelings and national discipline' (Act 21 of 1982, article 5D), being 'constructive in character' (Act 21 of 1982, article 7), being 'responsible' (elucidation on Act 21 of 1982, amendment I), 'carrying out social control functions' (elucidation on Act 21 of 1982, amendment II:14), and not publishing 'writings which affect the nation's morals, damage national integrity or create inter-tribal, inter-religious, inter-racial or inter-group controversies' (elucidation on Act 21 of 1982, amendment II:17).

For Indonesian citizens, only registered members of the Indonesian Journalists' Union (PWI) have been allowed to work as journalists since 1966. Like other unions, the PWI 'has been tightly regulated and directed by the New Order Government' (Hill 1994, p. 67). This arrangement was challenged by the establishment of an independent journalists' union in 1994. It should be noted that, a year later, the president and a senior member of the new union, Achmad Taufik and Eko Maryadi, who also published the monthly magazine *Independen*, were sentenced to thirty-two months' imprisonment each for 'spreading hatred' against the Indonesian government (*Time*, 18 September 1995, p. 27).

Broadly, the subject areas considered 'off-limits' to the Indonesian news media include anything that could be interpreted as seditious, insinuating, sensational, speculative, or likely to antagonise ethnic, religious, racial, or 'group' (class) tensions. These subject areas, which may include anything from reporting on separatist movements, religious clashes, or anti-government activity, are grouped under the acronyms 'MISS' and, more commonly, 'SARA'.[2] As well as these areas, there are other subject areas that are regarded as 'unprintable', such as anything other than the most innocuous affairs of the president's family (Hill 1994, p. 45).

To avoid any loop-hole in this far-reaching and highly interpretable document, through which the news media could act against the wishes of the government, Chapter IX, article 36 says: 'Matters which have not as yet been arranged in this Regulation shall be regulated by virtue of a special Decision by the Minister

---

2   'MISS' is an acronym for subjects that journalists should not report, allow to be reported, or encourage through reporting: *menghasut* (provoke agitation), *insinuasi* (insinuation), *sensasi* (sensation), and SARA (to spread racial or religious hatred). 'SARA' is an acronym for *suku* (ethnic group), *agama* (religion), and *ras* (race).

of Information'. There is, in effect, no legal redress against government intentions to control the news media, be they foreign or domestic, to suit its own interests:

Government considers the press an ally, a kind of outside 'insider' to whom the giving of special privileges and status in society comes naturally in the context of a Javanese version of a corporate state. The social responsibility attributed to the Indonesian press finds a different interpretation than in the West. In the Javanese 'central court' concept of the corporate state, social responsibility is vested in the president and his government. The press is expected to support and promote the carrying out of this social responsibility of the state. In this conceptual framework there is not much place for open dissent and criticism, let alone the denunciation of policies or public figures (Nono 1978, p. 269).

Consequently, 'The New Order's exercise of power over the press was demonstrably less selective, less open to conciliation, and more authoritarian. Borrowing from New Order rhetoric, the press had "freedom", increasingly constrained by "responsibility" as defined by those who had the power to ban and imprison' (David Hill, as quoted in Tickell 1987, p. 34).

Although it is clear, from the language and structure of Indonesian legislation, that control of the media is primarily aimed at securing political compliance, this does not then mean such compliance is agreed to in principle. Of the numerous Indonesian journalists I spoke to, there was broad agreement that regulation of the Indonesian media was repressive and undesirable. Further, there was a marked desire to see significantly greater media freedom, including the ability to criticise the government. This desire is perhaps best summed up by the following quotation: 'The radical political transformation that took place in late 1965, and the following destruction of the PKI and the birth of Suharto's New Order, have not stopped state repression against the human need for free expression and difference. If anything, the change has often created a more ruthless kind of coercion' (Gunawan 1995).

9

UNITY IN DIVERSITY?

Assertions of difference

In a state as geographically and culturally diverse as Indonesia, it has always been a tenet of faith that national cohesion can only be achieved through embracing difference. This has led to the nationalist catch-cry and oft-espoused *Pancasila* principle of 'unity in diversity'. In one sense, the state has little choice but to adopt such a policy if it is to survive in its present form. In another sense, the idea of achieving consensus from disparate cultures well matches a syncretic Javanese world view (as discussed in chapter 2), which seeks to find a convergence of otherwise contradictory elements.

Yet the non-Javanese regions that comprise Indonesia do not always wholly accept incorporation into the unitary state. This lack of acceptance has been demonstrated not least by the three provinces of Aceh, Irian Jaya, and East Timor, while other forms of political dissatisfaction have increasingly made themselves felt towards the end of the 1990s. One of the most violent clashes, reflecting ethnic, religious, political, and economic causes, was between the Dayak[1] peoples of West Kalimantan and transmigrants from the island of Madura.

Dayak defiance

In West Kalimantan, since the middle of the eighteenth century, there has been an established Chinese mining and business community, initially invited there by the local sultan. The Chinese

---

1   The term 'Dayak' has a slightly pejorative tone and is not used by them. Rather they identify themselves on the basis of their cultural group.

formed *kongsi*, which was a mixture of secret society, mine management, and government, with total control over the area they
occupied. While the ethnic Chinese and local Dayak peoples have
managed to live in relative harmony,[2] more recent waves of immigrants, in particular from Madura, have led to outbreaks of significant levels of violence.

The violence of early 1997 was attributable to a number of
causes, probably all of which could be regarded as connected. In
the first instance, the economic displacement of the local Dayak
people by the Madurese has led to considerable Dayak resentment. Land leased to Madurese transmigrants was not being
returned to Dayaks when the leases expired, and this has been a
major cause of economic displacement. The Dayaks also claim
that the education system discriminates against them. There are
few teachers for large classes; their education and qualifications are
consequently poor, and they are increasingly being pushed out of
jobs in gold, tin, and coal mines, and on the rubber and palm
plantations. The traditional Dayak swidden, or shifting dry rice
cultivation, has also been disrupted through the establishment of
plantations and extensive logging.

There are about 50 000 Madurese in West Kalimantan. They
are transmigrants shifted from the overcrowded island of Madura,
just off the coast of north Central Java. While the Madurese live
in territory traditionally occupied by Dayaks, they are not particularly tolerant of them, considering them to be both uncivilised
and unclean. This intolerance is exacerbated by the fact that the
predominantly animist Dayaks eat pork, as they have always done,
and keep dogs, while the strongly Muslim Madurese regard eating
pork and keeping dogs as offensive. The Madurese are also
regarded as less tolerant of other religions and peoples, and have a
tradition of frequently settling disputes by fighting with knives.
The Dayaks have their own traditions of waging war against outsiders and each other. The Dayaks also believe that an offence
against one member is an attack on the tribe and must be avenged
through 'pay back'.

---

2   There were cases of Dayaks killing Chinese in 1968, and there were further tensions
    in the 1980s, but conflict has been at most sporadic, especially when compared with
    other anti-Chinese rioting in Indonesia. Rioting against Chinese, especially by
    Muslims, has a long history in Indonesia and was at one of its cyclical peaks in the
    period leading up to the 1997 DPR elections and the 1998 presidential 'election'.

There is also some belief that local resentments have been stirred up for more overt political reasons, with local politicians attempting to gain advantage by manipulating these tensions (Feith, pers. comm., 3 February 1997; van Klinken 1997a). In any case, in the first few weeks of 1997, officially more than 300 people were killed in Dayak raids on Madurese homes, predominantly in the north of West Kalimantan. Unofficial though widely reported sources put the number of dead at up to 3000. A singularly grisly aspect of the killings was that the Dayaks reverted to traditional methods of warfare, in which the heads were taken from victims and parts of the flesh were eaten. Before the effective Dutch suppression of head-hunting in the early 1900s, the Dayak peoples were widely known for their head-hunting and cannibalism (as were many ethnic groups in the eastern islands). While the practice of taking heads effectively ended, it remained alive as a custom through songs, some of which had been traditionally sung during battle or in the process of decapitation.

Although head-hunting and cannibalism strikes great fear into those who believe they might be its victims, its primary purpose is ritualistic. In traditional Dayak belief, eating the flesh of the 'enemy' endows the eater with the strength of that enemy. Those whose heads are taken will become the slave of the head-taker in the afterlife. In an environment in which the Dayaks feel they have become the economic 'slaves' of the foreign Madurese, as well as defeating the enemy, head-hunting restores a 'balance' to existing socio-political relations. That is, to paraphrase the Dayak view, 'We are your slaves now, but you will be our slaves later'. This is but one example of where diversity did not imply unity.

Rebellious Aceh

Muslim separatists in Aceh Province at the northern tip of Sumatra have been battling the central government, be it Dutch or Javanese-dominated, since late last century. The local tradition of resistance to outside authorities was rekindled in the mid-1970s, when the armed independence group Aceh Merdeka (Free Aceh) unilaterally declared independence on 4 December 1976. There was considerable local support for the independence movement, reflecting a desire of a significant number of the province's three and a half million people for political separation. However, by 1990 counter-insurgency operations struck at Aceh Merdeka's military capacity, and a year later, with many field commanders killed or captured, the Jakarta government claimed the movement had been 'crushed'.

Government reprisals, usually carried out by non-Acinese troops, were wide-ranging, and it has been claimed that more than 2000 civilians were killed and many tortured between 1989 and 1993. In relation to this, it was claimed that the army engaged in the arbitrary mass killing of civilians in at least two instances (Amnesty International 1994, pp. 55–6). This strengthened resentment against rule from Jakarta and continues to fuel the separatist movement. There have been sporadic attacks on police and the army since 1990.

By 1997, military tensions in Aceh had again escalated after police found caches of weapons. The weapons, consisting of AK47 and M16 assault rifles, and thousands of rounds of ammunition, were discovered after a policeman attempted to search a heavily laden taxi. The occupants of the taxi shot at the policeman, sparking a gunfight and later a search of the vehicle. This was followed two weeks later by military raids on the home of a village witchdoctor in the North Aceh regency, in which further weapons were seized. The Indonesian government acknowledged that more than 120 weapons had been captured between May 1996 and early 1997, indicating that Aceh Merdeka had been building up for a further offensive. The Acinese have traditionally had close links with their Muslim counterparts on the Malay Peninsula, and it is believed that the arms came through Malaysia across the lightly patrolled Malacca Straits.

Transmigrasi, development, and displacement

In Irian Jaya, the Free Papua Movement (OPM) has waged a limited guerilla war against the Jakarta government since 1965 and particularly since formal incorporation in 1969, although there has been opposition to incorporation within Indonesia since the Dutch granted Indonesia *de facto* control of the province in 1963. While the OPM is opposed to incorporation within Indonesia, it also resents the government's transmigration and mining policies. The transmigration policy has brought thousands of Javanese and Balinese families to Irian Jaya to help relieve overcrowding on those islands. But the migration is viewed by OPM as colonisation, and the settled agricultural methods of the colonists have taken land that traditionally belonged to the indigenous Papuans. Government mining leases have also caused bitterness among many local people, with the loss of their land to mining companies with no compensation, and the destruction of large areas of habitat, including the polluting of major waterways upon which many local people relied.

Lowry outlined it thus:

The process of integration and modernisation in Irian has also been inhibited by cultural insensitivity. This has stretched from the widespread use of unnecessary violence and force to the alienation of land without compensation or inadequate compensation, the failure to involve locals in development projects, large-scale transmigration projects in the border areas which have encroached on indigenous lands and resources, and the imposition of a national administrative system which ignored indigenous social structures and norms (Lowry 1996, p. 174).

The best known case of a mining company causing resentment among indigenous people is the American majority-owned Freeport copper, gold, and silver mine, which covers an area of 2.6 million hectares in south central Irian Jaya. The agreement for Freeport to start mining in Irian Jaya, signed on 7 April 1967, was the first result of the New Order government's attempts to lure investors back to Indonesia after the economically disastrous Sukarno years. Since then, the Freeport mine has become the world's single biggest gold mine and the third largest copper mine. It is one of Indonesia's top ten tax-payers and produces total receipts for Indonesia of in excess of US$200 million a year. Freeport was crucial to regaining the confidence of foreign investors and remains important as an ongoing source of government revenue. Because of this, the Indonesian government, through the army, has acted to repress local discontent. Such discontent has in a number of cases been supported by the OPM, particularly through flag-raising ceremonies. The view within the Indonesian army in Irian Jaya is that if anyone unfurls the OPM flag, they can be shot. This has resulted in numerous cases of human rights abuses, including the killings of dozens of local people. In 1995 Indonesia's defence minister, Edi Sudrajat, told the MPR that as the OPM's support base is ordinary people and that as 'bullets have no eyes', the deaths of ordinary people are unavoidable (IRIP News Service 1995, pp. 17–20). Lowry simply describes the events as 'ABRI personnel [indulging] in indiscriminate killing and torture of suspected rebels and sympathisers [which reflects] continuing reliance on the excessive use of force and extrajudicial procedures' and the 'indiscriminate use of terror and force rather than [the building of] social structures and networks which would produce more enduring and self-sustaining results' (Lowry 1996, pp. 176, 178).

In a more personal account of conflict between Indonesian soldiers and the indigenous Papuan people, a soldier known as 'Krisna' said soldiers 'often shoot and eat pigs and poultry belonging to the local people. Sometimes the local people are shot. Occasionally Irianese women are raped. These are the sources of tension between locals and the army' (Krisna 1995).

Conflict between the OPM and the Indonesian army has continued to flare sporadically, which has also created tensions with neighbouring Papua New Guinea (PNG). While the PNG government is linked by ethnicity to the West Papuans, it has rejected calls to support them, fearing Indonesian reprisals. OPM attacks on government troops peaked in 1977–78, when about forty government soldiers and perhaps hundreds of poorly armed OPM guerillas were killed. The ABRI response was 'savage' (Lowry 1996, pp. 171–2). Events escalated and, from 1983 and into 1984, another OPM-led uprising resulted in government reprisals, with about 12 000 Irian Jayan refugees fleeing to camps across the PNG border. The Indonesian army has on several occasions entered PNG in 'hot pursuit' of OPM guerillas. In order to placate the Indonesian government, in 1990 the PNG government arrested one of OPM's leaders, Melkianus Salosa, and handed him to Indonesian authorities. He was convicted of subversion and sentenced to life imprisonment, during which he was tortured (Amnesty International 1994, p. 73). In 1992, Salosa was found dead outside the high-security prison he had been held in. Hundreds of others have died in military custody in Irian Jaya, as well as in attacks on non-military targets. In what was believed to be a reprisal raid in 1993, Indonesian forces crossed more than 10 kilometres into PNG and killed thirteen people and wounded eight others in Yapsie village.

There are currently a few hundred OPM guerillas still active in Irian Jaya, although they enjoy the support of a large number of indigenous Papuans (see Lowry 1996, p. 41). As well as armed insurrection, the OPM has organised peaceful resistance to the government, through demonstrations, flag-raising ceremonies, political discussion groups, and appeals to the United Nations and other international bodies.

The mouse that roared

Of all the dissatisfaction with incorporation into a unitary state, East Timor is by far the best known case of opposition to rule by Jakarta, and conflict there, of varying levels of intensity, continues to this day. Probably the most important aspect of the East Timor question is that, according to the United Nations, East Timor is not actually a part of Indonesia, but is occupied by Indonesia in contravention of repeated United Nations calls for it to withdraw. Most of the international community[3] and the UN understand the occupation of East Timor by Indonesia to be illegal. As such, it is tempting and probably legitimate to identify the East Timor issue not as a matter between a province and the state, but as a matter between a state and a region that still has the status of a colony, albeit a colony that has proclaimed independence. However, from an Indonesian perspective, East Timor *is* a province of the state, known as Timor Timur, and it is difficult to find, even among Indonesians opposed to New Order policy on East Timor, an acceptance of the idea that East Timor could or should be entirely independent. Within the politics of Indonesia, then, East Timor is a troubled and troublesome province, a reluctant member of the greater family, but a member nonetheless. It is only from the greater international perspective that East Timor has, or should have, an independent existence. As this discussion is focused on Indonesia as such, East Timor will be regarded as a reluctant province. However, I do acknowledge that occupation and political domination, as a fact of history, does not necessarily, or even often, accord with what is lawful, fair, or right, as vividly demonstrated by this situation.

East Timor, as a 'province', is far from settled and still constitutes a military challenge to the central government. Conflict between the armed forces and local people—including the armed

---

3   Apart from statements of protest by individual and collected countries, international concern over East Timor was reflected in the Nobel Peace Prize being awarded jointly to East Timor's Bishop Carlos Belo and C.N.R.M. international spokesman, Jose Ramos Horta.

resistance, Fretilin, through its armed wing, Falintil—has continued since Indonesia invaded East Timor in 1975. Although there have been reports of killing on a massive scale, probably the best known (and certainly the most widely reported) incident was the Dili massacre at the Santa Cruz Cemetery in 1991.

Indicating the intractable nature of the conflict, then head of ABRI, Try Sutrisno, said that 'It is necessary to fire on those who do not follow the official line. Abri is determined to eliminate whoever disturbs stability' (Vatikiotis 1993, p. 185) and that East Timorese separatists would be 'wiped out' (Thatcher 1991). The disruptions in Dili were the work of 'ill-bred people who have to be shot', Try is reported to have said. 'In the end they had to be shot . . . And we will shoot them' (as quoted in Hill & Sen 1991; see also Schwartz 1994, p. 213) More than a year later, Try was still taking a hard line with those who 'disturbed the peace' (Reuter 1993).

Apart from issues of succession, the issue of East Timor is perhaps Indonesia's greatest problem—'disastrous', according to Schwartz (1994, p. 195)—combining both considerable international opprobrium and internal dissent in a country noted for its emphasis on maintaining cohesion. Early one morning, during a visit to East Timor in 1995, the windows in my Dili hotel room began rattling as the air shuddered under the heavy thud of the rotor blades of an Indonesian army helicopter passing low overhead. On Dili's street corners, grey-shirted police stood guard in shaded concrete boxes while various hues of green throughout the town reflected the different army battalions stationed in East Timor. Companies of armed troops marched along the main road from the Comoro airport, along Jalan Fatu Mada, or were seated in open trucks leaving town. One truck-load of troops was dressed in riot uniforms and helmets with face guards and neck protectors, and were armed with perspex shields and batons. Military patrols out from Dili were routine.

The military was the most obvious feature of Dili, a run-down, relatively nondescript, and otherwise slow-moving provincial town of just under 200 000 people, perhaps half of whom come from elsewhere, mostly Java. But apart from the military, the Indonesians, like the Portuguese before them, had a minimal presence outside Dili, with a few officials holding administrative posts in the larger towns. The Indonesian government claimed that East

Timor was, by the 1990s, a peaceful region, with thirty or so Falintil guerillas left in the remote mountains of the eastern Los Palos regency. However, it was widely acknowledged in Dili that the security situation in East Timor was not what the Indonesian government claimed it to be. The Indonesian claim to peace was belied by the continuing presence of what Fretilin representatives estimated to be around 18 000 Indonesian troops, including a large number of Indonesia's paramilitary police.[4]

The high Indonesian military presence implicitly acknowledged there was still a significant 'security problem' in East Timor. According to a Fretilin[5] spokesman in Dili, there were about 400 armed Falintil guerillas in the Los Palos region in the east. And he said that up behind the steep mountains near Maliana, close to the West Timor border, Falintil's main guerilla force of about 750 operated, protected by impassable terrain and very few passable roads.

The Fretilin spokesman said that the guerillas were formed into twenty-two companies, which operated semi-independently. He said the guerillas were supported by a base of about 8000 Falintil members. After twenty years of fighting and a consistently high casualty rate (as admitted by the Fretilin spokesman), these numbers seemed inflated. But sources in the Catholic Church supported the Fretilin claim, estimating that there were about 2000 Falintil fighters in the mountains. An aid worker in Dili said that probably half that number would be under arms, the rest being unarmed activists associated with the Falintil bases.

The Fretilin spokesman said there were regular clashes between Falintil guerillas and the Indonesian army, though mostly at the instigation of the Indonesian forces. Falintil had neither the numbers nor the technology to engage the Indonesian army in any meaningful sense. But Fretilin claimed that the persistence of its

---

4   The actual number has been open to considerable dispute, with the Indonesian government consistently claiming that the number of troops stationed in East Timor is lower than the actual figure. Based on government information, Lowry put the number of battalions as low as eight by September 1993, estimating that each battalion had about 700 troops (1996, p. 156). Other common estimates at this time put the total figure at between 12 000 and 15 000 troops.

5   Fretilin had by this time actually made an alliance with the UDT to form the Council of National Maubere Resistance (CNRM). However, in East Timor itself, Fretilin supporters maintained an independent political identity.

armed opposition helped keep the issue of East Timor alive in international forums and thus maintained pressure on the Indonesian government to negotiate a settlement. The official Fretilin position, such as outlined by CNRM spokesman Jose Ramos Horta, was that a gradual, monitored transition leading to a referendum on incorporation would be acceptable.

With the 'Sabanese'[6] dominating the local economy, supporters of Fretilin wanted Indonesia to leave the province entirely. 'We have nothing', said the Fretilin spokesman: 'The Sabanese own everything in East Timor'. Virtually all of the shops and businesses in Dili were owned by non-East Timorese Indonesians, while senior army officers controlled its limited industry of exporting coffee and importing consumer goods directly from Singapore.

The resentment felt by many, particularly young East Timorese, also continued to feed Fretilin's armed base. Fretilin's numbers received a boost after the 1991 Dili massacre and after riots in 1994. Until 1992, the recruitment of young East Timorese from Dili into Fretilin was planned by the now gaoled Fretilin leader, Xanana Gusmao. East Timor's youth, particularly the generation born since the 1975 invasion, have been radicalised by both their economic and political circumstances, as well as through a campaign by Fretilin. This being the case, it appears that East Timor will remain an intractable problem for Indonesia.

Young East Timorese I spoke to were vehement in their opposition to Indonesia. This opposition motivated regular beatings of Indonesians, particularly lone soldiers, by East Timorese youths. As if to underscore the point, while I was talking to two youths, an off-duty Indonesian soldier was attacked at a street stall less than 50 metres from us. He tried to escape the kicks and punches of two youths only to run into the blows of two others. Assaults by young East Timorese against non-East Timorese have become increasingly common in the 1990s, as a means of venting anger and frustration and, in a very basic way, of making a political protest. From time to time, these youths would be caught and detained, but in most cases they tended to get away with the assaults. These attacks reflect a Fretilin campaign to instil in East Timor's youth an implacable opposition to Indonesian domina-

---

6   'Sabanese' is an East Timorese colloquialism for 'Javanese', but in this context is
    intended to include all other non-Timorese Indonesians.

tion. Judging by the regularity of protests in East Timor, the occasional riots, the assaults and, not least, the stream of youth into the
Falintil force, this campaign appears to have been successful.

One favoured meeting place for East Timorese youths and
other supporters of independence was the infamous Santa Cruz
Cemetery, the site of the 1991 massacre. In a country where un-
authorised public gatherings remain illegal—especially in East
Timor—large numbers of people could still legally gather at
Dili's main cemetery with the ostensible purpose of visiting
deceased family and friends. However, the cemetery itself received few visitors, while groups of people congregated in the
street to the south of the cemetery, between it and a military
cemetery across the road. The rows of headstones in the military
cemetery indicate that the Indonesian army has not always had
military matters its own way.[7]

Foreigners were most unwelcome near the cemeteries, as was
clearly indicated to me by an Indonesian official, and while East
Timor was open to tourism, the very few foreigners who visited
were treated with deep suspicion, which was the common currency of East Timor. Dili is a town filled with informers, mostly
immigrants from West Timor attracted by the money they could
earn from the Indonesian government. The East Timorese could
pick their West Timorese cousins by dialect or accent.

Like other parts of Indonesia, there was disquiet in the lead-up
to the 1997 DPR elections. But unlike other areas, armed guerillas actually launched attacks against police soldiers in the lead-up
to, and just after, the elections, leaving no doubt that they represented the most militant opposition to Suharto's rule. Police said
that, before polling booths opened on election day, twenty-one
people, including five attackers and a former member of parliament and his wife, were killed in guerilla assaults in the regional
towns of Los Palos and Bacau, as well as in Dili itself (Williams
1997c). Two days after the elections, a further eighteen police and
a soldier were killed by guerillas when hand grenades were

---

7   Lowry says that 'McDonald's estimate of about 1800 killed in the four years to 1979
     is probably close to the mark' (1996, p. 154), although this seems low and is probably
     an 'official' figure. Adam Schwartz says some estimates put the number of Indo-
     nesians dead at up to 10 000 in the period to 1980 (1994, p. 204). A journalist for
     Time magazine claims that between 15 000 and 16 000 Indonesian soldiers have been
     killed in East Timor (Church 1995).

thrown into a truck travelling from Bacau to Dili (*Sunday Age*, 1 June 1997, p. 12). Well over twenty years after the Indonesian invasion, a resolution to the political situation in East Timor was not even looking close.

Indonesia, or Greater Java?

Ignoring the overt rebellions (or resistance) of East Timor, Irian Jaya, and Aceh, and the massacres of West Kalimantan, it could still not be asserted with absolute confidence that Indonesia would remain a unitary state. Throughout the provinces of Indonesia, most people are willing to acknowledge that they are Indonesian. But in doing so, many associate themselves with other minorities in the archipelago rather than associating themselves directly with the central government or, more generally, the Javanese. As far apart as the spidery arms of Sulawesi, Flores, Bali, and Sumatra, people resent Javanese dominance of Indonesian politics, and in most cases identify themselves primarily on the basis of their cultural group. The Mentawai of Siberut Island off Sumatra's west coast resisted cultural incorporation until, according to a non-government aid organisation worker based there, Indonesian soldiers shot some villagers as an example to the others. The Batak peoples of northern Sumatra converted to Christianity as a consequence of Dutch evangelism, but also (like the Mentawai) to oppose the dominance of Islam and to provide a vehicle for preserving their traditional, often animist, beliefs. The traditionally matrilineal Minangkabau of central Sumatra similarly regarded Java as an alien place and its people as cultural aggressors, while in coastal northern Sumatra, the ethnic Malays looked more to their cousins on the other side of the Malacca Straits for cultural affiliation than to Jakarta. Not surprisingly, Sumatra was the home of the PRRI rebellion of 1958, which began in the West Sumatra hill town of Bukit Tinggi. Although the PRRI rebellion was fairly quickly quashed (along with the associated Permesta rebellion in Sulawesi), centralisation and regional representation have continued to play on the minds of government strategists.

A new structure?

As the period of Suharto's New Order government has come to a close, at a time when regional dissatisfaction with increasing centralism is palpable, government strategists have been looking more closely at potential new forms of regional representation for the post-Suharto period. The concern is that, unless some flexibility is offered to the outer islands, the structure of the state could begin to crack at a time of pressure, such as the transition from Suharto to a new president. This presents a vision of Indonesia's 'Balkanisation', which, as an end of the state, is every Indonesian political thinker's greatest nightmare.

To counter both this fear and the potential reality, a return to a federal state has been considered by some in Golkar (although, it must be noted, with considerable misgiving). But this idea was hampered by its constitutional complexity and its seeming inability to satisfy both the outer islanders and the Javanese at the same time. A more likely outcome would be the granting of greater representation to the outer islands, particularly Sumatra, at the upper reaches of government. This is expected to come from two sources, both within ABRI and both of whom are well positioned at the close of the Suharto regime.

Suharto's authority was vast, especially by conventional Western political standards. Yet opposition, which has never completely disappeared, has been more obvious towards the end of his rule. The plans being laid for his succession reflect concerns only with the maintenance of the state after his political demise. In the period after Suharto, with the loss of his enormous personal power, the centre will necessarily be weakened and the periphery will, by definition, be relatively stronger. The logic of this cycle, however, is that, as power is eventually consolidated at the centre, the periphery—the outer islands—will decline in terms of their autonomy. Within the dynamic of Indonesia's 'unity in diversity', the only questions would relate to how much more representation or autonomy the outer islands would receive and how long such a state of affairs would last.

10

HUMAN RIGHTS, ABRI, AND THE LAW

Like any other state in the world, Indonesia is subject to international pressure and influences. In Indonesia's case, perhaps the most pressure is applied over issues of human rights violations in the rebellious provinces of Aceh, Irian Jaya, and East Timor, and also among labourers who are no longer content to work for less than a livable income, among religious groups, and among political dissidents. No other aspect of Indonesian civil and political life so clearly demonstrates authoritarian rule as does the country's record of human rights violations. Various international governments have limited or cut off aid or military supplies to the Indonesian government in recent times, most notably after the 1991 Dili massacre, which went some small way towards encouraging the Indonesian government to rethink its approach to how it deals with dissent.

Whose rights? What rights?

The Indonesian government almost universally rejects specific claims of human rights abuses, although it has begun to acknowledge that a problem does exist. Against each specific claim, though, it disputes both the detail and the causes of such claimed abuses. In broader terms, it also argues that issues of human rights need to be understood within the specific context of each country's history and circumstances. Since about 1994, representatives of the Indonesian government have been less fervent in arguing for an Indonesian version of human rights, and the previously heard, illogical calls for respect for 'state's rights' have almost entirely disappeared. Having noted that, human rights issues are still a major point of contention within Indonesia and continue to dominate its diplomatic relations. In 1997, for instance, the Indonesian government cancelled the purchase of F-16 fighter aircraft from the USA in response to vociferous criticisms of Indonesia's human rights situation and its electoral process. Meanwhile, the United Kingdom was pressuring the states of the European Union to ban the sale of weapons used for internal repression to a numbers of governments, including Indonesia's.

To differentiate it from the Indonesian government's earlier use of the term, the sense in which 'human rights' is used here relates specifically to the role of government and, in this context, refers to civil and political rights. There are other rights—such as the right to development, which is acknowledged by the United Nations and has been identified by the Indonesian government as taking precedence. But these are certainly less critical—so-called 'second-generation rights'—and do not go as directly to the core of an individual's immediate well-being. Indeed, they are often used as a smokescreen for the abrogation of political and civil rights.[1] Further, individuals or non-government groups can and do abrogate the rights of others. But these cannot be understood within the same context as state-related civil and political rights. Where they do occur, they are beyond the authority of the state and constitute illegal activity, which is a matter for criminal law. It is government abrogation of human rights that is of most concern, for the government, as a normative expression of the political values and concerns of its people, is supposed to offer them protection.[2] When a government, or its agents, becomes predatory in its behaviour towards the people under its care, civil and political matters have reached a truly parlous state.

When discussing issues of human rights, it is also important to note that criticism of foreign observers for their lack of cultural understanding or sensitivity does beg the question of cross-cultural interpretation: How well or otherwise are outsiders able to distinguish cultural authenticity from political manipulation? And, in

---

1 Although the right to development is perfectly legitimate and reasonable, authoritarian governments often use it as a means of denying political and civil rights, in much the same way that 'development journalism' (or '*Pancasila* journalism') is used as a method of imposing censorship on the news media.

2 This is the predominant view of the role of the contemporary state as expressed by organisations such as the United Nations and goes to the heart of discussions of political legitimacy.

turn, how does this impact on notions of rights? If one accepts the idea of fundamental cultural difference, then cultural misunderstanding is likely to take place, or cultural offence is more likely to be caused (inadvertent though it may be). Furthermore, a method that might be employed to overcome such difference would also itself be culturally located and, consequently, compromised.

Such cultural relativism would mean that no one could offer any critical analysis within any other cultural context without being at least insensitive and probably ignorant. Hence, when Indonesian government representatives claim, as they have frequently done, that human rights issues in Indonesia need to be understood within that country's particular cultural and historical context, and that expressions of concern over human rights issues are cultural imperialism, they are effectively denying outsiders the legitimacy of their concerns. By the same logic, Indonesians who do not agree with the government on this point are 'un-Indonesian'. However, this is a difficult position to sustain, partly because Indonesia is, as a composite state, heterogeneous by definition, and especially because the Indonesian government has difficulty proving that it actually represents the views of its constituents.

This is not the most appropriate place to initiate another skirmish in the 'Asian values' debate, but it must be said that claims to cultural relativism are usually made by those with vested interests in such claims (politicians claiming cultural acceptance of authoritarianism, for example). Further, broader claims to 'Asian values' (or sometimes 'Confucian values') are nonsensical. 'Asia' —by definition, a European imaginative construct (Said 1991)— is, from Afghanistan to Japan, vastly too heterogeneous to lay claim to even the broadest type of cultural singularity without completely losing meaning. Similarly, a political interpretation of Confucianism is applicable only to a limited number of states (not including Indonesia), implies cultural stasis, and almost completely subverts the benign intentions of Master Kong (latinised as 'Confucius').

While it must be acknowledged that cultures are different, they are not radically so (see Ricoeur 1981, pp. 49–50; Todorov 1986, p. 374). The quality of being human underpins culture, and supersedes it. Hence, human rights are, by definition, universal rather than culturally specific. If issues of human rights are, as claimed by Indonesia's representatives, culturally specific, then what is being referred to is 'Indonesian rights', not rights that are founded on the quality of being human. For those who do argue for the cultural specificity of human rights, experience in countries where such abuses take place—including Indonesia—has overwhelmingly confirmed that ordinary people do not like being killed, gaoled, tortured, or otherwise repressed, no matter what their cultural or political affiliation. In this respect, what constitutes human rights cannot be determined by the very individual or group accused of their violation (a government or its representative), but can only be understood as a set of principles pertaining to all people at all times in all places. The United Nations Charter on Human Rights, while not perfect, certainly goes a long way towards codifying what human rights are, in particular the most contested and most abused of human rights, civil and political rights.

As someone who was regularly engaged with the international community, Indonesia's foreign minister, Ali Alatas, was consistently the strongest advocate for a more 'gentle' policy towards dissidents in Indonesia, although he was also among the least influential in government. Similarly, although not doing so uniformly, the international community is encouraging Indonesia to move towards a more open democratic process. This is intended to redress civil and political grievances, as well as to provide more accountability within the political process. Against this, there remains the argument that, as a developing country, Indonesia cannot 'afford' open political participation.

Rights and development

The issue of 'development' is one of the most difficult for outsiders to address when discussing human rights in developing countries. It can be persuasively argued that people care little about abstract rights when they are hungry, or that a sense of social order, indeed social discipline, is necessary to achieve economic growth. Yet a majority of Indonesians could not have been regarded as living in absolute poverty before the 1997–98 crisis, if the inflated income claims of the government could have been believed, and presuming a relatively equal distribution of income. Of course, there was still considerable poverty in Indonesia, in absolute terms, even before the crisis, and the distribution of income is so skewed as to render the economist's conventional per capita GDP equation meaningless. But more importantly, a number of surveys have shown not only that authoritarianism and the human rights abuses it engenders are unnecessary to achieve development, but also that authoritarianism and its attendant human rights abuses can be counterproductive (Howard 1983, p. 478; Donnelly 1984, p. 258; Goodin 1979).

Apologists for authoritarian governments often argue that economic development can take place within an authoritarian environment, with countries such as China, South Korea, Taiwan, Malaysia, and Singapore cited as examples. What they usually fail to note is that, in some cases (such as South Korea and Taiwan), industrial infrastructure was already in place before economic growth, that distribution of income is usually poor (arguments about the need for capital accumulation notwithstanding), and that growth could have occurred or indeed have been greater in a participatory political environment. Taking the right to freedom of expression as one example, a free flow of information is necessary to generate productive ideas, to limit corruption, to reduce wasteful spending on a military designed for domestic repression, and perhaps most importantly, to ensure an adequate distribution of wealth. Conversely, where serious human rights abuses do take place, it is common to find a shortage of productive ideas, a proliferation of corruption, high levels of spending on a military designed to quell expressions of dissent, and an unequal distribution of income. Indonesia was in the unhappy position of finding itself burdened with all of these problems, many of which had specific focuses.

East Timor

In a number of arenas in which Indonesia is active, the issue of East Timor looms large. If the country's leaders could have known the difficulty it would have caused them, they would have had to give the idea of invasion and incorporation a very serious second look, if not abandon it completely. Apart from being a financial drain, a constant military obligation, and having the potential to act as a catalyst for the disintegration of the state (according to the Indonesian government), events in East Timor also continue to be the focus of much world attention. This is no more so than in regard to issues of human rights violations.

Already burdened with a poor human rights record in conventional domestic matters, the full-scale 'counter-insurgency' campaign conducted by Indonesia's armed forces could not help but result in human rights violations on a massive scale. Although the exact figure will never be known, a wide range of very credible sources estimate that up to 200 000 people have died in East Timor since the Indonesian invasion of 1975 as a direct result of that invasion, mostly within the first decade after the invasion. The prime causes of death have been starvation caused by compulsory relocation, preventable disease caused by lack of otherwise available medicine, and the killing of combatants and more commonly civilians, often on the scale of wholesale massacres, by Indonesian soldiers.

Although various representatives of the Indonesian government have been prepared to concede that there have been human rights violations in East Timor—particularly a high level of deaths during the earlier period of Indonesian occupation—they have claimed that the extent of such violations is exaggerated. The then home affairs minister, Rudini, said that foreign assessments of the Dili massacre, made it 'sound like the massacre committed by Pol Pot'. This incident alone, in which up to 270 defenceless protesters were gunned down by soldiers, cannot be compared to the genocide in Cambodia between 1975 and 1978. But, over the same period in East Timor, the deaths of a quarter or more of the total population offers a chillingly close parallel to the experience in Cambodia.

The problems associated with human rights in East Timor stemmed in the beginning from a perception, real or invented, that Fretilin was in effect a communist-front organisation. Given the rabid anti-communism of the New Order government, this was regarded as extreme provocation. When the Indonesian government began sending in troops in covert operations from September 1975, it embarked on what was to be a long history of illegal and internationally unacceptable activities. That it chose to invade overtly, on 7 December that year, only confirmed that the New Order government generally, and ABRI in particular, was not concerned about the niceties of respecting self determination, human life, or international law. When the first paratroops landed in Dili, the indiscriminate killing began and, in the following days, took on a more methodical approach. One cannot visit Dili without being reminded that the pier at the centre of town was where innumerable East Timorese, arbitrarily arrested in the days after the invasion, were lined up and summarily executed, their bodies dumped into the sea. One cannot visit the officially promoted Panti Pasar (also called, though not literally, 'the White Beach') nearby, where most of their bodies washed up days later, without being further reminded.

In the period after the invasion, the Indonesian army conducted a bitter campaign against Fretilin's armed wing, Falintil, and anyone who might be suspected of being a supporter of the 'resistance'. Perhaps the most notorious feature of this war against the East Timorese people was the 'fence of legs' campaign of the early 1980s, whereby East Timorese were forced to walk in front of Indonesian soldiers so that they would be shot first if the Falintil guerillas opened fire. There were summary and often arbitrary executions of East Timorese suspected of supporting Falintil, with reports of whole villages of suspected Falintil sympathisers being killed, their bodies buried in mass graves or dumped in the sea.

While direct killings accounted for most of the large numbers of deaths in the period immediately after the Indonesian invasion, starvation and related diseases took the greatest toll. In a bid to cut off popular support for Falintil guerillas, the Indonesian military authorities in East Timor initiated a campaign of removing people from their villages and resettling them in 'secure' compounds far away from their homes. East Timor is, at the best of times, a hard and only semi-hospitable environment, and apart from a few more fortunate areas in the centre of the island, agricultural cultivation is a slow and difficult process. When villagers were removed from their homes, they were rarely allowed to take farming implements with them and had little or no store of food or grain. With Indonesian military authorities in East Timor less concerned about the well-being of these people than defeating Falintil, minimal effort was made to ensure that they were fed. The direct consequence of this campaign, particularly in the late 1970s and early 1980s, was widespread starvation. Most observers believe that this policy alone accounted for most of the deaths in this period.

The incident to have attracted most international attention, although not nearly the worst in terms of its outcome, was the Dili massacre on 12 November 1991. In this incident, Indonesian soldiers opened fire on protesters at the Santa Cruz Cemetery in southern Dili. Amnesty International believes that 270 protesters were killed at the cemetery or while attempting to flee. Witnesses said they saw soldiers then beating wounded people with truncheons and rifle butts (Amnesty International 1994, 50–1). Dozens more were reportedly killed in the days and weeks after the incident, including some in hospital, as the military authorities punished the dissenters. Between sixty and eighty people involved in the protest were believed to have been killed on 15 November. East Timor was very much a province under military occupation, where the indigenous people were regarded by Indonesian soldiers with contempt and hostility.

The causes of human rights complaints in East Timor can no longer simply be explained in terms of an invading force repressing the indigenous population. Most East Timorese have been born in the years since the Indonesian invasion and have grown up with the Indonesian presence. The East Timorese are treated as second-class citizens in their own land and are increasingly economically marginalised. In addition to the Indonesian dominance of the local economy (see p. 172), Indonesian government workers receive a 99 per cent pay loading for being stationed in East Timor. Along with East Timor's relative remoteness, this loading is reflected in the fact that most goods and services are about double the cost of those in Java. Given that East Timor is the poorest province in the archipelago—a poverty that is almost exclusively borne by the East Timorese—this only contributes another volatile ingredient to the cocktail of East Timorese resentment against Indonesians. Both these issues lead to resentment, which spills over into anti-Indonesian activity and the destruction of non-East Timorese owned property, in particular shops and market stalls. The Indonesian authorities respond, too often with a heavy hand, with further abuses of human rights as a result.

In December 1994 this resentment spilled over into rioting in Dili, during which most of the town's Indonesian owned restaurants were burned down. Rioting and subsequent deaths became increasingly common. The large market at Maliana, near the West Timor border, burned down in one such incident, and there have been regular subsequent reports of East Timorese being shot in demonstrations or other scenes of conflict. Reports of conflicts between Indonesian troops and East Timorese residents are continuing unabated as this is being written, and it certainly seems as though the issues that caused such conflict, including the cyclical nature of repression and dissent, are a long way from being resolved.

The resentment felt by many, particularly young East Timorese, also continues to feed into Fretilin's armed base. The regeneration of support for Falintil that resulted from the Dili massacre and riots in 1994 provoked the expected response: Indonesian military officials stepped up the campaign to isolate and root out the guerillas. Predictably, this campaign was partly directed against civilians, again resulting in further human rights abuses, such as arbitrary arrest and detention, torture, and killings.

East Timorese who felt able to speak to me claimed that Indonesian soldiers still abuse them, beating, torturing, and sometimes killing unarmed people, particularly outside Dili. There have been trials of Indonesian soldiers on charges of murder, but many East Timorese regard these as token gestures to placate international concern over abuses of human rights. The actual punishment meted out to soldiers convicted of murder—four years 'imprisonment'—was mild by the more usual standards of punishment for this level of offence and reflected Indonesia's elastic, pro-government legal code.

While there is hope that some resolution to East Timor's problems might be found, the Indonesian government remains fixed in its position that the region will remain under Jakarta's direct control. The head of ABRI at the time of the Dili massacre, General Try Sutrisno, went on to become Indonesia's vice president, representing the majority 'red and white' faction of ABRI. If Tri's comments on the Dili massacre are anything to go by (see p. 170), whatever moves the Indonesian government might make towards reconciliation in East Timor, there will still be considerable resistance within ABRI towards such a settlement.

Aceh

At the other end of the archipelago, the military situation was only slightly less difficult. Rebellion and repression have, as already noted, been a long-standing feature of Acehnese political life, rising and falling with almost predictable regularity. Tensions in Aceh Province escalated in the late 1980s, when the separatist group Aceh Merdeka launched a military operation against the

Indonesian government. Over the following three or four years, around 2000 people died, many in public executions, others secretly, their mutilated corpses being left in public places. Many had their hands and feet bound, had been shot at close range, and showed signs of torture. Most of those killed by special counter-insurgency troops lived in rebel-held areas, and the extra-judicial killings were partly an effort to terrorise local inhabitants into helping authorities track down Aceh Merdeka members.

Amnesty International also received unconfirmed reports of mass killings, in one case of fifty-six detainees on 12 September 1990 at Bukit Panglima, while another 200 bodies were discovered near the village of Alue Mira in mid-1990. A regional military commander later confirmed the existence of the grave, although he said the number was indeterminate because 'It's hard to tell with arms and heads all mixed up' (Amnesty International 1994, p. 56). While the scale of killings reduced after 1991, there have continued to be sporadic clashes between Aceh Merdeka members and police and army units. There have been no investigations into any of the extra-judicial killings by soldiers or police, nor has the practice been halted, much less condemned, by the Indonesian government.

The Acinese independence movement is again on the rise in the late 1990s, if the number of arms captured is an indicator. It could reasonably be expected, then, that there will be further incidents of human rights abuses. Like other cases in which human rights abuses have taken place, those in Aceh reflect a deep-seated opposition to the Indonesian government or its policies, the response to that opposition being repression rather than resolution.

Irian Jaya

Irian Jaya has faced a similar situation to that in Aceh, where those killed by soldiers include non-combatants as well as guerrillas of the OPM. There have been numerous incidents in which individuals suspected of OPM membership or support have been summarily executed, even for the 'crime' of raising the OPM flag as a symbolic gesture. Often victims of the Indonesian army were beheaded and their heads used as proof of their death. There have been other reports of government soldiers firing indiscriminately at villages suspected of supporting or being sympathetic to the

OPM. There have also been numerous unexplained deaths in custody of people arrested on charges related to membership or support of OPM. In all, OPM claims that around 13 000 people have been killed in 'massacres', while aerial bombardments have killed a further 80 000 since 1969 (OPM 1997).

The root of these immediate problems was the issue of Irian Jaya's incorporation into Indonesia. In simple terms, the Indonesian government conducted a plebiscite of especially selected village leaders in 1969. However, the people of Irian Jaya, or 'West Papua' as the OPM calls it, were not given the opportunity to vote on the issue in a free and open act of self-determination, despite a United Nations-brokered agreement that they would be. The ability to conduct such a vote is a fundamental political right, yet it was disallowed primarily because it would have been unlikely to have returned the Indonesian government's required response.

Furthermore, although a few indigenous Papuans have been incorporated into the economy of Irian Jaya, most do not even receive the supposed benefits of development, which according to the rhetoric of the Indonesian government is at least as important as, and may take precedence over, political and civil rights. The culturally conscious Javanese often regard ethnic Melanesians, the indigenous peoples of Irian Jaya, as being less 'human', and their treatment, particularly by government authorities, tends to reflect this superior view. Such a culturally superior view is manifested in many of Indonesia's outer islands, but perhaps Irian Jaya offers the most extreme example.

Unionists

Working conditions in Indonesia are, for most people, very poor. For those who work in factories or other places of large-scale employment, conditions often reflect a status that is well below the average, even with Indonesia's modest levels of overall economic development. In this sense, many Indonesian workers' 'right to development' was not being met, and when workers have banded together to seek change, which is an inherently political exercise, they have confronted a range of mechanisms designed to stifle such moves.

To its credit (limited though it is), the Indonesian government has recognised the problem of often unrealistically low levels of income[3] and has moved to implement a minimum wage. But this minimum level of income was still the lowest of any ASEAN country in 1992 (*Jakarta Post*, 1 December 1992, p. 2) and not enough for most families to adequately sustain themselves. In many cases it was simply not recognised by employers. A survey by the International Labour Organisation (ILO) in 1989, for example, showed that half of all factories in the Jakarta area were paying less than the minimum wage, and that 88 per cent of women workers in Jakarta factories were malnourished (Bourchier 1994, p. 53). For those people lucky enough to have a full-time job (unemployment and underemployment being rife, at about 48 per cent), workplace conditions are often also very poor, with few safety practices or procedures and very often long, compulsory hours of work. The conventional response to such situations is for workers to join together to request improved pay and conditions, but this implies the creation of a trade union, and trade unions in Indonesia are not allowed an existence independent of the government.

As with other so-called 'functional' organisations in Indonesia, trade unionism may only be represented through the official, government-sponsored trade union organisation, the All-Indonesia Workers' Union, (Serikat Pekerja Seluruh Indonesia, or SPSI). It is through SPSI that all workers' demands and concerns are channelled, and it is this organisation that has the sole discretionary power to call for strike action, which is only allowed when all other avenues have been thoroughly explored. In practice, striking is only very rarely permitted, virtually 'nullifying . . . the right of workers to strike' (Hadiz 1994, p. 66). Even then, the police and army are allowed to intervene to stop the strike if they see fit to do so (on the grounds of 'national security') (see Lambert 1993, pp. 15–18). This tends to militate against the

---

3   Some critics of this view suggest that the only 'realistic' wage level is one that does
    not encourage foreign capital to go offshore to cheaper labour markets. That view
    begs a number of responses, the first of which is that there are not many labour mar-
    kets that are cheaper than Indonesia (south-east China, for example, was about four
    to five times more expensive in terms of labour before the radical devaluation of the
    rupiah). Further, labour costs can, and probably should, be measured as 'realistic' only
    when they meet minimum living requirements, not the requirements of international
    capital. The link between labour costs and the high level of underemployment or
    unemployment is a difficult one to sustain in any case, but especially so in Indonesia.

government's apparent concern for the well-being of workers, limiting as it does their ability to press for the government-sponsored minimum wage levels. The state of industrial relations in Indonesia is neither new nor significantly changed. As long ago as 1980, it was noted that 'The suffering of the workers is so clearly terrible. But even though there is the FBSI,[4] there are Pancasila labour relations, there are slogans saying this and that, yet still the plight of the workers does not change. Crushed, suppressed, and without help' (*Merdeka*, 4 September 1980).

In the late 1980s and into the 1990s, as a consequence of the limitations imposed on workers' industrial action by the government, individuals and smaller, non-official organisations organised a number of industrial campaigns. In 1992, about three-quarters of 155 recorded strikes in East Java related to poor pay and working conditions, with military intervention rising from 61 per cent of cases in 1992 to 73 per cent of cases in 1993 (Waters 1993). From 1989 to 1990, the number of strikes rose by 300 per cent (Bourchier 1994, p. 54). These campaigns met with varying degrees of success and varying degrees of repression. In all cases, undertaking strike or other industrial action was a risky business, indicating both desperation and determination on the part of employees (for further discussion on labour conditions and rights, see Bouchier 1994; Lambert 1993).

Partly out of these labour struggles and partly through helping organise them, the independent Indonesian Labour Union for Prosperity (SBSI) rose in the early 1990s to become one of Indonesia's highest profile and most viable genuine points of opposition to the New Order government. At its peak in 1994, SBSI claimed a membership of 500 000, but was soon hit by a wave of repressive government action. The union, which was banned by the New Order government, had been campaigning for better conditions for workers, including actual payment of minimum rates of pay, a lift in the minimum rate of pay, and the ending of labour exploitation. When a series of strikes turned violent in 1994, the chairperson of SBSI, Mochtar Pakpahan, was arrested on a charge of 'sedition' (Williams 1997b) and sentenced to four years' gaol. He was released nine months later after winning a

---

4   Federasi Buruh Seluruh Indonesia, or the All Indonesian Labour Federation, a forerunner to SBSI.

Supreme Court appeal, but after coming under much official pressure, the Supreme Court overturned its own decision to free Pakpahan and reimposed the original sentence. He was free and awaiting the resolution of this action when he was again arrested and charged with subversion related to the July 1997 riots, although this was widely seen more as an opportunity to suppress a difficult union activist than having anything to do with the riot itself.

Perhaps the most celebrated example involving the suppression of workers' claims was the Marsinah case. A young factory worker from PT Catur Putra Surya in Porong, Sidoarjo, near Surabayawho, who had helped to organise a strike was found dead after disappearing following a workers' and company meeting on 3 May 1993. The strike had been called to force the company into paying the government's minimum wage of Rp2250 a day, which had been implemented by law two months earlier. Marsinah was one of fifteen workers' representatives at a meeting with officials from the company, SPSI, and the Department of Labour. Marsinah took an active part in the discussion, which saw company management accept the workers' demands for the minimum wage, as well as the creation of an independent trade union. Following the meeting, sixteen worker activists received summonses to report to the local military headquarters, where they were threatened and forced to sign letters of resignation, which included admissions of being involved in illegal meetings and intimidating other workers. Marsinah was not one of those forced to resign. However, she did obtain a copy of the resignation document. She was last seen at 9:30 p.m. as she headed off to find her evening meal. Her body showed signs of having been beaten and raped when it was found five days later over 100 kilometres from her home. Although not charged with murder, an army captain was subsequently court martialled as a consequence of the case. According to Legal Aid Foundation lawyer Rambun Tjajo, who was one of a team requesting repeal of the law allowing military intervention in industrial disputes, 'The Marsinah murder is a clear cut example of the way violence is used by the state against the peaceful actions of workers who, in most cases, are making legitimate demands such as payment of the minimum wage' (as quoted in Waters 1993). Although this was not the only time that worker activists were killed or otherwise mistreated, it did manage to attract considerable international attention and at least gave ABRI pause to consider its heavy-handed approach to resolving industrial disputes.

In 1996 ABRI went through more conventional channels to suppress non-official industrial action when it arrested the President of the Indonesian Centre for Labour Struggle (PPBI), Dita Indahsari. Dita had been leading a strike of 20 000 workers in Surabaya, East Java, at the time of her arrest under Indonesia's subversion laws. The PPBI is the trade union organisation affiliated with the banned PRD, and the move against Dita was at least as much an effort to break the PRD as it was to break the strike. However, strikes are not necessarily motivated by party ideology; they can often be understood simply as workers taking direct political action over real, immediate issues.

Dissidents and protesters

The Indonesian government takes a very dim view of political dissent and, under its useful but ambiguous laws, can arrest anyone it believes is opposing government policy. For example, criticism of government policy can be interpreted as subversion, a 'crime' that can carry a range of penalties, including the death penalty. It should be noted that, apart from the events following 30 September 1965 and the subsequent ousting of Sukarno, the death penalty has been used more as a threat than as an applied punishment. However, it does act as a considerable deterrent and does allow an extreme range of punishment, which is applied at the discretion of the (usually government-influenced) judge. Like opposing government policy, criticism of the president is not allowed and can attract very severe sentences. If the government is really enthusiastic about pursuing a dissenter or group of dissenters, it will label them as 'communist', which again is a crime punishable by severe sentences.

The usefulness of these 'codes' of 'criminal' law is that there is almost no defence against them, as what is interpreted as subversion, defaming the president, or communism is very much in the eye of the beholder. To that extent, attempting to establish an independent political party or other politically oriented organisation can constitute 'subversion'. Expressing concern about Suharto's tenure in office being a result of a rigged political system constituted 'defamation'. And calling for a greater redistribution of the nation's wealth, even through officially sanctioned projects such as education or health schemes, can be called 'communism'. Indeed, Suharto himself used the term 'communism' to describe anyone who opposed him, including, while returning from a trip to India in December 1993, members of ABRI (in relation to support for Megawati's chairing of the PDI).

Dissent and political opposition is usually firmly under control, but when it has boiled over, it has often been in the form of street marches or riots. Sometimes a street march, when confronted with police or soldiers, has turned into a riot. The response of the police and army was often indiscriminate and violent, and there were numerous reported cases in which protesters were either beaten severely or killed. The alleged 'riot' at the Tanjung Priok port area in Jakarta in 1984 was a case in point, with perhaps 200 people being shot by soldiers after they protested against the arrest of Islamic leaders (see pp. 111–12). In July 1996, the worst riots since 1984 broke out in Jakarta, with widespread destruction of property in response to the storming of the Megawati-controlled PDI headquarters by police and soldiers (see pp. 137–8). The chairperson of the PRD, Budiman Sujatmiko, and PRD secretary general Petrus Haryanto were arrested and charged with subversion as a consequence of the riots, even though they claimed not to have been involved. In effect, Budiman and Petrus were arrested because they had spoken out against Suharto at the PDI headquarters and, at least as importantly, because they had helped organise an anti-government political party that had an overtly left-wing agenda. In May 1997 Budiman was convicted and sentenced to thirteen years' imprisonment. The pair had earlier dismissed their legal council on the grounds that the lawyers would be susceptible to official harassment after the trial and that, in any case, the outcome was a forgone conclusion. Fellow PRD activist Dita Indahsari was sentenced to six years' imprisonment, and Coen Hussein Pontoh was sentenced to four years. Another eleven PRD members are being tried for 'subversion' as this is being written, with prosecutors asking for sentences of between twelve and fifteen years each.

Amnesty International has listed a large number of prisoners of conscience in Indonesia, particularly in relation to the ABRI raid on the PDI office but also in connection with union activities, with 'defaming' the president or expressing other anti-government sentiments, with defending land or farms against large-scale government-backed projects, and, still, with the events following the suppression of the PKI in the mid- to late 1960s. Amnesty International has expressed concern for the personal health and safety, particularly in relation to torture, of a number of political prisoners associated with the PDI riot.

Criminals

Given the government's attitude towards political dissenters, it is not surprising that more conventional law-breakers are often treated in an equally off-hand manner. Indonesia's gaols have many short- and longer term residents, indicating that, conventional crime is socially unacceptable, although it does not present a threat to the state. Even so, Indonesia's police and armed forces have often taken short-cuts in dealing with real, suspected, and claimed criminals.

One method of dealing with criminals without reference to the legal apparatus is simply to kill them. Semi-official death squads have operated in Indonesia since the first days of the New Order government, initially to dispose of remaining and suspected communists and their sympathisers and, more recently, to remove leaders of anti-government riots. But by the early 1980s, known criminal figures were being summarily executed in increasingly large numbers in what was known as *penembakan misterius* (*petrus*), or the 'mysterious shootings'. About 5000 people were killed between late 1982 and 1984, starting in Yogyakarta and eventually spreading to the outer islands. These mysterious killings were the work of security services and were believed to have been undertaken by Kopkamtib, at the behest of Murdani, who at that time directly controlled Kopkamtib and was also commander of ABRI from 1983. Just before Ali Murtopo, the former head of the intelligence network, died in 1984, it is thought that, upon assuming much of that responsibility, Murdani opted to close down Murtopo's unofficial intelligence network, which employed many known criminals or allowed agents to employ criminal behaviour.

The killings ended what was widely regarded as a worrying rise in violent and increasingly organised crime. But they also showed, yet again, that the New Order government would not hesitate to use absolute force to deal with any problem it regarded as presenting a threat, or indeed just to tidy up a few loose ends. In his official memoirs, published in 1989, Suharto acknowledged that these 'mysterious killings' had been conducted by members of the security establishment in a deliberate government attempt to break established crime through a sort of 'shock therapy' approach (Suharto 1989, p. 364). Of course, Suharto did not acknowledge any involvement in closing down Murtopo's old intelligence network.

Although the *petrus* campaign ended in 1986, it set a precedent for police and other security forces in dealing with difficult criminal matters. A 'shoot on sight' policy was initiated after 1986, so that fleeing suspected criminals could be shot without official repercussions. As a consequence, hundreds of suspected criminals were shot dead, allegedly while trying to escape custody or lawful apprehension.

Suspected criminals are also routinely tortured, primarily to extract confessions to facilitate the 'legal process'. Sometimes the torture goes too far and they die in custody, although many are also shot while allegedly trying to escape. That is, the explanation of 'death while allegedly escaping' covers for the reality of 'death through beating or other causes while in custody'.

The legal system

Indonesia's legal process operates very much to suit the interests of the government, its associates, and ABRI. It retains a poor system of legal codification and scant regard for a consistent rule of law, and is openly susceptible to government and ABRI influence and interference, as well as corruption in less politically sensitive cases.

In the first instance, Indonesia's legal process is subject to the country's constitution, which has been changed three times since the proclamation of independence. In each case, the changes were intended to be provisional. The first version, the 1945 Constitution, was short, with thirty-seven articles, and ambiguous. Its dominant feature was that it provided for a strong presidency, with wide-ranging discretionary powers. Soon after coming into force, it was changed by decree to a parliamentary system. In 1949, partly to placate Dutch concerns about the well-being of nominally pro-Dutch parts of the colony, a new constitution was drawn up for the federal 'United States of Indonesia'. This constitution was considered, not unreasonably, to be overly influenced by the Dutch, and a new constitution was drawn up in 1950. This was a far lengthier document than the 1945 Constitution, with 146 articles. It guaranteed individual freedoms, put in place a parliamentary democracy, and limited the role of the president to being largely ceremonial. Article 134 of the 1950 Constitution called for a constitutional assembly to draw up a more permanent document, but while work commenced on a lasting constitution, it was never finished. The 1945 Constitution was put back in place in 1959 as a part of the process of implementing Guided Democracy. Indonesia's legal system operates within the framework of the 1945 Constitution, which is characterised by a strong central authority in the office and person of the president and an ambiguous account of what is guaranteed under the Constitution.

In formal terms, Indonesia's judiciary is independent of the executive, yet in practical terms it is very much subordinate to the executive and other powerful groups, such as ABRI:

Judges are civil servants employed by the executive branch, which controls their assignments, pay and promotion. They are subject to considerable pressure from the military and other governmental authorities that often determine the outcome of a case . . . Corruption is a common feature of the legal system and the payment of bribes can influence prosecution, conviction and sentencing in civil and criminal cases (United States Department of State 1997).

In particular, charges can be, and often are, brought by ABRI. In politically sensitive cases, prosecutors represent the government position and judges invariably accede to the government's preferred outcome, very rarely delivering judgments that embarrass the government (and when they do, such judgments are often subsequently overturned). The position of prosecutors and judges is partly a consequence of their appointment and promotion being directly determined by the Ministry of Justice, which links them to the executive. Further, the president may intervene in judicial matters by making note of those cases he wishes to see pursued. And the Supreme Court, which in most other countries has the power to determine the constitutional validity of laws passed by the legislature (or through the president by decree), in Indonesia can only make recommendations and does not have the power of full judicial review. In a practical sense, then, judges, prosecutors, and the legal system are simply another branch of executive government, rather than an independent institution.

The compromised position of Indonesia's judiciary is further skewed in favour of the government through a range of repressive and widely interpretable legislation, most of which focuses on political 'crimes'. In particular, the Anti-Subversion Law is one of the most widely interpreted and used articles of Indonesia's criminal code and, potentially, the most draconian. Any act or statement can be interpreted as socially disruptive if it is in contravention or critical of the tenets of the *Pancasila* (themselves highly interpretable), or critical of the president, the government, its institutions, or its policies. The logic of this law is that if a case is brought against an individual, the prosecution only need prove that what has been interpreted as subversive took place to secure a conviction. It does not need to prove that what took place was itself subversive. As a consequence, individuals can be convicted of subversion on the flimsiest of grounds. Conviction under this statute attracts penalties up to and including death.

Similar to the Anti-Subversion Laws are a series of articles (154, 155, and 160) that forbid the 'spreading of hatred' against government officials. Punishment under these laws ranges from four and a half to seven years' imprisonment. Related to these laws, article 134 of the criminal code imposes sentences of up to six years for 'insulting the president'.

Indonesia did implement a Code of Criminal Procedure in 1981, which was intended to provide certain rights to detainees and defendants. However, the code has been regularly ignored or obstructed, particularly in relation to detainees having access to legal representation during interrogation. Further, there are no effective legal sanctions against non-compliance with the code (Amnesty International 1994, pp. 40–1).

Government initiatives

In 1993, largely in response to criticism over the Dili massacre, but also acknowledging Indonesia's poor international standing on more broad human rights issues, the government established a National Human Rights Commission. Consequently, discussion of human rights issues was cautiously elevated to the national agenda, particularly through some of the media, and the commission has become increasingly bold in reporting and commenting on alleged abuses. However, the commission received less than full endorsement from large sections of the government, is treated with some suspicion by ABRI, and is unable to rely on the independence of the legal system to prosecute those cases it is able to bring to court. The establishment of the commission also means that human rights issues are 'localised', with Amnesty International and the International Committee for the Red Cross being increasingly restricted.

One clear example of how the commission has failed, despite its own best attempts, is the placing of the commission's East Timor office opposite an ABRI base, where it and the people entering and leaving it can be easily monitored. This proximity means that people with legitimate complaints are hesitant to lodge them, for fear of further retribution, and the numbers of complaints to the office have consequently been low. The commission has lodged a request to have its office relocated and, at the time of writing, this is still under consideration by the Indonesian government. Further, although Dili remains by far the biggest centre in East Timor, travel to Dili from other parts of East Timor is still difficult and time consuming,and often attracts undue attention. The ICRC's office in Dili remains open, but is engaged in a constant struggle to maintain, much less expand, its services.

In any discussion of human rights issues in Indonesia, what needs to be considered first and foremost is that the country's style of government, almost by definition, will continue to find itself at odds with claims to human rights. Human rights issues remain a critical aspect of political life in Indonesia, representing some of the real and immediate issues faced by many ordinary Indonesians on a daily basis, as well as a movement to address such issues. But in a broader sense, the issue of human rights abuse in Indonesia is intrinsically linked to the type and process of government in that country. In simple terms, superficial attempts to address human rights issues are little more than tinkering around the edges while the wellspring of repression remains firmly intact. In this sense, the chairperson of Indonesia's Legal Aid Foundation, Adnan Buyung Nasution, was correct when he told me that, for example, the problem of East Timor would be resolved if and when Indonesia became a genuinely democratic state. Of course, this ignores the distinct possibility that a majority of East Timorese might choose to secede regardless of the political composition of Indonesia. But it does recognise that most, if not all, of Indonesia's wide range of problems with human rights are a direct consequence of its political system and could be addressed by instituting fundamental political change, including genuine self-determination through a representative political structure. Unfortunately for Indonesia's human rights activists, such a change is a very long way from being realised, and as a consequence, despite a superficial acknowledgment of the problem, human rights issues are likely to remain high on both Indonesia's domestic and its international agenda.

11

CORRUPTION AND THE FIRST FAMILY

'The most corrupt country in Asia'

The initial official response was silence. Then came the protestations, notable for their lameness. It was a broadside the Indonesian government had apparently not expected (though it probably should have, given that similar observations had been made before) but that, apparently, it increasingly deserved. A survey conducted by the Hong Kong-based Political and Economic Risk Consultancy Limited showed that Indonesia was 'the most corrupt country in Asia' (*Jakarta Post*, 31 March 1997, p. 1).

The survey, which was based on interviews with 280 business executives, said, 'A series of high profile cases highlighted the extent to which politically influential individuals were able to arrange matters to their own financial benefit. Growing nepotism . . . was thus probably equated with corruption' (*Jakarta Post*, 31 March 1997, p. 1). An Indonesian government spokesman protested weakly that the survey had not included Pakistan, which was said to be more corrupt than Indonesia. This was cold comfort indeed for those who had been on the receiving end of Indonesia's myriad forms of corruption.[1]

Apart from the views of foreign business people, the issue of high-level corruption has also been creating increasing concern

---

1   An earlier index of world corruption, before Tommy Suharto's Timor car deal, noted that Indonesia had slightly improved its corruption 'rating'. The index was based on ten separate surveys of international corruption. On a scale of 0–10, from total corruption to total integrity, Indonesia scored 2.65 (number forty-five of fifty-four countries listed). In Asia, China (2.43), Bangladesh (2.29), and Pakistan (1) were regarded as more corrupt than Indonesia (Transparency International and Goettingen University 1996).

within Indonesia, with regard to its cost to local businesses and to ordinary Indonesians, and its direct influence on the country's currency crisis, not to mention its moral bankruptcy. 'Corruption' is a pejorative term in Western political culture, implying that a person is influenced by personal gain in contradiction of a stated principle, particularly where profit can be gained at the expense of responsibility to third parties (such as a political constituency). In Java, however, there is a tradition of buying favours, and of political leaders accumulating wealth as a consequence of their authority.[2] It could therefore be argued that the values ascribed to corruption are in fact culturally located and hence relative. Given that the buying of political favours meets with a considerable degree of acceptance in Java, there is a difference between the Western and Javanese meanings of 'corruption'. However, this difference must be clearly understood.

In the first instance, the ability of Java's traditional leaders to sell political favours rested in large part on their autocratic power. Simply, there was no court of appeal in such matters. Second, without a well-established system of taxation, selling political favours was a method of raising capital for maintenance of the state. And third, even though such practices may have been tolerated, they generally were supposed to be in keeping with the ability of subjects to pay, were subtle in practice, and were never just the accumulation of wealth for its own sake. Like other aspects of Indonesian political culture, the attempts to relativise the idea of 'corruption' by Indonesian apologists overstates traditional practice and fails to acknowledge that Indonesia is a modern nation-state rather than a feudal sultanate: 'In many cases [corruption] is socially tolerated. In others, not' (Schwartz 1994, p. 135).

Suharto and corruption

Suharto's two primary methods of receiving non-official payment have been through *yayasans* (charitable foundations) and joint business ventures. Suharto was once removed from a military position as a result of his corrupt use of *yayasans*, a fact that is lost in much contemporary discussion. Perhaps, as I was frequently told in Jakarta, the *yayasan* front is publicly accepted because it is

---

2   Of course, corruption exists elsewhere in Indonesia, but as Javanese political tradition dominates Indonesian politics, I have focused on that source.

officially promoted as being for ethical purposes. This accords with (and, in Javanese tradition, parallels) both the limited avenues of appeal on such matters and the requirement for public deference. Yet it was his reputation for being 'shamelessly greedy' (Vatikiotis 1993, p. 99; see also Schwartz 1994, pp. 77–8, 110–13, 133–61) or financially *kasar* (rough, coarse) that also earned Suharto the opprobrium of Java's most important traditional leader, Sultan Hamengkubuwono of Yogyakarta, in early 1966. Asked if he would support Suharto in his bid for power, the Sultan reportedly laughed and asked if 'he was still in the habit of stealing' (as quoted in Vatikiotis 1993, p. 17). The Sultan considered Suharto's methods 'rough and prone to corruption' (as quoted in Vatikiotis 1993, p. 99; see also Schwartz 1994, p. 137).

Corruption generally, and within the first family in particular, has been on the public political and economic agendas since at least 1986,[3] when Australian journalist David Jenkins published the story of links between Suharto and Indonesia's biggest businesses (Jenkins 1986). It has been claimed, correctly, that Jenkins's information was already widely known among Indonesia's elite and a few Indonesian specialists. But the information had not been made public within Indonesia or in the international community, and the story led to a string of similar reports in the following years. Its publication was allegedly so sensitive that Indonesia came close to breaking off diplomatic relations with Australia.[4]

Of course, corruption is not the exclusive preserve of Indonesia's elites, and in terms of corrupt individuals, they comprise a small minority. However, the small-scale corruption that was endemic in Indonesia, such as by state officials, had by the mid-1990s begun to be reined in. Concerned about both local and foreign complaints, the Indonesian government instituted a number of anti-corruption measures, which seemed to be cleaning up the lower echelons of the public service. Having said that, the experience of being pulled over by a police officer for an arbitrary traffic

---

3   Corruption had been a public issue from the late 1950s and again after the Pertamina collapse in 1974. However, before 1986 it did not openly include the involvement of Suharto and his family.

4   I have suggested in a previous publication that Indonesia's response to the 'Soeharto Billions' article was predicated on a complex range of criteria, of which the article itself was only one factor (see pp. 114–18 of this volume).

offence—in a country where there are effectively no road rules—and of paying the 'fine' directly to the officer in cash is still common in the late 1990s. Similarly, a good job in the public service after leaving university still requires a significant cash payment to the right officials. This sort of corruption is annoying and, for poorer people, debilitating. But the type of corruption that led by example, and which helped bring the economy and perhaps the political process undone, was on a massive scale and was practised by a few people at the top of the political and economic heap.

Since 1986, corruption in Indonesia, and particularly in relation to Suharto and his family, has been widely reported (outside Indonesia) and discussed. In fact, by 1988 the issue was regarded as so potentially debilitating to Indonesia that apparent Suharto loyalist and head of ABRI, General Benny Murdani, suggested to Suharto that he might think about limiting his children's questionable business activities. Their growing wealth was unseemly and—in a number of ways, including damaging local banks, pushing local businesses out of the market, and scaring off foreign investment—such naked nepotism was hampering Indonesia's economic development. Suharto already believed that Murdani had played a role in opposing the planned appointment of Sudharmono as vice-president. Given this, it is not surprising that Suharto's response to Murdani's suggestion was to sack him as head of ABRI and appoint him to the significantly less powerful position of defence minister, from which he was removed at the next opportunity five years later. The alienation of Suharto from Murdani was probably the most significant shift in Indonesia's political landscape since Suharto came to power, although in some senses the split was probably overdue, as Suharto had already begun to distance himself from ABRI. But Suharto continued to rely on ABRI to maintain the political status quo. The split with Murdani not only ended Suharto's ability to rely on ABRI as a cohesive force, but it set in train a process that could well ensure that Suharto's successor as president in the longer term will not be of his own choosing.

All of Indonesia's current political problems can be seen as coming to a head over the issues of corruption and the first family, both separately and combined. In particular, the increasingly unequal distribution of income—between Java and the outer islands, between rich and poor (in which economic elites often get richer through corrupt means while the poor, generally, do not), and in favour of those close to the president or other powerful members of the elite—all of which is exacerbated by the economic crisis, has cemented a mood of political dissatisfaction among many Indonesians. This can vary from perceptions among senior army officers that they are being kept away from the spoils of office to riots in Dili over exorbitant prices foisted on the local population by non-Timorese-owned businesses, and riots throughout the country against Chinese businesses.

The issue of what many see as an inadequate distribution of income within Indonesia is symbolised by corruption, as it exacerbates the rich/poor divide as well as excluding or penalising legitimate businesses. Corruption exists from the very lowest levels of government bureaucracy all the way up to the first family. Indeed, Suharto's close associates and family have made an art form of creaming off many of Indonesia's most profitable ventures (from the media to property, agriculture, manufacturing, banking, high technology, and so on), while being protected by monopoly regulations and their relationship to the president. At the upper reaches, the magnificent wealth of Suharto's family and his cronies stands in appalling contrast to Indonesia's tens of millions of genuinely poor. As discussed, living standards had improved in Indonesia between the 1960s and the crisis of the late 1990s, but inadequate access to education and health care is still widespread, and the measures and methods of analysing what comprises absolute poverty do not bear close scrutiny (see p. 89). The rich, by contrast, are not just wealthy by Indonesian standards, but many are very wealthy by any international standard. According to Golkar sources, Suharto's personal wealth was about US$9 billion before the currency depreciation. However, as long ago as 1989, the United States Central Intelligence Agency (CIA) estimated Suharto's wealth to be as high as US$20 billion, including funds tied up in Suharto-controlled 'charitable foundations', while other estimates put it at US$13–16 billion. The CIA estimated that his family was worth about the same figure (Grant 1996, p. 113). Suharto is not merely rich; he can claim to be among the world's super-rich. Not only is this increasingly a source of considerable disquiet within Indonesia, but it has also hindered the country's economic development and continues to concern foreign investors.

'After Marcos . . .'

Not surprisingly, the level of corrupt wealth possessed by Suharto, his family, and his cronies has drawn direct comparisons to the former Philippines dictator Ferdinand Marcos. However, the extent of Suharto's wealth and that of his clique makes Marcos look amateurish in the corruption stakes. As Vatikiotis noted,

While the Marcoses in the Philippines were content to fritter their wealth on property and material goods at home and overseas, Suharto has erected an imposing financial edifice which puts the money to work—both on his and the nation's behalf. The web of Suharto's investments through holding organisations and 'charitable foundations' or *yayasans*, is wide, encompassing the country's most profitable enterprises, but also funding some of the lowest levels of society. Through a network of such foundations Suharto and his family hold stakes—and a share of profits—in a dozen large enterprises, including the fourth largest private bank (Bank Duta), an insurance company (Asuransi Timur Jauh) and rice, textile and flour milling concerns controlled by Liem Sioe L[i]ong (Vatikiotis 1993, p. 51).

In an ironic twist, business interests close to Suharto moved in to buy up many of Marcos' assets after the collapse of his government to a military revolt, thus channelling their own ill-gotten gains into the Philippines. Those interests were Suharto's business partner Liem Sioe Liong (also known as Sudono Salim) and his step-brother Sudwikatmono, and their purchases were valued in 1986 at around US$50 million (Byrnes & Abueg 1986).

According to a well placed government source, Suharto's wealth resides in two main areas (apart from direct business interests), the first being Swiss bank accounts and the second being *yayasans* (charitable foundations). The bank accounts speak for themselves, but the *yayasans* are a peculiarly Indonesian way of diverting money from public scrutiny. The *yayasans*, a number of which were controlled by Suharto's late wife, Tien, are essentially slush funds into which money can be paid without being open to the public gaze. Also, because the *yayasans* are supposed to be non-profit charitable organisations, they are not audited and do not attract tax:

The foundations are a remarkable vehicle for those with excessive personal wealth, since they provide both a means of accumulating riches and disguising or atoning for the fact by doing good works . . . using *yayasans* as a way of marshalling wealth under a philanthropic banner, Suharto docks as much as Rp500 a month from every one of the country's four million civil servants as a compulsory contribution to a mosque-building foundation he heads. The estimated Rp200 million a month this nets goes unaudited (Vatikiotis 1993, pp. 51–2).

The first family

Other family members, though not as rich as Suharto himself, are still extraordinarily wealthy and have business interests that reflect more than just their business acumen (Murdoch 1996; *Jakarta Post*, as quoted in the *Age*, 18 March 1997, p. 10; Loveard 1996; Butler 1996; Huus 1997; *Indonesia Times*, 16 February 1997). The oldest Suharto child (born 1949), Siti Hardiyanti Rukmana, known as 'Tutut', was involved in over 100 companies including toll roads (her biggest source of direct income), contracting, broadcasting, telecommunications, manufacturing, and banking. In one case, Tutut bought and then resold F16 fighter aircraft for the military. Tutut also has the contract to build Jakarta's subway system (US$1.3 billion) and received the first commercial television licence in the country. The extent of her interests is not fully known, although her net worth was estimated in 1997 to be at least US$2 billion.

Son Sigit Harjojudanto (born 1951) has been involved in about twenty companies, including a plastics manufacturing plant, and owns 17.5 per cent of the giant Bank Central Asia (which is controlled by Suharto crony Liem Sioe Liong). Sigit's net worth was around US$450 million in mid-1997.

The third oldest child, Bambang Trihatmodjo (born 1953), was chairperson and 60 per cent stakeholder in the publicly listed Bimantara Group (most of the rest is held by other family members). He has had interests in at least 140 companies, dealing, among other things, in electronics, telecommunications, broadcasting, car production, property (including Jakarta's Grand Hyatt Hotel), construction, and shipping. Bambang's 60 per cent-owned Satelindo company took control of Indonesia's state-owned satellite service in 1993 at no cost. The arrangement has cost the Indonesian government about US$100 million a year in lost revenues. In 1997 Bambang and a business partner, Johannes Kotjo, bought most of the dissolved assets of the Bank Summa through their consortium PT Bhakti Karya Indah Permai. Most of the assets were in property, including the Darmo Satellite Town (a 53-hectare housing and commercial development in Surabaya), the Jakarta International Trade Centre on 44 hectares in East Jakarta's Kemayoran district, and Jakarta's Peranusa Sari-Garden Hotel (*Jakarta Post*, 11 April 1997, p. 12). Bambang's net worth was about US$3 billion (*International Business Asia*, 30 June 1997, p. 16).

Siti Hediati Herijadi, known as Titiek (born 1959), has been involved in about eighty companies, including telecommunications, finance, property, and forestry companies, as well as being a partner in Jakarta's elite Plaza Senayan shopping development with brother-in-law Hashim Djojohadikusomo. In 1997 Titiek was also given the go-ahead to construct a bridge between Sumatra and the Malay Peninsula, a grandiose idea that dismayed many and challenged the government's austerity measures following the mid-1997 currency collapse and associated rising national debt. Titiek's net worth was estimated to be around the US$200 million mark in mid-1997, but also importantly she is married to General Prabowo Subianto, who is expected to figure significantly in the post-Suharto period. Titiek is also a member of the board of commissioners of the Jakarta Stock Exchange.

Hutomo Mandala Putra, better known as 'Tommy' (born 1962), has been involved in at least seventy companies. The industries he has been involved in include an airline (Sempati Air) bought from a holding company controlled by ABRI, importing liquefied natural gas, toll roads, wood manufacturing, fertiliser production, construction, advertising, the media, gas exploration, timber, sugar and palm oil plantations, clove concessions, and car importing. Tommy's net worth in 1997 was at least US$600 million.

The youngest Suharto child, Siti Hutami Endang (born 1964) is involved in about twenty companies including telecommunications, property, contracting, and trading companies. With a little less than US$100 million, she is the poorest of the Suharto children. The third generation of the presidential family is also getting into business, with Sigit's eldest son, Ari Sigit (born 1972), involved in importing rock phosphate, a monopoly on selling fertiliser pellets, and trades in electrical goods and brewing. He has also identified himself as the unnamed person who a number of Indonesian publications have called the 'godfather' of Jakarta's multi-million-dollar trade in the illegal drug 'ecstasy'. Ari Sigit said the media claims were 'exaggerated' (Murdoch 1996). His net worth in 1997 was about US$25 million.

Suharto's half-brother, Probosutedjo, has interests in construction, glass-making, and agribusiness, while Suharto's cousin, Sudwikatmono has a monopoly on the importation and distribution of movies, as well as having investments in, and acting as a front man for, the giant Salim Group.

The cronies

Beyond the first family, Suharto's close business associates have also grown extremely rich as a consequence of their association. His closest business associates include Liem Sioe Liong, head of the Salim group, and Bob Hassan. Hassan was Suharto's regular golfing partner and, from March 1998, trade and industry minister. He made his fortune by helping deforest Kalimantan, which returns about US$4 billion a year (*International Business Asia*, 30 June 1997, p. 16). Apart from becoming a minister, Hassan is primarily involved with Suharto through his role in *yayasans* headed by Suharto and in business with the Suharto children. Hassan is also head of the export associations in the rattan and timber industries, and is the self-styled king of Indonesia's timber industry, through his business Apkindo. Apkindo fixes the prices of exports and of finished products, organises markets, and takes an extraordinarily large proportion of profit for itself.

The Salim group is estimated to turn over about US$9 billion a year, with about 60 per cent of that figure coming from its Indonesian operations. Like Bob Hassan (Schwartz 1994, p. 28), Salim head Liem's relationship with Suharto goes back to the 1950s, when he became an important supplier to ABRI's Diponegoro Division in Central Java. In the 1950s, the Diponegoro Division's chief supplier and financial officer, and later head, was Lieutenant Colonel Suharto[5] (Schwartz 1994, p. 109; Robison 1986, p. 296). In 1959, as a consequence of his dealings with Liem and Hassan (particularly a sugar smuggling scheme), the then ABRI chief General Nasution removed Suharto from heading the Diponegoro Division as a part of an anti-corruption campaign.

Although Liem's business was slow to develop, it jumped ahead with Suharto's political ascension, and by 1990 the Salim group

---

5   The division's financial assistant at this time was Sudjono Humardhani, who later rose to become a leading 'financial' general and one of Suharto's top 'fix-it' men during the early period of the New Order government.

returned US$8–9 billion a year, accounting for 5 per cent of Indonesia's gross domestic product. Liem was Indonesia's single biggest owner of private banking and controlled a number of key commodities, as well as having stakes in other major industries, including chemicals, automobiles, other manufacturing, processed foods, and property. He is also moving into telecommunications, electronics, and timber. Liem's foreign interests accounted for about 40 per cent of his holdings, which, before the economic crisis, were between two and three times as large as their nearest private competitor in Indonesia.

Another businessman, Prajogo Pangestu, is also close to Suharto. Pangestu has concessions for about 5.5 million hectares of forest and associated wood processing facilities, estimated to be worth at least US$5–6 billion and returning over US$1 billion a year. It was these timber holdings, and those of Hasan and Sinar Mas group head Eka Cipta Widjaya, that were in large part held responsible for the forest fires in Indonesia from mid-1997, which devastated large tracts of Sumatra and Kalimantan and cast a hazardous pall across the archipelago for months. As well as his own extensive timber holdings, Projogo is in partnership with Tutut in sugar plantations and a US$1.2 billion pulp and paper plant in Sumatra. Prajogo was also involved in a controversial US$1.6 billion petrochemical plant that he was developing with Bambang Trihatmodjo. Prajogo's closeness to Suharto stemmed partly from the fact that he did Suharto favours. For instance, he financed the publication of Suharto's autobiography and in 1990 pitched in US$220 million to bail out Bank Duta, a bank controlled by Suharto through three *yayasans*, after it lost US$420 million on foreign-currency speculation. Suharto's other crony, Liem put forward another US$200 million. For his trouble, when Prajogo wanted an unsecured loan for $550 million from the state-owned Bank Bumi Daya, Suharto personally intervened twice with the bank's president, Surasa, to ensure that the loan was made (Schwartz 1994, pp. 140–1).

One (although not always the most reliable) way of assessing the wealth of individuals is through their tax contributions. Topping the list, Liem was Indonesia's biggest individual tax-payer, while one of Liem's partners, Sinar Mas group head Eka Cipta Wijaya, was second. Anthony Salim (Liem's son) was eighth, Prajogo Pengestu ninth, Bambang Trihatmodjo tenth, Tommy

Suharto thirteenth, and Sudwikatmoto fourteenth on the list. Not surprisingly, Suharto was connected to companies that occupied some of the highest places on the tax list, including Bambang's Indosat, which was the third highest tax-payer, and Liem's PT Indocement, in sixth place. The highest tax contributor, PT Freeport Indonesia, which operates the enormous Freeport gold and copper mine in Irian Jaya, was the single biggest tax-payer in 1996.

As with human rights and democratisation issues, there has been increasing pressure, especially from foreign banks (including the IMF) but also from investors, for monopolies, competition, and requirements to conform to international accounting practices. In large part, this has occurred as Indonesia has moved towards opening its economy to the outside world, and is the result of global requirements for standardised business and legal practices. After the oil-price shocks of the 1980s, the Indonesian government realised that it had little choice but to diversify its economic base, which it has done with reasonable success. In large part, this required foreign capital to establish new industries. However, foreign capital was concerned about investing in a country that did not offer investors adequate security within an open market context. Yet contrasting with this increasingly open economy are the monopolistic business interests of those close to Suharto, including his family and powerful supporters. The business practices of the president's family and friends deter foreign investment and were at the heart of the run on the rupiah in 1997–98, yet Suharto was unable or unwilling to take hard decisions in this area. The changes in this field that will come now that Suharto has left office will have implications not just for the Indonesian economy, but also for the aligning of factional differences and the potential for post-Suharto conflict.

The cases that concern local and foreign business people and Indonesians run into a long and seemingly never-ending list. Perhaps no single survey could take into account the multitude of economic and business deals that have favoured individuals at the expense of the wider economy. But any discussion of such issues inevitably identifies Suharto and his children as the most outstanding examples of nepotism and corruption. This is partly a consequence of their association with the presidency, and partly reflects the massive levels of wealth that they have accumulated almost exclusively as a result of their proximity to power. Of these cases of corruption, one stood out above the rest, especially at a time when Suharto might have been considering finally limiting such behaviour. It concerns Suharto's youngest son, Tommy Suharto, and what has been promoted as Indonesia's 'national car'.

The Kia-Timor—Indonesia's doubtful 'national' car[6]

International Grand Prix watchers have increasingly noticed the unusual name 'Timor' appearing on strategically positioned billboards behind many of the world's race tracks. If people know the name at all, they tend to associate it with lingering problems in Indonesia's most recently acquired and most troublesome province. Yet 'Timor' is also the name of Indonesia's 'national car', and the billboards are there to promote it. Why 'Timor'? A car for the American market might be given a name that suggests the frontier, such as 'Sierra'. An Australian car could conceivably be called the 'Kimberley', or a European car after one of the continent's more exotic locations. In official Indonesian thinking, Timor is also a frontier and slightly exotic. Rather than recalling images of conflict and horror, it summons up images reminiscent of the wild west. This might be a reason for this otherwise odd name.

Nevertheless, 'Timor' *is* an odd name. Most astute business people would still understand that the name 'Timor' is problematic. Only the strongest supporters of official Indonesian policy would disregard the symbolism that the name could carry. The relationship between the car's name and this most official Indonesian view of East Timor seems less surprising in light of the fact that Tommy Suharto is the major shareholder of the company that produces the Timor. Indeed, Suharto has made it extraordinarily simple for his youngest son to enter the otherwise competitive automobile business.

There is a belief among Indonesia's more nationalist technocrats that the nation needs to establish a local car-manufacturing

---

6   Much of the material in this section is taken from an article I wrote entitled 'Motor Industry in Indonesia Follows a Different Road', which appeared in *Business Motoring*, May 1997.

industry in order to honour its commitment to scrap its 65 per cent car tariffs by 2003. If it is not established by then, either Indonesia will have to change its commitment to tariffs or watch its fledgling car industry collapse and miss out on the economic development that can flow from such an industry. Car manufacturing has the potential to offer Indonesia a number of advantages. In the first instance, it could provide a significant source of employment in a value-added industry, including among component suppliers. It is also believed that a domestic car manufacturer would provide technological transfers for other areas of Indonesian manufacturing. With worrying high foreign-debt levels, a locally produced car could also help settle the balance of trade, first in the area of import substitution and later in the export field.

Finally, a number of developing countries regard having their own car manufacturer as a matter of national pride; a nation cannot be said to have achieved 'tiger economy' status until it is a large-scale heavy manufacturer (of cars, for example). Malaysia has gone down this route with the Mitsubishi-based Proton, which set up a challenge for Indonesia.

The Timor was born as 'Indonesia's national car' on 26 January 1996, when Tommy struck a deal with the South Korean Kia Motor to supply knocked-down sedans for assembly in Indonesia. The intention was that the Timor would use a proportion of locally produced parts, rising from 20 per cent to 60 per cent over three years, in order to qualify as locally manufactured. On 28 February, two days after the deal between Tommy Suharto and Kia, President Suharto announced, by presidential decree, generous new concessions for so-called 'pioneer' car manufacturers in order to ease the start-up of the new 'national car'. These included exemption from import duties or luxury taxes. Import duties on a car are worth 65 per cent of its value, while luxury taxes add a further 25–30 per cent, or a total of about 63 per cent of a car's retail price. To qualify for 'pioneer' status, the car has to have an Indonesian name, be manufactured by a company that is Indonesian-owned, and provide technological benefits for Indonesian industry. The goal that the Timor would have 20 per cent Indonesian content in its first year was later put aside.

The Timor is owned by Kia-Timor Motors, which in turn is 70 per cent owned by Tommy Suharto (through two of his companies, Timor Putra Nasional and PT Inauda) and 30 per cent owned by Kia Motor. As such, it qualifies as Indonesian-owned, although it is not wholly owned as initially required.

Tommy Suharto was given this golden opportunity to break into the car market even though his only previous experience with cars was helping his friend Setiawan Djody to purchase the prestigious Italian sports car manufacturer Lamborghini, in which Tommy was given a stake. The details of Tommy Suharto's involvement in the Lamborghini purchase are, like most such deals, scarce. But it is believed that Setiawan, through Tommy Suharto, secured loans from banks that were beholden to or under pressure from Tommy through his influence with his father. The Lamborghini deal was one minor example of how Tommy Suharto's business ventures have worked. Tommy Suharto has the highest profile of Suharto's six high-profile and enormously rich children. He has used his closeness to Suharto not only to benefit himself, but to deny his siblings in their attempts to compete with him for a slice of Indonesia's then lucrative automotive pie.

The sibling who most lost out over the Kia-Timor deal was Tommy's older brother, Bambang Trihatmodjo, who owns the Bimantara Cakra Nusa car company, which manufactures Hyundai cars in Indonesia. Angry at being cut out of the 'national car' deal, Bambang publicly noted that Tommy had no previous experience in the car business, no plant for the car's construction, and despite numerous other business interests, no core business. He also noted that, despite being extremely wealthy, Tommy had no capital with which to set up a car manufacturing plant. Instead, Bambang offered to manufacture a 'national car' himself. He said at the time that he could 'launch a car by the end of the year if we get the same facilities as Timor'. Such support, however, was not forthcoming.

Bambang's idea, at least in retrospect, was to open up the new manufacturer to Indonesian investors and component suppliers. Bimantara has produced thousands of Hyundais a year since its US$50-million production line was started up in July 1995, with target production originally expected to reach 20 000 cars a year when a new US$700-million production line opens in 1998. Bimantara had given itself until just 1999 to reach a 60 per cent local-content rate, while Hyundai boss Chung Se Jung had promised to provide for rapid technology transfers.

When he heard there was to be a 'national car', Jongkie Sugianto, the president of Bambang's company Bimantara, thought Bimantara had it in the bag. Instead, when President Suharto announced the deal would go to Tommy, Jongkie was shocked. 'We really couldn't believe it', he said. Sales of the Bimantara Hyundais immediately fell by 20 per cent ahead of the arrival of the new, cheaper Timor. The shock of the decision was felt more widely than by just the Bimantara group, too, as other car manufacturers, in particular Toyota, were sent reeling. Toyata's Indonesian company, Astra International, shed almost half of its Rp5000 share price when the Kia-Timor deal was announced, although it did recover later (but this was before the share market collapse that followed the currency collapse).

Also feeling the pinch from Tommy's privileged access to the car market was his older sister, Siti Hardiyanti Rukmana ('Tutut'), who imports Malaysia's 'national car', the Proton Saga, which is a locally produced Mitsubishi. Similarly, Suharto's step-brother, Probosutejo, was affected by Tommy's perceived advantages, having been involved in a joint venture with General Motors to produce Opel and Chevrolet cars. One of Bambang's public comments about losing the 'national car' project was that there was no guarantee that the new national car manufacturer would run well. This was a veiled criticism of Tommy's ability to run such a business. Tommy Suharto's other businesses, notably through his Humpuss group, have been run in conjunction with other business people who have had long and close business links to the president.

Tommy's earlier business experience

Tommy's one major foray into a business of his own—the clove market for Indonesia's aromatic *kretek* cigarettes—ended in failure. Tommy was granted a monopoly over the sale of cloves for the cigarettes in 1990, but by early 1992, despite being given loans for US$350 million by reluctant (though powerless) state-owned banks, Tommy admitted the business had failed. As a consequence, the farmers were obliged to submit to a scheme that dropped the price of cloves to US$2 a kilogram to help shift accumulated stock. Meanwhile Tommy's monopoly business retained its original selling price of US$6.50–$7.50, the difference, in effect paid by the farmers, being to cover Tommy's debt. This was but one venture of the many in which the commercially adventurous young Suharto has been involved.

Given the pressure that the elder Suharto could ordinarily be assumed to be under regarding issues of nepotism and corruption, many observers wondered why he gave Tommy the Timor deal. One answer is that Tommy was always Suharto's favourite child, and that of all his indulgences, the most fulsome were saved for Tommy. Tommy has also bragged about his influence with his father, and it may be this influence that gave him Indonesia's most prestigious new project in years. There is also the likely scenario that Tommy's desire to enter the car market, supported by his mother, Tien, precipitated a family feud. Tien was known to be very influential with the president, especially regarding business matters, and she undoubtedly supported the deal. At the height of the feud, Suharto came down against Tommy's older brother, Bambang, and presumably opted to give Tommy the commercial advantage. One story has it that a family argument over this issue precipitated the heart attack that killed Tien in April 1997, and that Suharto never forgave Bambang for that.[7]

Some observers also view Suharto's extraordinarily generous concessions to his youngest son as a means by which Tommy might have amassed a cash fortune quickly, which could then be easily moved off-shore. According to a source close to an anti-Suharto group within ABRI, the more hard-line of the armed forces factions had indicated that the Suharto family would not be allowed to keep their amassed fortunes after Suharto left office. After three decades in power, and having been born in 1921, his hold on the presidency was unlikely to last a lot longer. In late 1997 it was believed these officers and Suharto had reached a new agreement, which could protect Suharto family business interests, although Tommy was widely viewed as having few genuine friends either in the military or among Jakarta's business leaders. So, it could be that Indonesia's new 'national car' was intended as little more than a lucrative superannuation scheme for Tommy. Suharto did not himself need further funds. It may even be, as he

---

[7] In Jakarta such stories are significant for their symbolic value and as a reflection of public perceptions of 'palace politics'.

has said in the past, that Tommy Suharto really did believe he had the competence and experience to run a business without recourse to his father's influence. It is common wisdom, however, that one should not believe one's own propaganda.

To further guarantee the Kia-Timor project's advantages over its competitors, on 15 March 1996, just weeks after the project was announced, the government declared that the 'pioneer' concessions introduced to give the Timor its initial advantage would not be extended to any other manufacturer for a minimum of three years.

Without production facilities up and running, and under pressure to actually begin selling cars, it might have been thought that Indonesia's new 'national car' had some initial logistical difficulties. In a turn of logic that reflected a traditional Javanese disposition for projecting appearances as reality, the answer to this problem was simple: import the cars from Kia already assembled and rebadge them in Indonesia. The effect was that Tommy Suharto was able to import cars fully and sell them at about half their normal retail price. President Suharto even announced, under a new presidential decree on 4 June 1996, that the Timor would be fully imported for a year. Some 45 000 completely assembled models would be brought in to allow time for production facilities to get up and running by March 1998, but this did not eventuate. Yet months after the car went on sale, the Timor's Surabaya plant in Central Java still had no more than a small handful of workers employed to attach badges to the car. Needless to say, a bid to have the Timor assembled by one of Indonesia's two existing car plants was turned down by those manufacturers. One observer described the concept of accepting that proposal as being like 'allowing your competitor to sleep with your wife'.

The time taken to establish the factory could have reflected the difficulty Tommy had in raising the estimated US$300 million required for start-up from Indonesia's banks, which is not surprising given his previous borrowing history. Facing closer international scrutiny, the days of Indonesia's banks acting as a source of liquidity for the country's well-connected entrepreneurs has come to an end. None of this initially stopped the Timor from selling, however. At a retail price of Rp3.5 million, or a little less than US$10 000 for the 1500 cc model to around US$13 000 for the 1800 cc model at mid-1997 prices, the Timor was initially cheap enough to tempt many of what was then Indonesia's emerging middle class.

A new market for new cars

As Indonesia's per capita GDP rose, so too did its car sales. When per capita GDP was US$900 in 1992, fewer than 200 000 new cars were sold. By 1997, with per capita GDP at US$1100, new car sales were expected to top 550 000. This indicates that basic wages remained static, while small middle and higher income groups were increasingly able to afford expensive consumer items such as cars. Up until September 1995, more than 18 per cent of cars sold in Indonesia were at the prestige end of the market, reflecting the fact that Indonesia's very rich were becoming very much richer. Honda accounted for a further 14 per cent, while Mitsubishi took just under 9 per cent. Toyota, with its popular, locally produced four-wheel drive Kijang, claimed 32.5 per cent of the market, leaving the others to divide up 27 per cent between them. Priced competitively, the Timor could have expected to take a significant share of this market. But the secretary general of the Association of Indonesian Automotive Industries, F. Suseno, said that the Timor should really have sold for about Rp105 million including taxes, or about US$30 000. At this price, no one would touch it.

Once the hype of the new car had settled down, the Timor's sales slumped to about a quarter of their target of 4000 units a month. Despite going against its own Finance Department's rules, government departments and authorities were ordered to buy the car. Meanwhile, in order to cover the short-fall in returns from the low sales, three state banks and ten private banks were ordered to lend US$1.3 billion to PT Timor Putra Nasional. A dispute had arisen within government ranks over whether the government should guarantee Timor's bank loans, no doubt reflecting the tension that this blatant and potentially very costly act of nepotism had created within the government (Tuckey 1997).

International objections

While Indonesian customers initially queued up for the new, cheap cars and then changed their minds and stayed away in droves, international trade representatives were queuing up at the doors of the World Trade Organisation. When the cars were released to the Indonesian public, the USA, the European Union, and especially Japan immediately expressed their deep concern. Potentially debilitating complaints were lodged by Japan, the USA, and the European Union with the World Trade Organisation under the provisions of the Uruguay Round of the General Agreement on Tariffs and Trade. A United States trade official went so far as to describe the Kia-Timor development as being 'one of the bigger bilateral issues at this point'.

The Timor deal also did not sit well with President Suharto's vocal commitment to free and fair trade in the Bogor Declaration, which was the high point of the Asia-Pacific Economic Cooperation (APEC) summit meeting in Indonesia in 1994. It is not just the complaint itself that is at stake, but also how the international community views Indonesia's commitment to free and fair trade. It may also determine whether Indonesia's word on investment and economic issues will be trusted in future. This in turn can influence foreign capital inflows, which was the prime source of Indonesia's economic growth in the decade before the collapse. The Kia-Timor deal has scared potential investors in Indonesia, including the Toyota-backed Astra, which was to have invested US$120 million in upgrading local content. That investment, along with possible investment from a number of other manufacturers, including Ford, General Motors, and Chrysler, has since been put on hold.

To help address the long-standing concerns of investors about the propriety of aspects of doing business in Indonesia, Suharto appointed the seemingly incorruptible Satrio Budihardjo 'Billy' Joedono as trade minister. But when the Timor project came up, Joedono was unceremoniously sacked, the first such sacking to have taken place outside of a Cabinet reshuffle following a presidential election. The industry minister, Tunky Ariwibowo, took Joedono's old position as trade minister, combining the portfolios, but was replaced in 1998 by Suharto's business partner Bob Hassan. Ariwibowo is viewed as one of President Suharto's closest cronies. After assuming responsibility for the Trade portfolio, he was widely described as a travelling salesman for the Timor car, taking every chance to talk it up.

Given the difficulties that the Kia-Timor project waded into and that such difficulties were apparent from the start, not to mention Tommy Suharto's highly questionable business record, the question has to be asked: why did Kia Motor enter into the agreement in the first place? Of the three Korean car companies, Hyundai, Daewoo, and Kia, Kia is the smallest and least profitable. In a country where many in the industry believe there may only be room for two major automotive manufacturers, it is also the most vulnerable. The director of planning at Kia, Kim Woon Keun, said simply, 'To keep our company alive, we have to go abroad.'

In his bid to set up his youngest son, Suharto might have over-stepped even Indonesia's own flexible mark. He has done so once before when he used his friendship with Ibnu Sutowo, the head of the national oil company, Pertamina, in the late 1960s and early 1970s, to milk the company as a cash cow, almost bringing the economy undone. This time, though, the person at the centre of the storm was his son, and Suharto is widely thought to be blind to the sins of his children. As a single issue, the Tommy Suharto–Timor national car saga is a national scandal of huge and poten-tially crippling proportions, outraging international investors, domestic businesses, ABRI, and even members of the First Family. But more importantly, perhaps, it also shows ordinary Indonesians that the economic system that has been constructed under the New Order government is not there to meet their needs or aspirations:

'If Suharto were to step down, a lot of people would forget and forgive,' says Marzuki Darusman.[8] 'But the longer he holds out, the closer we get to a point of no return where we will have a backlash.' Unfortunately, with Suharto's family sitting on billions in dubious wealth, with rebellion on the streets and open political and moral defiance, many believe the point of no return already has passed (Butler 1996).

As a consequence of IMF pressure related to a proposed US$43 million bail-out package for the Indonesian economy, Suharto finally relented and withdrew most of Tommy's Timor car privi-leges. Tommy thereafter became a 'car importer', and in early 1998 the 'national car' project effectively died. However, the

---

8 Deputy chairperson, Indonesia's Human Rights Commission.

scandal it had caused was indicative of, and in part led to, the run on the Indonesian currency from August 1997, culminating in its effective collapse in February 1998. Similarly, more general high-level corruption and the capital flight it engendered as the rats began to desert the sinking Indonesian ship was the prime cause of downward pressure on the value of the rupiah. That Suharto seemed so incapable or unwilling to rein in such corruption only worsened Indonesia's international economic standing. It was this issue, then, that precipitated a significant political change in Indonesia.

12

COMPETING INFLUENCES

This chapter brings together the competing influences in Indonesia's political composition and discusses how they arranged themselves ahead of Suharto's inevitable retirement. Suharto won the presidency again in 1998, but his advanced age (seventy-six years in 1998) and economic problems did not allow him to complete this term. The primary factions competing for the longer-term succession are divided between Suharto's immediate family and a small coterie of political and business supporters on one hand and, on the other, the 'red and white' faction of the armed forces. Although, after the events of 1996, the PDI did gain some popular support, it no longer appeared capable (or desirous) of launching a concerted effort to challenge Suharto for the presidency. Megawati was keeping her options open, but she was unlikely to be allowed to participate in the formal political process.

Factional manoeuvring

By around the middle of 1997, after considerable manœuvring, it appeared that the 'red and white' faction of ABRI had established a framework for determining who would be the next president (van Klinken 1997b). With that person almost certainly one of its own group, ABRI intended that the next strongly established president of Indonesia would again be a general and that ABRI would continue its dominant role in Indonesian politics. Within this, there was some belief that faction leaders had made a deal with Suharto to secure his family's business interests in exchange for one of their own eventually succeeding him as president. The succession would thereby be given Suharto's stamp of approval and, therefore, some legitimacy, and would retain and reinforce the political integrity of the office of the president. In effect, this was a replay of a deal Murdani offered to Suharto in 1989 (according to a confidant of Murdani), which was not taken up at that time.

However, while such a deal might have been reached, it has not been made public as this is being written, nor is it guaranteed to come to pass, even if it has been made. There are certainly individuals and groups beyond Suharto himself and the 'red and white' faction who would not welcome such an agreement and who could be expected to attempt to unsettle it. The appointment of Habibie as vice-president and eventually as president, and son-in-law Prabowo's rise through ABRI ranks certainly complicate this scenario. But the 'red and white' faction, and in particular Murdani, who has close links with a number of faction leaders, had plans in place for the succession for some four years previously, so they are not likely to be easily deterred.

In 1993 Murdani reached an agreement with Try Sutrisno to support Try for the presidential succession in opposition to Habibie's candidature and then engineered support for Try's election among the various factions of the MPR, including Golkar. Try had the singular political advantage of having been commander-in-chief of ABRI, a position held by Murdani from 1983 to 1988, and received the official endorsement of ABRI before ABRI informed Suharto, which was previously unheard of. Though formerly close to Suharto, as his adjutant, Try was later seen to be aligned with Murdani. In terms of his public profile, Try had the advantage of having been very close to both Suharto and Murdani, which enhanced his appearance of legitimacy. As long ago as 1986, and despite his lack of outstanding talent or intellect—Try has listed his favourite pastimes as practising martial arts, gymnastics, and weight-lifting—Try was recognised as having the potential to take Indonesia's top job (Byrnes 1986c; Crouch 1988b). However, having been dropped as vice-president in 1998, his chances of succeeding Suharto in the longer term have diminished very significantly, even though he would still be a suitable 'red and white'-sponsored candidate.

Some contenders

In the early 1990s, Suharto had appeared to prefer his family rela-tive, Major General Wismoyo Arismunandar,[1] as his successor, and by 1993, when he was promoted to army chief of staff, many observers considered him the front-runner for the succession. But by 1995 Wismoyo had been dumped from presidential favour and from his position as army commander. The falling-out between Suharto and Wismoyo came to a head over Wismoyo's moves to distance ABRI from the president and, in particular, from Suharto's loyal ministers, including Habibie, Harmoko, and the newly appointed head of ABRI, Raden Hartono (Grant 1996, p. 108). Having risen rapidly through the ranks at least partly because of his family association with Suharto, Wismoyo appeared to regard Suharto as having been too long in power. As a result, he destroyed a strong chance of attaining ABRI command, the vice-presidency, or even the presidency itself. Wismoyo was well aware that his effective opposition to Suharto would jeopardise his political standing, yet chose to align himself with the ABRI group associated with Murdani. Perhaps Wismoyo was counting on a quick transition of presidential power, through which he would personally benefit. But, if so, he gravely miscalculated, quickly joining the ranks of former generals who have crossed Suharto and have lost out as a consequence.

Suharto's son-in-law Prabowo looked like being the next most favoured candidate and, moving to head the army's strategic reserve unit (Kostrad) in 1998, was well placed to support his claim (or to back another claim) to the presidency. Prabowo had only just won the confidence of sections of the 'red and white' faction of ABRI (having earlier been regarded as suspect because of his family-assisted rise through the ranks) when, in early 1998, he verbally attacked Murdani, indicating strongly that any rap-prochement between Prabowo and the 'red and white' faction was finished. Most importantly for Suharto, for a while at least, Wismoyo and Prabowo looked likely to best secure the great for-tunes amassed by the Suharto family.

---

1   Wismoyo was often referred to as Suharto's brother-in-law, but is only a brother-in-law by marriage, being married to a sister of Suharto's late wife, Tien.

As Try is widely perceived to have been forced on Suharto as vice-president by ABRI (Schwartz 1994, p. 286), Suharto's failure to stymie the appointment was widely interpreted as his first major political failure and heralded a string of disasters for the ageing leader in 1993. The rift between Suharto and ABRI was pushed out into the open in late October 1993, when Major General Sembiring Meliala, a member of the MPR and a serving member of the armed forces, bluntly said that the military would be the arbiter of presidential succession. This did not accord at all well with ABRI's at least nominal deference to the president. There were also initial indications that ABRI could, for shorter term tactical purposes, switch allegiance to a minor party, such as the small Indonesian Democratic Party (PDI), rather than support Golkar. Golkar was increasingly seen as having become a presidential vehicle rather than an organisation that represented ABRI and other 'functional groups' (Schwartz 1994, p. 285). This move followed the success of Suharto's protégés in being appointed to senior positions within the government organisation Golkar, and within ABRI.

ABRI got its own back, delivering a major personal blow to Suharto while he was out of the country by banning the state lottery, ostensibly to assuage student protests. The head of Indonesia's Legal Aid Foundation, Adnan Buyung Nasution, said of the lottery banning: 'The army didn't take action against the students. Suharto understood that very well, that the demonstrations, the demands of the students were only possible because of the support, indirectly, of the army' (1993b). Nasution claimed that the Suharto family directly received between seven and ten million US dollars a week from the lottery.

Along with the demise of Suharto's previously unchallenged leadership was the effective end of the government's 'openness' and 'democratisation' programs, such as they were. These were seemingly designed to give vent to growing middle-class frustrations, as well as to put a better post-cold war face on the often repressive government. But such 'openness' or 'democratisation' suited neither a president under pressure nor a military intent on getting its way. Manifestations of this 'openness' included greater freedom for dissent and a relative freeing of the previously tightly controlled media. But on 14 December 1993, twenty-one students were arrested at the DPR for 'defaming the president'.

The students had called on Suharto to account for a range of problems that beset Indonesia. Although the demonstration was neither large nor threatening, the students were later gaoled. Following widespread reporting of these arrests and of other political issues, the heads of the Indonesian media were called into the Ministry of Information a week later to be reminded of their 'responsibilities to *Pancasila* journalism'. The next day, the Department of Education called in senior academics from Indonesia's universities for a similar 'briefing' concerning protests on campus by restive students.

Two days after the media's briefing on responsibility, Indonesia's Director General of Press and Graphics in the Department of Information, Subrata, said: 'I think everybody must know that it is very hard now to make more openness'. Subrata outlined the constraints applying to both local and international media, reasserting the requirement to promote the 'national interest'. The protest by the twenty-one students and the subsequent reporting of it were publicly portrayed as the democratisation process getting out of hand. But a number of senior Indonesian journalists regarded these events as a ploy by Murdani to embarrass Suharto. They described the arrest of the students as a small tactical sacrifice by Murdani in a larger strategic game.

A leading Jakarta academic and political analyst said that Murdani has widespread support within the armed forces among high ranking officers, despite being retired. The officers were said to resent the declining political power and prestige of the military, reduced opportunities for advancement, and the excessive corruption of Suharto's family, particularly of his children, who are now officially listed among Indonesia's richest people (see also Schwartz 1994, pp. 297–305). Nine of the thirteen wealthiest individuals in a 1993 *Info Bisnis* list, based on tax information, were either close relatives, including his children, or family associates. Yet Suharto, at least on the surface, remained confident.

In response to growing pressure at home, on returning from a conference in India on 17 December 1993, Suharto lashed out at 'demands for more freedom', likening such demands to the tactics employed by the PKI. The blood-letting of 1965–66 still horrifies those old enough to remember, and Suharto's 'PKI' comments raised the stakes in his confrontation with the pro-Murdani ABRI faction by recalling the memory of the blood-letting. Yet even these comments could not turn the tide of events. Less than a week later, Sukarno's daughter, Megawati Sukarnoputri, was elected as head of the PDI. The PDI was electorally insignificant and effectively controlled by factions within the government. But Suharto strongly opposed the election of Megawati, and her victory was seen as a major symbolic defeat for the president. Megawati was popularly seen to represent Sukarno's relative economic egalitarianism, as opposed to the opulence surrounding Suharto's family and friends. The pro-Murdani faction in ABRI was also seen to be behind Megawati's victory. Three days after her election, Megawati was photographed with Jakarta's military chief, Major General A. M. Hendropriyono, at the forty-fourth anniversary of the City Military Command. In a country where symbolism is important, their posing together for the photograph was seen as a clear sign of the military's support (see also Schwartz 1994, p. 285). Hendropriyono was appointed as transmigration minister in March 1988, reflecting a chess-game style of manœuvring rather than Suharto's genuine acceptance of this general.

In 1993 Siti Hardiyanti Rukmana ('Tutut') was 'elected' as one of Golkar's vice-chairpersons, while Bambang Trihatmodjo was elected as Golkar treasurer. Management of Golkar's board of management was entrusted to B. J. Habibie, while Harmoko was 'elected' as party chairperson, the first civilian to take Golkar's top job. There were some objections within Golkar, but the purpose of this structure was to ensure that Suharto was re-elected in 1998. Through careful manœuvring and judicious appointments, Golkar's forty-five-member executive board was filled with Suharto loyalists. As the party of government, Golkar remained crucial to post-Suharto succession, though its influence was limited by a split between its civilian and military wings. As a creation of ABRI, there was some question about Golkar's viability without either Suharto or ABRI to support it.

Of all the various clusters that make up ABRI, and of the streams of political patronage that comprise the other main political groupings, there were seven main groupings around which the political process was coalescing. The first of these groups coalesced around former ABRI commander-in-chief General Feisal Tanjung. Feisal was very much a straight Suharto appointee, did not reflect ABRI's own desires, and is not well liked within ABRI (nor, if it came to a crunch, could he count on being able to muster a majority of the armed forces in opposition to competing generals). As a Suharto man, Feisal was close to Habibie and received support from ICMI. He was very much what has been referred to as a 'green', or Islamic, general. Feisal retired as commander of ABRI in 1998, thus opening the way for a less pro-Suharto general, Wiranto, to take that position.

The next major figure was former army commander General Hartono, who was allied with Suharto's daughter Tutut. Hartono was also very much a Suharto appointee, although he is reported to have had a difficult relationship with Feisal. Hartono's role was to control what Suharto perceived to be unreliable elements within ABRI. His link with Tutut could be seen in this light, although her endorsement of Hartono as a possible future vice-president was unsubtle. While Hartono remained as army commander, Tutut's future in a post-Suharto environment looked relatively secure. However, Hartono lost whatever clout he might have had within ABRI when he was appointed information minister in June 1997. The position of information minister has been a powerful one, as the influence of its former incumbent Harmoko attests. But Harmoko's influence rested very much on Suharto's patronage, and Hartono's position in a post-Suharto environment looks weakened, having been moved to the Ministry of the Interior in 1988. Hartono is identified as being within the camp that supported the status quo, which for the short term included support for Suharto. Hartono's position in a post-Suharto environment is less predictable, although he is likely to pursue a 'steady as she goes' course, with minimal disruptions to the economy and hence to those business interests that have benefited from Suharto's patronage. Harmoko himself was named as Minister of State for Special Affairs in the reshuffle of June 1997, giving this Suharto loyalist greater freedom to pursue the maintenance of the Suharto family's interests ahead of the post-Suharto period. By 1998, however, Harmoko had outlived his usefulness to Suharto and was quietly dropped from the Cabinet.

Hartono's initial replacement as army commander was the commander of Kostrad and former Suharto adjutant (1989–93), Lt General Wiranto. One of the rising younger generation, Wiranto leap-frogged to the position of commander of ABRI upon Feisal's retirement and in 1998 also assumed the position of defence minister, giving him an unusual amount of political power. Wiranto is also touted as a possible presidential candidate in the post-Suharto period.

Perhaps the next main grouping surrounding an ABRI figure is around Major-General Susilo Bambang Yudhoyono, who was regional commander of South Sumatra before being moved to the position of Assistant and then Director of ABRI Social and Political Affairs. The role of ABRI's Social and Political Affairs office is to advise on policy and to manage the secondment of ABRI staff to government positions. This places Yudhoyono in a central position from which to influence ABRI policy on its role in government. But, more importantly, Yudhoyono is seen as being closely linked to, and influential with, a rising group of younger senior officers, even being regarded as their intellectual leader. Yudhoyono is touted as a future vice-presidential candidate, especially if Wiranto succeeds Suharto, but in any case is expected to wield considerable political clout in the post-Suharto environment.

Beyond Yudhoyono is Suharto's son-in-law, General Prabowo Subianto. Prabowo's main advantage is that, as Suharto's son-in-law, he has had a spectacular rise through the ranks, and has overseen a number of significant military operations, including in East Timor and in Irian Jaya. Prabowo was appointed as commander of the influential Strategic Reserve (Kostrad), which was Suharto's military base when he took power in 1965–66. In a country that counts lineage as important, Prabowo is the son of Sumitro Djojo-hadikusomo, the founder of the Indonesian Socialist Party and an able finance minister during the 1950s. In this sense, Prabowo provides a link to an effectively disenfranchised part of the electorate. Prabowo's brother Hashim is the controller of one of Indonesia's larger conglomerates and has extensive interests in coal mining, banking, cement, financial services, and power generation, which places Prabowo in a position to be involved in the 'power financing' of the political process. Hashim is also beginning to figure in a possible post-Suharto environment. Prabowo is understood to have a number of links to businesses in the USA and Japan.

Although Prabowo is very well placed to take advantage of the post-Suharto period, there are some factors that count against him. The first is that he is widely perceived to be a Suharto loyalist, having married into the family and having had a spectacular rise through the ranks to become Indonesia's youngest general, which is largely attributed to his closeness to Suharto. Any future government that is not dominated by Suharto loyalists, as it seems will be the case, would be at pains to distance itself from the Suharto period of government and would probably move to delegitimise aspects of the Suharto period of rule. Prabowo could suffer as a result of this. Indeed, Prabowo could be at the forefront of any pro- and anti–Suharto conflict.

While Prabowo's rise through the ranks has been spectacular, some observers have questioned whether it was based on his actual military performance. In particular, in mid-1996 Prabowo led ABRI's elite Kopassus 'Red Beret' troops into the jungle of Irian Jaya to free hostages seized by OPM guerillas, which had been causing the Indonesian government much international embarrassment. Four English, two Dutch, and three Indonesian members of the scientific team that had been captured by the OPM guerillas were freed unharmed, but two other Indonesian prisoners were hacked to death by the OPM guerillas. And it was revealed, after the hostages were freed, that although they had been moved to eighteen or more campsites during their ordeal, they were never more than a few kilometres from the point of their abduction. Prabowo was popularly regarded as having succeeded in freeing the hostages, but as a campaign it was not regarded as a great military achievement. Similarly, his performance during postings to Aceh and East Timor was not regarded within ABRI as a great military achievement, although the media lionised his involvement in the Irian Jaya hostage release. Prabowo was the officer in charge during other doubtful events, including a helicopter crash in Irian Jaya that killed five soldiers preparing for the hostage release, and a massacre of fifteen Irian Jayans by a crazed junior officer. Prabowo's promotion in early 1998 was a clear sign that he was very much in favour with Suharto and was, while Suharto remained in power, earmarked for greater things. Prabowo, it seems, is Suharto's primary investment in using the military to secure his longer term goals.

Beyond ABRI

Outside ABRI, the main political groupings that are manœuvring to have a stake in Indonesia's political future revolve around Habibie and the economy and finance minister, Ginanjar Kartasasmita. Habibie, as already mentioned, was out of favour with many ministers and with sections of ABRI, and was finding it difficult to attract high-level government officials to his speeches and other programs. Indeed, a number of the political elite actively avoided Habibie, as he was perceived to have the stench of political death about him, despite his elevation to the position of an activist vice-president and then to president.

Habibie's problems stem from a number of sources, perhaps the most important being that, without the support of Suharto, Habibie has no genuine power base. Habibie is also widely held responsible for the purchase in 1993 of a group of East German warships at a cost of US$12.7 million, but which required a fit-out estimated by Habibie to cost US$1.1 billion. The purchase was not discussed with the armed forces. Although Suharto backed Habibie, he was embarrassed by the response, particularly the airing of disagreement over the purchase between ABRI and Habibie and Suharto in the media. In a rare display of anger, Suharto lost his temper with the media and promptly closed three major publications, causing a storm of protest both in Indonesia and abroad. More recently, in 1997 Habibie finally backed down on a proposal to build a nuclear reactor in Java. This long-standing proposal had generated significant local protest and, given the geologically unstable nature of the region, had perturbed Indonesia's neighbours, who could be affected by fall-out from an earthquake-damaged nuclear plant. The idea had not been perceived as a good one to start with, and Habibie's admission of defeat helped neither his standing nor that of the government.

Beyond these two high-profile cases, Habibie has also been keen to push Indonesia as a high-technology base and has attempted to launch a number of experimental or difficult industries, such as an aerospace industry. None of Habibie's high-technology projects have been a financial success, and all have cost the government dearly, both in terms of financial support and in terms of standing (see Robison 1997, p. 52). When one also considers his idiosyncratic flamboyancy and his ability to make enemies within ABRI, Habibie's political future looks positively black, despite his elevation to the vice-presidency. One assessment of Habibie's vice-presidency was that, upon succeeding Suharto as president, he would be among the easiest targets for factions in ABRI to unseat. Such a move to depose him would attract a lot of domestic and international support, the latter coming mostly through diplomatic and financial means.

Harmoko was another of Suharto's favourites yet not having the breadth and depth of enemies that Habibie has encountered. A good Muslim and a competent, if slightly repressive minister, Harmoko was the type of civilian Suharto would have liked to have seen retain office. However, Harmoko was also without a genuine power base apart from Suharto's support and is therefore not well equipped to enter the post-Suharto era, a fact seemingly recognised by his dumping. He later turned on Suharto, demanding that he resign.

Ginanjar Kartasasmita is regarded as very loyal to Suharto and he is unpopular with ABRI. Perhaps Kartasasmita's biggest crime in the eyes of ABRI is that he is seen as the protégé of Sudharmono, whom ABRI openly opposed as vice-president. He was also vice-chairperson of Sudharmono's Team 10, which through its allocation of government purchases to favoured, usually *pribumi*, clients was later identified with Suharto's shift in patronage away from ABRI. Ginanjar was educated in Japan and trained as an engineer, but is regarded by both Indonesia's technocrats and ABRI as belonging to the group that favours *pribumi* business people. Ginanjar is also linked to Habibie, through one of his former assistants being appointed as Ginanjar's senior deputy of planning.

As the coordinating minister for economy and finance, Ginanjar was responsible for approving many of Indonesia's major business deals, and was implicated in at least some of the less savoury activities of Suharto's family and cronies. Having said that, Ginanjar is said to have been slow to act on implementing some of the more obviously shady arrangements which favoured Suharto's ethnic Chinese partners, Liem and Pengestu, over *pribumi* interests, finally being forced to do so by Suharto. Ginanjar looks set to continue to receive support from and indeed represent *pribumi* business interests, strategically locating him close to a major economic group yet opposed to the politically unpopular Chinese business people.

The *Pendawa Lima*

While these political players featured significantly on the political landscape towards the end of Suharto's rein, another group of younger army officers, including Yudhoyono, is emerging as the real force in a post-Suharto Indonesia. This group is known by Golkar insiders as 'the *Pendawa Lima*', or the five Pendawas, after the victorious Pendawa clan of the Mahabarata epic. The *Pendawa Lima* has established links with most, if not all, of the major players in Indonesia, is powerful within ABRI, and is young enough to carry its own vision into the twenty-first century.

Yudhoyono is one of the most interesting of the rising group of players on Indonesia's political field, at first appearing to exercise more influence than his slightly obscure military position would indicate but being more centrally positioned by mid-1997. Yudhoyono's greatest strength is his intellect and his ability to bring others along with him, both of which contribute to a very well-developed leadership style. Among his peers, in particular the Magelang Military Academy's Class of 1973, Yudhoyono is the brightest star and, short of a political mishap, appears destined for great things. In terms of political alliances, Yudhoyono is regarded as the protégé of ABRI commander-in-chief and defence minister Lt General Wiranto and is linked to the former defence minister, Edi Sudrajat, who in turn is linked to Benny Murdani. While Edi's days as an active political player are over, Yudhoyono's are just beginning to reach their full flower.

The next *Pendawa* is former Jakarta military commander Major General Hendropriyono, who is seen as being linked to the former vice-president, Try Sutrisno, and to Suharto's son Bambang Trihatmojo. Through his link with Hendropriyono and his associates, Bambang is helping to ensure that his own personal fortune is not jeopardised in the post-Suharto shake-up. Hendropriyono was also influential in having Megawati Sukarnoputri elected as chairperson of the PDI in 1993, explicitly against Suharto's wishes. This damaged Hendropriyono's position in relation to Suharto, having him thrown out of the Jakarta command in 1994. But, strategically, it put him in good standing with many of his army colleagues and ensured that he would play an influential role in any post-Suharto political process. His elevation to the ministry in 1998 was widely regarded as a concession to ABRI's 'red and white' faction. Another Megawati supporter is

Yudhoyono's former commander and, briefly, chief of ABRI's Social and Political Staff, Major General Yunus Yosfiah. Yunus invited Megawati to speak at the ABRI staff college when he was the commander there between 1995 and 1997.

Lt General Wiranto is an especially well-placed member of this group, having become head of ABRI. Wiranto, a Suharto adjutant from 1989 until 1993, continued to be trusted by Suharto, even though he has links with 'red and white' officers who are not so favourably disposed towards Suharto. In this sense, Wiranto had he potential to act as a bridge between disaffected senior ABRI officers and Suharto loyalists. If nothing else, Wiranto can probably be relied upon to ensure that in the period of the transition to a post-Suharto government, ABRI does not get drawn into the political bickering by either participating as it did in 1965–66 or, worse, splitting and fighting within itself. Some observers in Jakarta suggested that Wiranto might eventually be a suitable replacement for Suharto as president, given his high standing within ABRI. Wiranto is also originally from Yogyakarta, close to where Suharto grew up, and shares a similar sense of decorum with Suharto, or at least an awareness of the type of propriety favoured by Suharto. Such a move would be popular within ABRI and would reflect Wiranto's strong position. In Indonesian politics, nothing is ever certain, but Wiranto is among the better placed officers to influence Indonesia's post-Suharto future. His main competitor within ABRI to influence the post-Suharto environment is Prabowo, and the two are seen as becoming increasingly antagonistic.

The head of the military district of South Sulawesi, General Agum Gumelar, is number four of the five officers referred to as 'the *Pendawa Lima*'. Agum brought to this group both the loyalty and control of Sulawesi, which has significant strategic implications for the maintenance of the state, and he is a trusted colleague of the other four. Agum was closely associated with Hendropriyono in having Megawati elected to the chair of the PDI and, for his trouble, was shifted out as commander of Kopassus. His elevation to Sulawesi regional commander in 1996 confirmed, however, that his career was not in permanent decline.

The fifth colleague in this group is Farid Zainuddin, who briefly took over as head of army intelligence, the BIA (Badan Intelijen ABRI), from Major General Syamsir Siregar in early

1997. Since Murdani's period as commander-in-chief of ABRI, military intelligence has assumed a significantly more important role in political affairs, even though Suharto and Feisal had moved to downgrade it in the wake of Murdani's dismissal first from the army and then from Cabinet. As head of BIA, Zainuddin was in charge of the organisation responsible for strategic and internal security intelligence collection and analysis, counterintelligence and security, special operations, and the security aspects of international relations. It was a most powerful position within ABRI. But perhaps for this reason, Zainuddin was quickly deposed from this position and replaced by Major General Zacky Anwar Makarim, who, however, is also regarded as being very close to this group. Farid was also associated with Hendropriyono and Agum in their support of Megawati for the PDI chair. Interestingly, Wiranto was a key figure in organising the physical ousting of the pro-Megawati group from the PDI headquarters in 1996, which perhaps indicates just how much senior ABRI officers viewed Megawati's political rise and fall as merely tactical considerations within a larger strategy.

Each of the *Pendawa Lima* is associated with the five individual Pendawa from whom the group derives its collective name. Yudhoyono is identified with the most famous Pendawa, Arjuna, who is both delicate but an unsurpassed warrior, capable of great self-discipline and iron willed, yet tender and loyal. Wiranto is identified with Kresna, first cousin to the Pendawa and part-god, intellectually brilliant, and a great politician, diplomat, and military strategist. Kresna is unscrupulous if the outcome is victory, and it is he who makes final victory for the Pendawas possible. Hendropriyono is associated with Gatotkaca, the son of (and a smaller and more attractive version of) Wrekudara, the most merciless and feared of warriors, who bows to no one, but who is unswervingly honest and loyal. Interestingly, Sukarno identified Gatotkaca as the model for the new Indonesian man. Agum is seen as Prabu Judistira, who being the eldest Pendawa is their king. He is the most pure of the Pendawa, spending his time in meditation and the accumulation of wisdom, ruling with perfect justice and aloof benevolence. Farid was portrayed as Abimanju, nephew of Judistira and son of Arjuna. Abimanju is traditionally regarded as having his hard *satria* ethics compromised by tenderness, but has more recently been viewed with popular sympathy (see Anderson 1965).

The *Pendawa Lima* is closely identified with former defence minister Edi and, through him, with Murdani. Through Edi they are also associated with, or seen as allied to, Suharto's son Bambang Trihatmojo. Edi himself has interesting links, particularly to politicians in the USA, which could be very useful in gaining endorsement for a change of leadership in Indonesia. Edi could offer future strategic and economic stability to his United States political contacts. Edi also has contacts in Japan, whom he could use to ensure future investment, in return for Indonesia's support for Japanese trade and investment policies. Beyond that, the group also has significant links to a number of major Indonesian investors, ensuring a ready supply of funds, should it be needed, as well as securing their own economic future.

To further cement this group's links, Murdani, a Catholic, also promises to accommodate Indonesia's Islamic community. In particular, the NU's Abdurrahman Wahid is understood to be very close to this group, and until his stroke in 1998, this association ensured a significant bloc of Islamic support for the group and also reinforced the NU's future political influence.

Strategic alliances

One of the major factors in the alliances that could be formed in the post-Suharto period is the relationship between the Suharto siblings. In simple terms, if Bambang Trihatmojo and Tutut could become close or even cordial, there is likely to be sufficient cohesion between their respective alliances to steer a stable political course. However, since the death of their mother, Tien, in 1996, they have not been close, and the associations that were being made before Suharto's departure are, to a significant degree, aimed at constructing some sort of workable relationship between the factions.

In this shifting of allegiances and balancing of alliances, Abdurrahman Wahid (Gus Dur) was perhaps the most influential player. Suharto is understood to have told Tutut that he does not trust Gus Dur and that the NU is not a reliable political ally. However, in the shorter term, Suharto was prepared to take on Gus Dur as a temporary ally and to have him publicly support Tutut in her own political and financial career. For his part, Gus Dur said he would support Suharto in his 1998 election campaign, although this is fairly clearly understood to have been a move towards offering Suharto an opportunity to step down soon after. With Gus Dur's health now so poor, his future in politics is doubtful.

Behind the *Pendawa Lima* and their associates is the shadowy hand of a *dalang*, who in this case is former ABRI commander-in-chief and former defence minister Benny Murdani. Should the *Pendawa Lima* be successful, Murdani could hope to come back to government as a senior adviser or special minister, largely to acknowledge his role in coordinating this group. However, he might choose to stay outside, preferring not to sully his standing with the practicalities of day-to-day politics. Murdani may well be, for want of a better term, the 'godfather' of the post-Suharto period.

In part, the issue of the presidential succession rested on who was to become vice-president. The vice-president would appear to be Suharto's obvious successor, but if that person is not favoured by the prevailing military group (presumably the *Pendawa Lima* or some similar alliance), then that group would simply request that the MPR reconvene and either confirm or deny the legitimacy of the succession. As there has been no precedent for the process of succession—Sukarno's ousting hardly represents a desirable model for any of the players—it is quite possible that the vice-president will simply be a seat-warmer until a person more acceptable to ABRI is appointed.

To this end, Habibie became vice-president, allegedly at the suggestion of Murdani. The idea is that Habibie would be so unpopular that those who actually decide the succession (this does not mean the DPR or any other elected body) would panic and opt for the main alternative, who would, of course, be a Murdani person. This analysis seems to give Murdani more power than many observers credit him with, and taking this view, it would be easy to overstate his importance. He will not be Indonesia's modern Gajah Mada, the prime minister who welded together the old empire of Majapahit. For one thing, Murdani is now too old. But he may be in a position to play the last piece on the chess board of succession, and that will be his achievement. If Suharto is still alive when this happens, Murdani's satisfaction will no doubt be the greater.

Problems with dismantling corrupt businesses

One of the more interesting aspects of the post-succession period will be what happens to Suharto's children and associates, as well as the financial empires they have built. Given the immense wealth of Suharto's family and business cronies, dismantling the fortunes of the family and the close associates would pose serious implications for the structure of Indonesia's already damaged economy. In simple terms, the combined wealth of this group is equal to a very significant proportion of Indonesia's total national wealth. Their respective incomes are a major part of Indonesia's total national income, and in many cases, they have established substantial foreign links. To pull the rug from under the first family and the close cronies would be to pull the rug completely from under the Indonesian economy.

In a society and economy in which corruption is so fundamentally ingrained, there is also the further question of the point at which an anti-corruption crusade stops. If such a crusade was thorough (and feasible, which it probably is not), it would have to spread throughout much of the senior echelons of the armed forces, throughout most of the upper levels of the ethnic Chinese business community, and to a large extent through the *pribumi* business community. The effect on the ethnic Chinese could be devastating, given the hostility that is already felt towards them throughout the country. An anti-corruption campaign could, and probably would, turn rapidly into an anti-Chinese campaign, with considerable destruction of property and loss of life. Ethnic Chinese businesses have been consistently attacked on the slimmest of pretexts, and there is no reason to believe that this would not be accelerated by an anti-corruption push.

Further, Indonesia's economy is fragile, as events from August 1997 and into 1998 showed, and growth is largely predicated on foreign investment and aid inflows. Political and more particularly economic instability has already deterred that investment. In early 1997, one seasoned observer believed that a foreign investment strike was inevitable, that the Indonesian economy would collapse, and that this would bring tensions to the surface that were only shallowly buried, particularly in relation to more fundamentalist Muslims and perhaps the urban poor. The collapse of the rupiah seems to have validated his concerns and has seriously complicated an already highly complex political problem.

However, there will probably only be a token gesture made towards the redistribution of Suharto's family's wealth, perhaps with the public floating of a proportion of the more obvious companies, such as Tutut's toll roads. Such a float would place shares in the hands of other members of the elite, including family members and friends, and would not effectively diminish either their wealth or their influence over the economy, but this objection could be easily swept aside in the interests of preserving economic stability. If a token Suharto family member must be humiliated in public and/or stripped of assets, Tommy Suharto is the most likely candidate, having few friends or allies and most obviously flaunting the value of his position as Suharto's son.

The pro-democracy movement

Indonesia's pro-democracy movement received extensive international coverage in the period between the election of Megawati Sukarnoputri as chairperson of the PDI in late 1993 and her forcible removal from office in mid-1996. It was partly just the name of the PDI that gave it its democratic credentials, and it was partly that Megawati was increasingly perceived to provide a genuine political alternative to Suharto. Megawati's pedigree as the daughter of Indonesia's first president, Sukarno, gives her some legitimacy, while as a woman, she has been associated with the likes of the Philippines' Corazon Aquino, Pakistan's Benazir Bhutto, Burma's Aung San Suu Kyi, Bangladesh's Sheik Hasina Wajed, and even India's Indira Gandhi. Yet the pro-democratic enthusiasm that has greeted Megawati's leadership of the PDI has always been, to a very large degree, misplaced.

Angus McIntyre has noted that Megawati's primary credibility derives from her role as a symbol of her father, who apart from his disastrous economic policies and questionable political ideals, retained, in rhetoric at least, a fond regard for Indonesia's 'little people' (*wong cilik*) (McIntyre 1996, pp. 1–3). Sukarno, nominally at least, was a socialist and is perceived to have sought a redistribution of income and the well-being of ordinary Indonesians. Contrasted with what is widely perceived to be Suharto's excessive corruption, and with the vast wealth of his family and cronies compared with the still very low incomes of most Indonesians, Sukarno represented a more equitable age, and Megawati has inherited that reputation.

In some senses, Megawati's political rise was a product of good luck. Not only is she a daughter of Sukarno, but her siblings also left the political door open for her. The other Sukarno children declined an invitation by the then chairperson of the PDI, Suryadi, to become involved in the party on the basis of its inclusion of the old PNI, which provided a link to Sukarno. One of Megawati's brothers, Guruh, did become involved in politics in a limited fashion, through his musical group Swara Mahardhika (Voice of Freedom), which supported a PDI campaign, but her sister Rachmawati said that Sukarno's children should, like Sukarno himself (allegedly), remain above politics and perpetuate Sukarno's teachings. The oldest brother, Guntur, who is most physically like Sukarno and who inherited a groundswell of support, opted to stay out of politics altogether, tending to his construction business (McIntyre 1996, pp. 12–14).

On 17 April 1987, more than five years before Megawati was to rise to the chair of the PDI, as many as a million PDI supporters gathered in Jakarta's main roads wearing red PDI T-shirts and giving the party's three finger sign. Many of those PDI supporters wore T-shirts bearing Sukarno's image, with one slogan reading, '*Oh Bung Karno . . . kamilah penerusmu* (We are your followers)'. Megawati yelled to the enthusiastic crowd, '*Hidup Sukarno* (Long live Sukarno)' (McIntyre 1996, pp. 14–15). Yet when Megawati finally achieved the position of PDI chairperson, positioning herself as a possible opponent to Suharto, she primarily had to thank a core group of senior ABRI officers. These men not only decided to back her in her bid, but also, in effect, placed her in the position of power she assumed. Sukarno was not a democrat, and nor were appeals to his memory predicated on democratic aspirations. In the last instance, Megawati came to power with the help of generals, not ordinary people.

Megawati's role in Indonesia's political future, if she is to have one, will continue to be based on her relationship to her father and her role as a channel for siphoning off the democratic aspirations of a significant proportion of ordinary Indonesians. It is possible that in a future government Megawati could be included in some largely nominal or ceremonial capacity, as this would give a nod to her backers in ABRI as well as acting as a pressure valve for democratic aspirations. But Megawati has not at any stage represented genuine democratic aspirations, any more than Cory

Aquino did in the Philippines (and it should be remembered that Aquino came to power only with the support of the army and achieved very little in office). In this sense, Megawati is very much a member of Indonesia's elite. Ultimately, any interests that she is finally allowed to genuinely represent will effectively be elite interests.

With the demise of Megawati, in the middle term at least, as an influential political player in Indonesia, much of the frustration felt towards Suharto's government was channelled into the PPP. Megawati's PDI supporters were given permission to vote for the PPP in the 1997 DPR elections, in effect to lodge a protest against the lop-sided election process. The PPP had already benefited greatly from Suharto's loosening of restrictions on public Islamic behaviour, such as the wearing of the *jelbab* (Islamic veil or head dress for women). It had also benefited from his broader support for Islam through organisations such as ICMI and through helping build mosques, making the hajj, and so on. Also contributing to the PPP's resurgence was the international rise of more fundamentalist aspects of Islam, particularly as a counter to what many non-Westerners perceived as the West's cultural and economic imperialism.

The PPP's strongholds were in Central and Western Java, Northern Sumatra, and Aceh. Travelling through Central Java in the politically volatile period of 1997, most of the kampungs one saw in the paddy fields flew flags of the black star on a green field on bamboo poles high above the houses. The image of the green and black flags flying defiantly from above the kampungs carried associations of rebellion, or the staking of territory, not just for a political party but for a political movement. But while there was extensive rioting throughout Java at this time, the flags were a statement of political affiliation rather than military banners. In simple terms, even the 'green' (pro-Islamic) generals of ABRI would have quickly and thoroughly quashed a rebellion had one appeared imminent. Still, it did indicate a growing strength of Islamic feeling, which in the past had been more fully suppressed.

The PPP's main advantage in the political process was its ability to attract and stir up large numbers of young people. This was demonstrated by its ability to attract large numbers to demonstrations and by the willingness of these demonstrators to riot if offence was perceived to be given to the PPP. Even the usual

Javanese tolerance of, and interest in, foreigners was modified by the upsurge in popularity of a more *santri* form of Islam and by support for the PPP. Graffiti in Yogyakarta called for a *jihad* (holy war), although its enemy was not specified, while many younger men and women took to insulting foreigners, who to them represented the decadent, imperialist West. This shift away from traditional syncretism and tolerance frightened and worried many older Javanese, indicating that formal Islam had become a political as well as cultural force.

But the PPP also faced a more daunting challenge to its longer term political aspirations: apart from its identification with Islam and internal support for an Islamic state, the PPP was largely bereft of political ideas. It had no think tank or policy foundation upon which to draw for its broader political and policy inspiration, nor did it have any figures who offered significant intellectual leadership. In large part, this was a continuing legacy of the NU's withdrawal from the PPP to pursue its ostensibly 'non-political' course. The NU's Abdurrahman Wahid (Gus Dur) had intellectual clout and had a relatively clearly defined position, which attempted to reconcile the interests of the *wong cilik*, or the 'grass roots' as he was fond of calling them, and Indonesia's central economic and political interests. Without Gus Dur and the NU, the PPP appeared inextricably linked to political conservatism, religious fundamentalism, and a lack of economic insight. These three factors appeared to ensure that, outside of its Islamic heartland, the PPP was doomed to minor-party status, regardless of the extent to which the political process was rigged:

To the extent that the Javanese 'Idea of Power' continues to predominate in Indonesia, the prospects of democratisation must be seen as slight . . . although pro-democratic sentiments are commonplace within the intelligentsia and sections of the urban middle class, there is little to suggest that the democratic culture has acquired deep roots in society. Traditional attitudes [in Javanese society] are still a problem (Crouch 1994, pp. 11–12).

In this sense, those individuals or groups who it appears will have most influence in the post-Suharto era are not united and, more importantly, neither dedicated to nor capable of establishing a significantly different political order from that which has dominated since 1966.

13

LOOKING AHEAD:
1998 AND BEYOND

Warning signs

Apres Suharto, le deluge? In the four months before the DPR elections in May 1997, protests and riots took place throughout Java, with rioting in Jakarta becoming an almost frequent occurrence. In a forceful display of defiance just before the elections, anti-government protestors confronted 20 000 police and soldiers, who had been sent in on top of the already significant military presence in Jakarta.[1] The death toll from the riots in Jakarta neared 100, with many more beaten and gaoled. Outside Java, election–related violence claimed more than 150 lives. Even though the Jakarta riots began as PPP gatherings, many protestors carried banners or wore T-shirts bearing the likeness of Megawati Sukarnoputri, the ousted leader of the PDI, indicating that there was common cause in opposing the government. And significantly, for the first time, some senior officers were saying off the record (but for publication nonetheless) that should the unrest against the government deepen they had a plan to 'replace the President'. This was Jakarta-speak for staging a coup, which had already been discreetly canvassed by some restive ABRI and Golkar members. This was beginning to become a recurring

---

1   By way of illustration, the number of extra police and soldiers transferred to Jakarta was more than the total number stationed in East Timor at that time. Jakarta had a standing army presence of three battalions of 700 troops each, as well as two cavalry battalions (about 700 personnel) equipped with armoured cars. Beyond this there are also about 3500 special forces (Kopassus) personnel, ABRI or Kostrad headquarters staff, the presidential guard, marines, Kodam (military region) III battalions, navy headquarters personnel, the Halim air force base, and police stationed in or near Jakarta (Lowry 1996).

theme in Indonesian politics in both the late Sukarno and Suharto periods. A coup was unlikely, but that it was being talked about more openly was an indication that some sort of political change was increasingly likely.

As these events were unfolding, the children of Jakarta's wealthy elite partied at the city's fashionable nightclubs—with many taking the hallucinogenic drug 'ecstasy', of which there was an embarrassing abundance—driving home in their parents' BMWs and Mercedes, and then spending the following days smoking heroine to ward off post-ecstasy depression until the next round of drinking, dancing, and ecstasy-taking at the nightclubs. Meanwhile, just a couple of kilometres away, families continued to live in slums built of cardboard and other refuse, often without enough to eat and usually without access to drinkable water.

Looking into the future is fraught with difficulty, and there is no place more certain to disappoint the soothsayer than Indonesia. More than anything, Indonesia's political landscape has been reluctant to change, but when it has, it has done so in ways that have defied all but the most insightful of predictions. This is exacerbated by the fact that the country's factions have gone to ground, very few sure of their position in relation to their opponents, and no one prepared to take a stand when the situation is so fluid and unpredictable.

Perhaps the biggest issue of the transition from Suharto to a post-Suharto government has been determining by what mechanism this transition would take place. The only precedent that Indonesia had to draw on—the removal of Sukarno—was an event that filled most Indonesians with loathing, primarily because of the associated bloodshed. Also, such a tightly controlled process allowed almost no room for the exercise of popular choice. Popular choice cannot reasonably be expected to have any significant impact on the outcome of the transition. However, many of Indonesia's political and economic elite are keen to ensure that there is at least a semblance of popular contribution to the final outcome, in order to enhance the political legitimacy of the next government.

But little is as it seems in Indonesian politics, and the growing amount of discussion about the succession in early 1998 could have been misplaced. Discontent with Suharto's rule, both public and official, reached an almost dangerously high level. And, of course, Suharto is mortal, and being born on 8 June 1921, he was starting to look like one of the world's oldest leaders. Yet Suharto first gave air to the issue of his retirement in the late 1980s, and discussion in the late 1990s about his departure from office sounded very much like an echo of similar discussion from a decade or more before. Suharto had even been off-side with ABRI since the late 1980s, yet no overt challenge had been forthcoming from that quarter. This is partly because even ABRI wanted to preserve the mystique of authority, partly because it was strongly suggested that, just ahead of the 1998 MPR 'elections', Suharto had arranged a deal with members of the 'red and white' faction of ABRI, and partly because such a challenge was not guaranteed to succeed.

Nevertheless, the issue of who was to become Indonesia's vice-president for the period beginning in 1998 was even more crucial than it had been in previous elections. The vice-presidential candidates whose names had been bandied about before the 1998 'election' included Suharto's daughter Tutut, Hartono, Wiranto, Prabowo, the incumbent Try Sutrisno, Habibie, and, surprisingly, the former vice-president, Sudharmono. This group could even have been expanded, to include some of ABRI's rising stars, although the settling of the vice-presidency on Habibie could itself also be a stop-gap measure ahead of more thoroughgoing reorganisation of the top echelons of power.

Tutut's effective nomination as vice-president was high on the list of talked-about possibilities because she was perceived to be the most politically astute and engaged of Suharto's children and was therefore best positioned to offer dynastic succession. Both her elevation to the Ministry of Social Affairs and the appointment of some of her supporters supported this possibility. Certainly the idea of dynastic succession was not out of keeping with what many had observed to be Suharto's growing sense of identification with Java's traditional rulers. Yet if Tutut had succeeded Suharto, the move would have been greeted with considerable opposition, which would probably have ensured a difficult transition. Similarly, Tutut had championed Hartono as a political leader, bringing together his ABRI connection and his loyalty to Suharto. Yet Hartono was not well supported within ABRI and would have been unlikely to have been able to count on its loyalty to him in a period of succession. Increasingly, after a period of political and military ascendancy, Hartono has been seen as a political lame duck, a position that has only increased the overtly political rise of Wiranto.

As a former Suharto adjutant, a good Central Javanese Muslim, and the person appointed as head of ABRI in 1998, Wiranto could be a front-runner for 1999 or beyond. Wiranto's chances depend on how long Habibie can hold on to the presidency. In this respect, Wiranto could provide the balance required to quell ABRI's rising resentment, through increasing ABRI's formal role in government, as well as by appealing to Muslim groups and maybe even giving a nod in the direction of pro-democracy agitators. Wiranto could also be expected to have the well-being of the country's economy at heart and would be unlikely to unsettle or depose its wealthy, Suharto-connected business magnates while managing IMF-proposed economic reform.

Suharto's son-in-law Prabowo, once considered very much an outside chance for succession because he was simply too young, firmed up his position as Suharto's tenure grew longer. Prabowo's rise through ABRI's ranks, while almost unseemly in its speed, gives him both military and political clout. His link to Suharto, through his marriage to Suharto's second daughter, Siti Hedijanti Herijadhi (Titiek), was both a strength and a weakness. The strength was obvious: it located Prabowo close to the family and hence imbued him with some concern for the protection of the family's interests.

Prabowo is also able to draw on his own political history, as the son of one of Indonesia's more capable politicians. Yet within the context of a political mood that is looking to create a break with the Suharto period, Prabowo is also seen as too close to Suharto and as too much a recipient of his direct good will. As such, his support within ABRI is at best uncertain and probably not well founded. Prabowo is perhaps beginning to believe that his successes have been of his own making rather than as a consequence of his family connections, although it still leaves him as one of the very few even vaguely realistic pro-Suharto options. But like Tutut and Hartono, making the transition to the presidency would most probably be an unrealistically difficult exercise.

The former vice-president, Try Sutrisno, acquitted himself well—which is to say quietly—in his term as vice-president. Try also has good Islamic credentials, has been one of Suharto's adjutants, and has the status of being a former commander-in-chief of ABRI. Yet Try was not a Suharto appointee and is seen as more firmly representing the Murdani faction of ABRI (and Murdani again lobbied for him, at least briefly, to be reinstated as vice-president in 1998). Although not a stupid man—he could not have risen to be commander of ABRI if he was—he is very widely perceived as having limited intellectual abilities and certainly not the breadth of vision or the political acumen that would be required of a future president. However, as president, Try could count on the very direct support of a senior group of current and former ABRI figures, not the least of whom would be Murdani himself. Indeed, if Try was to ascend to the presidency, Murdani could reasonably be expected to come back into the Cabinet as Minister of State for Special Affairs (a position formerly occupied by Harmoko after being replaced as information minister by Hartono), or in a similar position. Until being dropped, Try presented perhaps the most realistic option for a stable future in that he had already held the vice-presidency and he offered one of the best chances for peaceful succession in which the economic status quo would be largely retained.

Suharto's protégé Habibie was handed the vice-presidency, and later the presidency, primarily because he is a most committed Suharto loyalist. But Habibie is extraordinarily unpopular with ABRI and much of the wider population. He also has no effective power base of his own from which to sustain the presidency, and is perhaps too idiosyncratic, and too flawed in his political and economic judgment, to survive as president. Habibie's elevation appears only to have been accepted by ABRI as a precondition for installing its own candidate at a more opportune time.

Undermining any strategies regarding the succession is the problem, as already noted, of there being no adequate precedent for succession. Habibie might have succeeded Suharto in the short term only. ABRI could still request that the succession be reconfirmed by the MPR, perhaps a reconfigured MPR. This reconfirmation would then provide an opportunity to reject Habibie and appoint someone who might not be so obviously placed. Thus the new president could simply be a care-taker, or seat-warmer, while the real business of succession is resolved else-where. In this respect, although not limitless, the field for Indo-nesia's future president is far wider than it first appears.

The more things change . . .

But most Indonesian political observers seem to agree that there are a few outcomes in terms of Indonesia's political leadership that seem most likely, and that these would have their own broader implications. These would go a small way towards addressing, one way or another, some outstanding issues: corruption, the role of *pribumi* versus ethnic Chinese business people in the economy, a possible redistribution of localised wealth, the role of ABRI, and the extent to which Indonesia could move towards a participatory democracy. But even without Suharto, there is unlikely to be sub-stantive change in Indonesia's political make-up, the primary reason being that enough influential people have too much to lose. Indonesia's economy can not afford the shock of a further serious flight of capital, which would come with a wholesale clean-up of questionable businesses. Nor can it cope with a fur-ther drop in foreign investment, which would result from a radi-cal political change or the political instability that might accompany it. It hardly bears mentioning that such concerns are in part made redundant by the economic and subsequent political crisis, in which capital flight and falling foreign investment have figured prominently.

To a large extent, the broader political stability of the archi-pelago is based on its economic stability, marginal though that was in some of the outer regions even before the economic collapse. Further, while there might be disputes among the elites them-selves, none of them, including the alleged pro-democrats, seriously believe that real political power could or should be passed down to the *wong cilik*. Translated as 'little people' (literally *orang-orang kecil*), the term would be remarkably audacious and patronising in its tone if used in a Western democratic society. But this is precisely the term that members of the elite use to refer to ordinary Indonesians in their public discourse, including in news-papers and on radio and television. At least there is very little pre-tence in the way that the elites view the reality of the relationship.

Almost regardless of who occupies the position of president after Suharto, the most likely outcome is that, in practical terms,

Indonesia will be ruled by a triumvirate or perhaps small clique, at least for the short to middle term. For cohesion, this group would rely on or consist of senior figures from the armed forces. There has long been a sense that, after Suharto, ABRI will reassert what many within it believe to be its rightful place, under the *dwifungsi*, as an arm of government. This effectively precludes broader political participation, or the much-vaunted 'democratisation', although it is likely that there will be some acknowledgment of domestic and international concerns. Such an acknowledgment might include the divestment or floating of some, probably a minor, proportion of the major conglomerates, a redirection of at least some development funds towards health, housing, and education projects, and a period of greater freedom of expression. This last outcome could be expected to be especially encouraged where it offers a developing criticism of the previous government, which, *ipso facto*, would assist in the process of legitimising the new government. Such 'openness' has been seen before, particularly in the period of the changeover from Sukarno to Suharto. But realistically it would be likely to be a short-term phenomenon, as using the media for the purposes of legitimation is not the same thing as allowing genuine or fully fledged freedom of expression. As the new government consolidates itself, it will have less need for criticism of the previous government, and it will be particularly careful not to let the flow of criticism be directed back at itself (for example, in relation to its own similarities to the government that it has displaced).

Of the new ruling clique, one of the group could eventually be expected to assert himself as leader, retaining the support of the armed forces and subordinating the other members to ministerial positions, from which they could, if necessary, be dismissed. There is also the possibility that Habibie might not occupy the position of president for long, perhaps being acceptable only until a more appropriate candidate can be groomed for the position. Who might replace Habibi as a longer term president remains highly speculative and can not be judged until events unfold. But each of the *Pandawa Lima* could, short of some unforeseen catastrophe, be expected to want to play a role in the future government at least. Their respective manœuvrings can only be watched with intense interest.

Little hope for democracy

This scenario does not paint an optimistic picture for those who have pinned their hopes on Indonesia's eventual democratisation. Perhaps, it has been too easy to be drawn into Jakarta's 'palace' political culture, and to ignore the chanting angry mobs outside. But democratisation, desirable though it remains in normative terms, simply lacks sufficient support from those within the political structure for it to have a bright future. Some observers have argued that development will bring with it an associated push for democratisation. It is true that some of the smaller business people in Indonesia find the country's style of unresponsive and corruption-prone government bad for business, while others among the small 'middle class' desire more of a say in the running of their country. However, it is equally true that while democracy cannot exist (or at least so far has not existed) without capitalism, capitalism has shown itself to be very capable of existing without democracy. Indeed, if one accepts the 'Asian values' argument put by Singapore's government, full participatory democracy of the Western type is positively bad for economic development. But more importantly, what the argument for a deterministic link between economic development and democratisation fails to note in Indonesia's case is that, in many fundamental respects, its economy and its government still operate on a feudal basis (see chapter 2). This is alleviated by growing access to higher technology than is usually associated with traditional feudalism, as well as the growth of manufacturing industries and associated large urban areas. But the majority of Indonesians still live in rural areas, and access to technology, in so far as it is influential, is not evenly distributed,[2] and so this influence is limited. Democratisation is therefore not only uncertain, but its appearance, if it surfaces at all in any meaningful sense, would also seem fragile.

Certainly there have been angry mobs in the streets protesting about issues seemingly associated with democratisation, the July 1996 pro-PDI riot being perhaps the best example, along with

---

2   It would be interesting to diverge here into a discussion of print technology, literacy rates, levels of newspaper readership, media control, and the quality of information as a measure of access to potentially democratising influences. In part, though, this has been discussed in chapter 8.

serious protests in 1998. But as a proportion of the population, such protests have been small. More than anything, the July 1996 riot reflected a justifiable frustration with government's heavy-handedness, rather than any support for democratic principles as such, while in May 1998, the post-election riots reflected economic desperation as much as a desire for basic political change. We might wish for an open, participatory political process, as do many in Indonesia, from trade union activists, NGO and legal-aid workers, intellectuals, journalists, at least some students, general pro-democracy activists, and perhaps some regional separatists. They all see democratisation as a way to achieve some sense of political control over their own lives.[3] But wishing is a far cry from realising such a process.

One issue is kept off the agenda for discussion about Indonesia's political succession, but it looms increasingly large when trying to envisage a post-Suharto Indonesia: it is that of national unity (the term 'nation' being used here in its geographic and political sense rather than its cultural and community sense). In simple terms, Indonesia has been kept together on a number of occasions through armed force, and although a national consciousness has been developed, the unity of the 'nation' remains fragile. Resentment towards Javanese domination is rife in the outer islands, yet given that the Javanese comprise close to half the population, their political dominance could be expected. What most riles outer islanders, though—and this dates back in varying degrees of intensity to the 1950s—is the distribution of income between Java and the outer islands, their lack of representation in the political process and (to a considerable degree) within the armed forces, and an inability to resolve local issues without recourse to the central government. This is all pushing towards consideration of a different form of Indonesian unity, with the idea of a return to federalism even being discussed, though rarely accepted, in Jakarta.

If, however, Indonesia was to reconfigure itself in the post-Suharto period, there would be some tension within some regions over whether it would be worthwhile to stay within the

---

3   It could be suggested that some Indonesians do not want an open, participatory political process, especially where such a process would exceed their sometimes circumscribed grasp of the world. But even at a local level, based on my experience, it is far more common for ordinary people to want to have some say over matters that affect their own lives.

nation, but there could also be more scope for greater political representation at a local level. The decentralisation of authority from Jakarta, which would mean an abandonment of the unitary state in favour of a federalist state, could be Indonesia's greatest hope for a move towards participatory politics. However, any move towards federalism would encounter stiff resistance not only from almost any government likely to set up in Jakarta, but also from any Javanese people who care to think about its implications. Java generally, and Jakarta in particular, would be the poorer for such an arrangement, and Javanese conceptions of Indonesia as a representation of Javanese-inspired unity would disappear. The Javanese idealisation of Indonesia as the continuation of Gajah Mada's glorious empire would no longer hold true, although a federal system might in fact bear a greater similarity to the Majapahit empire. The reality is that only a government free from both ABRI's influence and the idea of Javanese centralism would countenance a return to federation. However, it is likely that any future Indonesian government will be more, rather than less, influenced by ABRI. Given this likelihood, democratisation, political participation, a regionally representative or federalist state, and meaningful free expression all appear to be mirages, or at best very distant goals.

EPILOGUE:
THE FALL OF
SUHARTO

Thick black smoke is billowing up from the south-east around in the direction of Tanah Tinggi, and from the south of the Atrium in the direction of Kramat. On the way back here from the office near the Monas we could see thick black smoke from the direction of Jalan Gadjah Mada where there were riots and looting early this morning as well as cars and shops set on fire. It seems that Jakarta is ablaze in every direction you look. As I glance out the window again a new plume of smoke has appeared from the direction of Gambir railway station.[1]

Ethnic Chinese were a favourite target of the rioting that gripped Jakarta in May 1998, but anyone with property was, it seemed, fair game. Troops and police had, for a while, lost control as the calls for the resignation of President Suharto grew louder from both the angry mobs and, increasingly, members of Indonesia's elite. No matter how the riots were interpreted at the time, it soon became clear that Indonesia's New Order government had entered its final phase, and Suharto's days in power were fast coming to a close.

Emboldened by shadowy support from high places, students as far afield as Yogyakarta and Medan, but especially those in Jakarta, had pushed the limits of what the New Order had regarded as acceptable dissent. Protests were allowed on university campuses, but when they moved outside the campuses they were met with ABRI opposition. Initially these confrontations were relatively non-violent. But then, in Medan, ABRI reaction turned nasty,

---

1 This is an extract from a letter received by the author from an employee of a non-government organisation, who was in Jakarta at the time of the May 1998 riots. The writer of the letter cannot be identified.

with students being severely beaten, rubber bullets and tear gas being used, and a number of female students being gang-raped by soldiers.

Then, in Jakarta, while Suharto was attending a meeting in Egypt, students at the private Trisakti University campus joined the protest movement. However, Jakarta was the direct security concern of Suharto's son-in-law and the person who had assumed effective leadership of ABRI's pro–Suharto 'Green' faction, Major General Prabowo Subianto. With Suharto out of the country, the stakes concerning political leadership were high, and Prabowo's men reacted with violence. As students began to run back to their campus, the troops opened fire. The rubber bullets soon gave way to conventional rounds, and fleeing students dropped before the gunfire. The final toll was six dead and many more wounded. What was perhaps most significant about the events of May 1998 was that troops loyal to Prabowo did not hesitate to fire on students and then other protesters as a core tactic of maintaining 'order'. That they should do so highlighted the essentially repressive nature of the Suharto government and the mechanisms it had put in place to ensure its own well-being, regardless of the wishes of ordinary Indonesian citizens.

There were more student protests, but increasingly Jakarta's poor and dispossessed joined in. What had started as a naïve but politically motivated protest soon turned into an orgy of anti-government rioting and looting. Looters were trapped in burning buildings, and the death toll quickly rose to over 1000, with the mayhem only being quelled when the army brought its armoured cars and tanks onto the streets.

This was the situation just a few weeks after Suharto had been sworn in for his seventh consecutive term as president and after he had announced his new, crony-heavy Cabinet. The public outcry for Suharto's resignation reached unprecedented levels, with former generals, academics, and ordinary Indonesians calling for him to quit. Major General Yudhoyono personally delivered a message from a number of retired generals, addressed to ABRI commander-in-chief General Wiranto, requesting that Suharto resign. A similar petition was presented to a special session of the MPR, in which, in an act of unprecedented defiance, half of that assembly called on Suharto to resign. Its repeated calls were spearheaded by former Suharto loyalist and MPR chairman Harmoko.

Despite Wiranto saying that the call was unconstitutional and advising against planned protests two days later, it was becoming increasingly apparent that Wiranto had done a deal with Suharto: 'agree to retire quietly and there will be no more violence'. On 19 May 1998, in a public speech televised live, President Suharto announced the formation of a 'reform committee' and a new 'reform Cabinet'. But more importantly, Suharto also announced that there would be new presidential elections and that he would not stand as a candidate. No date was given for the election and many believed it could be more than a year away, which did not satisfy the protesters. On 20 May 1998, with Harmoko now threatening to have the MPR impeach Suharto, the MPR building swamped by protesters, and all credible candidates refusing to join his 'reform committee', Suharto began to waver. When Harmoko again spoke against Suharto, and when the ABRI 'fraction' leader in the MPR, Syarwan Hamid, raised his fist in symbolic support, it appeared obvious that Suharto was alone. A visit to his home by three former vice-presidents—Try Sutrisno, Sudharmono, and Umar Wirahadikusumah—that evening further encouraged Suharto to resign. A visit later that night by Wiranto sealed the arrangement: Suharto and his family would be protected after his resignation. At around 11 p.m., Suharto summoned Habibie and informed him that he would become Indonesia's third president on the following day.

Suharto's resignation was initially greeted with great enthusiasm on the streets of Jakarta—at last the 'Old Man' was gone and the Suharto era was at an end. However, as Habibie was sworn in as president, there were other serious concerns. Habibie was not well liked; he was a direct Suharto beneficiary, and he had no power base of his own. Yet Wiranto supported Habibie's appointment, at least initially. In naming his new, very slightly more inclusive 'reform Cabinet', Wiranto was reappointed as commander-in-chief of ABRI and defence minister, while Tutut and Bob Hasan were dropped. Habibie had no choice in any of these decisions.

The appointment of Habibie to the vice-presidency in March had always been designed to allow Suharto to quietly step away from Indonesian politics during his five-year term of office. Habibie, a trusted ally of Suharto, was placed in that position in order to cover Suharto's back as he and his cronies made their exit. In that sense, Suharto's plan had worked: most of Suharto's wealth was believed to be already out of the country when power was transferred.

During the period of his vice-presidential nomination, it was said that Habibie was only acceptable to ABRI because he was so expendable. Being sworn in as president did not, therefore, automatically mean that he would survive in that position. Habibie remains very unpopular with many Muslims, with ABRI, and with ordinary Indonesians. Because of his mistakes while Minister for Research and Technology—such as his failed bid to develop an Indonesian aerospace industry—he is also unpopular with the IMF and international money markets.

While Suharto's resignation was greeted with enthusiasm—even Habibie was regarded as a better option than continuing with Suharto—real power appeared to be firmly in the hands of Wiranto. Wiranto said that ABRI would maintain order, reconfirming that he is first and foremost a traditional Indonesian general, rather than a democrat or populist as some had begun to believe him to be. Wiranto was supported in the 'reform Cabinet' by General Junus Yosfiah, former head of ABRI's Social and Political Affairs office, who is noted for his hard-line military position. The retention in the Cabinet of Hendropriyono and the Red and White supporter Juwono Sudharsono further indicated that ABRI was again in the ascendancy, and that the Red and White faction had won the day.

After a brief and somewhat ill-conceived show of power on 22 May, in which he told Habibie to appoint him as ABRI commander-in-chief, Prabowo was shuffled out of Kostrad to the staff and command college at Magelang. However, there was also the possibility that he could face charges over a bomb attack. Initially, suspicions regarding the attack had been focused on Sofyan Wanandi, the businessman brother of Jusuf Wanandi, who was an integral part of the Murdani-influenced Centre for Strategic and International Studies. Meanwhile, Prabowo's military allies were similarly moved from influential positions in what was beginning to look like a purge, to be replaced by Red and White loyalists. In particular, Kopassus commander Major General Muchdi Purwopranjono was replaced by Major General Sjahrir.

The Red and White faction had not only won in Cabinet; it had also won control of ABRI. Whether Habibie survives as president depends on whether it suits their interests, although Yudhoyono has indicated a more liberal response from ABRI towards politics in the future.

With Habibie's future less than certain, possible contenders for a future presidential contest have begun to appear. They include the leader of the Muhammadiyah, Amien Rais, although as a formal Muslim, he is unlikely to receive support from the majority of Indonesians, who are nominal Muslims. Rais has also previously expressed strong anti-democratic sentiments. The other major Islamic leader, Abdurrahman Wahid (Gus Dur), now blind as a consequence of his stroke, has also been unable to come to terms with Rais and his organisation. Former Democratic Party leader Megawati Sukarnoputri has no substantial support base for a presidential bid. The coordinating minister for finance and economic planning, Ginandjar Kartasasmita, looks somewhat better placed, having both international and domestic support, as does former minister Emil Salim, who appears closer to Wiranto.

In the days after Habibie took office, he made a number of moves towards establishing his reform credentials. Labor unions previously banned under Suharto were legalised; there were moves towards liberalising press regulations; there was a start to disassociating government and business, and resolving other conflicts of interest; and it was announced that all political parties could contest future elections, although no date was set for such elections. Another move was the selective release of political prisoners, and access to others was made much freer. One of the first results of this was that Abdul Latief—a former colonel, alleged 'gestapu' conspirator, and, for thirty-two years, a political prisoner—claimed that he had told Suharto of the plot against the army's six senior generals before the events of 30 September 1965 unfolded. Latief said that he told Suharto of this because Suharto was believed to be a Sukarno loyalist. This allegation pulls the rug from underneath the official history of the New Order government, and along with calls by Amien Rais that Suharto should be charged with corruption, it signals that the delegitimisation of Suharto has begun.

The moves towards liberalisation are heartily welcomed both within Indonesia and abroad. Such moves are to be expected as part of a new government's attempts to legitimise itself, but this liberalisation does not necessarily guarantee permanent political change. A reordering of Indonesian political society is certainly under way, but the final shape of that society is clouded by numerous competing interests—many, if not most, of which are hardly inclined towards liberalism. With the political demise of Suharto and the consequent overt moves towards liberalisation, there has, at least for a while, been a flowering of political hope in Indonesia. But it would be a brave person who predicted that hope will survive intact.

A Review of the
Literature

Many authors have been drawn deeply into the subject of Indonesia, reflecting its own complexity, richness, and self-absorption. Many acknowledge that they have fallen in love with the place. It could even be said, without malice, that many people who develop an interest in Indonesia are drawn in so far that they come to identify themselves by their Indoncsian affectations, sometimes even to the extent of having pretensions to 'polite' Javanese behaviour.

In part, this reflects what some have described as a sense of spiritual emptiness in modern Western culture. Many are seeking fulfilment in more 'traditional' (pre-industrial), arguably less materialistic, cultures, a phenomenon that is reflected in Western interest in Eastern religions and philosophies. But, the tendency of authors to become immersed in Indonesian culture is also a manifestation of some of the deeply engaging aspects of an intrinsically introspective and complex political culture. Like an addiction, it invites the casual participant to become ever more deeply involved in a logic that, it is often suggested, can only be understood in its own terms.

Yet this approach conceives of Indonesia and its politics as Javanese (as so often is the case). Even then, Indonesia is viewed as reflecting an idealised, high Javanese culture that has not remained static but has been reconstructed and reinvented to suit the changing needs of a particular political elite. The very best writing on Indonesia recognises this, and manages to retain a critical distance. This critical distance does not preclude sensitivity or even empathy, but it does recognise that ultimately observers have to make their own observations and not simply reiterate the observations of others.

The proposition that one can offer a useful critique across cultures immediately calls forth a range of theoretical debates. Not the least of these relates to the fundamental distinction between positivist and relativist analyses (what *is*, or is claimed to objectively be, and what is said to be a question of subjective judgment), between etic and emic (external and internal) perspectives, and related issues in cross cultural understanding. On the face of it, there would appear to be a basic interpretive division between these positivist and relativist positions, yet in the literature there is considerable agreement across the analytical positions, while division exists within each, most notably in positivist analysis. Although 'inside' and 'outside' perspectives have troubled many anthropologists, they have concerned political observers less; they simply argue that politics is politics. Some anthropological critics have questioned understanding that is based on an acknowledged external viewpoint, but the subjectivity of an 'insider's' perspective can similarly be questioned. None of this, however, has much bothered journalists, who face more immediate and sometimes more prosaic concerns, such as simply getting the story written by deadline. Interestingly, the two most important books on Indonesian politics in recent times have been written by journalists, who have been much less concerned about engaging in theoretical debates about perspectives than about simply telling a story as they see it.

The most influential recent book on Indonesia is Adam Schwartz's *A Nation in Waiting* (1994). Though the title anticipates the transition to a post–Suharto government, the book itself offers an account of Indonesian political life as it has been played out particularly since the early 1970s. Schwartz's book has attained a sort of cult status among students of Indonesian politics, being arguably the most comprehensive single account of the subject since the 1960s.

Indeed, this is the book that Indonesians travelling abroad most often seek out first, partly because it provides the type of account of Indonesian affairs that simply cannot be published in Indonesia. The fact that it has been banned in Indonesia means that it has achieved a certain notoriety on that basis alone. This says more about the political bravado and social daring of the reader than it does about the contents of the book, and again reflects the precedence of style over substance.

In practical terms, a close reading of Schwartz's book will provide the attentive reader with a solid understanding of the main issues in contemporary Indonesian political life. However, despite being closely written and full of useful detail, there is a sense in which the subject is a jumble. In large part this reflects the inherent difficulty in teasing out the strands of the subject and laying them out in neat, straight lines. The fact is that Indonesian political life is not simple, and it is effectively impossible to discuss one aspect without necessarily touching on others. A three dimensional matrix *might* illustrate it, but the writing of a book is constrained by a set of methodological abstractions that differ from those used to construct such a model.

At another level, because the author is (or was once) so clearly close to the subject, the book does not really succeed in welcoming readers whose understanding of the subject is effectively nonexistent. In a sense, as an introductory text, Schwartz requires his own, separate introduction.

Published a year before Schwartz's book, Michael Vatikiotis's book *Indonesian Politics Under Suharto* (1993) acts as such an introduction, yet it is more than an introduction in terms of the value of its subject matter. Also written by a journalist—they both worked for the *Far Eastern Economic Review*—Vatikiotis's book is not only two-thirds the length of Schwartz's tome; it is also written in a more accessible style. But more importantly, where Schwartz notes what might be interpreted as critical material on Indonesian politics, Vatikiotis is less coy and offers a sharper, more critical perspective. This is not so much a question of interpretation, as there is no disagreement in terms of substance between the two, but rather it reflects their different personal or perhaps journalistic styles: Schwartz is slightly more explanatory, while Vatikiotis is slightly more adversarial.

Not surprisingly, the issue of Suharto's succession haunts both books. While this issue has been critical in contemporary Indonesian politics, it has been the dominant issue on the political agenda since the late 1970s. Vatikiotis hinted that Suharto would be on his way out either in or soon after 1993, while Schwartz hinted that Suharto would be looking to step down in 1998, with possible democratisation to follow.

Taking far fewer chances than either, Bruce Grant's revised edition of his 1964 classic, *Indonesia* (1996), takes a more open approach to Indonesia's future. Having lived through Sukarno's fall, Grant benefits from the circumspection that comes from experience. Yet as history carries its baggage into both the present and the future, so too has Grant's *Indonesia*. The relevance of some parts, particularly the interviews, seems questionable. But the structure of this book is far more straightforward than either Schwartz or Vatikiotis, and if Grant's vision is slightly more limited, he brings to his work an eye for detail that reflects his own journalistic (and academic) training.

It is often said that many great works are produced early in the careers of their authors, who like radioactive material thereafter decline into a type of half-life. At one level, Grant has spoilt the reputation he built with the 1964 and 1966 editions of *Indonesia*, as his later effort simply could not live up to the impact of the earlier editions. Today the subject of Indonesia is not so poorly understood as it was then. A part of the impact of the 1964 and 1966 editions was that, as there was so little at that time to compare it with, almost anything would have been good, and so a book of its inherent integrity was especially well received.

Another recent critique of Indonesia is *Power in Motion* by Jeffrey Winters, which focuses on Indonesian economics, taking a special interest in how the state under the New Order government has responded to its needs and the needs of international capital. This is an interesting and most useful account of the development of the Indonesian economy and economic policy since the mid-1960s. However, as an overview of contemporary Indonesia, the book tends to take too little account of non-economic factors in the decision-making process—particularly that of cultural influences and the more universal desire for power. Its vision has been limited in order to expound only or primarily on the narrowly defined subject at hand.

If these four books are the most obvious 'actors' on the 'stage' of political commentary on Indonesia, not only is there a large supporting cast, but some of the 'bit players' and older actors are also challenging the leads in an attempt to steal the show. Herb

Feith's classic, *The Decline of Constitutional Democracy in Indonesia*, is undoubtedly the foundation stone upon which all other accounts of Indonesian politics are built. Less well known but perhaps equally as important is Feith's contribution, 'Indonesia', to Kahin's *Governments and Politics of Southeast Asia*. This 87-page account of Indonesian politics from the beginning until the early 1960s is concise, clear, detailed, and immensely readable. It is perhaps the ideal introduction to the subject for the period before the bloody events of 1965–66. Beyond that, almost anything Feith has written or edited on Indonesia is very worthwhile, especially his work with Castles, *Indonesian Political Thinking, 1945–1965* (1970).

Historically located between Feith and Grant, on one hand, and Schwartz and Vatikiotis, on the other, is Richard Robison's analysis of Indonesian economics and politics, *Indonesia: The Rise of Capital* (1986). Closer to Winters both as a study of the link between economic and political issues and, perhaps, from a 'political economy' perspective, Robison's work was one of the earlier sustained attempts to analyse the economic basis of the New Order government's political structure. Dated now, this work is expected to be republished in an updated, revised edition. At least ideologically if not methodologically sympathetic to Robison, the 'alternative history' of Indonesia offered by Malcolm Caldwell and Ernst Utrecht (1979) is not so much alternative as Marxist. This is a straightforward if critical account of Indonesian history, which tends to take a somewhat jaundiced view especially of the Dutch, the Japanese, and ABRI, from which the New Order government arose. Its Marxist perspective has left it open to some criticism, but the type of Marxism evident is not strident and probably not out of place with the kinds of views that might have been propounded by Sukarno himself.

More recent than any of these books, but similar to Caldwell and Utrecht's history, is Robert Cribb and Colin Brown's *Modern Indonesia* (1995), which is a history of the country since 1945. This is an especially good and clear account of Indonesia's political development up to recent times, although within its limited space, and given the scope of the subject, detail does sometimes tend to be overlooked. Not one to be called a Marxist, Merle Ricklefs, in his *A History of Modern Indonesia since c. 1300* (1993a), provides perhaps a more definitive text, although it does not offer quite the ease of reading of Caldwell and Utrecht. Similarly,

Ricklefs's *War, Culture and Economy in Java 1677–1726* (1993b) offers a useful insight into an important period of Javanese political development, although it is a specialised text that probably only a dedicated reader would wish to peruse.

Of course, any discussion about Indonesian politics must incorporate an overview of ABRI, and indeed an analysis of ABRI is a useful way to explore the *Realpolitik* of Indonesia. Robert Lowry's *The Armed Forces of Indonesia* is more an account of the purpose and structure of ABRI, although he does offer some observations that link it to the more explicitly political. Ian MacFarling's account, *The Dual Function of the Indonesian Armed Forces* (1996), is something of a 'bookend' to Lowry's work, focusing on the 'personality' of ABRI and its role in Indonesian politics. Better on this subject, though, is Harold Crouch's *The Army and Politics in Indonesia* (1988), which, happily, has been updated. Although structured as a history, Crouch's book is far more analytical than most and in some senses is the most incisive document on Indonesian politics. These three books were all prefigured by David Jenkins 1984 work *Suharto and his Generals: Indonesian Military Politics 1975–1983*. An account of the machinations of military politics, and particularly Suharto's consolidation of power, Jenkins's book offers close insights into the working of Indonesian politics at the time and stands well as a historical document.

Permanently banned from entering Indonesia for his 1971 account (with Ruth McVey) of the killings of six generals on 30 September 1965, Ben Anderson has been more reflective in his previous work. *Mythology and the Tolerance of the Javanese* (1965) is a product of his formative years in Java and offers a useful insight into some of the thinking on ethics at the centre of Indonesian political 'tradition'. His essay 'The Idea of Power in Javanese Culture' (1972) has been widely touted as the clearest exposition on this subject, not to mention the source of considerable debate, though his ideas have held up well. A later analysis, 'Old State, New Society: Indonesia's New Order in Comparative Historical Perspective' (1983) was a critical retort to those who Anderson views as either apologists or misguided defenders of Indonesia's political processes. His crowning work on Indonesia, *Language and Power: Exploring Political Cultures in Indonesia* (1990), is a definitive work on the subject and was followed by the widely acclaimed *Imagined Communities*, which while not exclusively about Indonesia, grew out of his interest in Indonesia as a post-colonial 'nation'.

Associated with Anderson through Cornell University's Modern Indonesia Project is Somarsaid Moertono, whose *State and Statecraft in Old Java* (1981) offers an extremely useful insight into Javanese political tradition. Most notably, Moertono acknowledges the influence of India, especially the idea of the mandala, in Javanese conceptualisation. This appears to have implicitly influenced Anderson's understanding of Indonesian political organisation. Interestingly, though, G. Moedjanto's *The Concept of Power in Javanese Culture* (1993) appears to be influenced by Anderson's 'Idea of Power in Javanese Culture', though he uses Moertono's specific use of history to illustrate his points.

Like Anderson, the anthropologist Clifford Geertz starts with Indonesia but thereafter works more broadly. His most notable, early work is *The Religion of Java* (1960), which like Feith's earlier work, went a long way towards explaining what was until then only poorly understood. In this sense, though, Geertz was looking at the influences of and in Javanese culture, rather than directly at politics, although his anthropology does slip into the political from time to time. In particular, *Local Knowledge* (1983) and *The Interpretation of Cultures* (1993) are both extremely useful in developing mechanisms for exploring what lies behind the facade of Indonesian, and particularly Javanese, life.

Also coming from an anthropological perspective, although with its emphasis on politics, is John Pemberton's *On the Subject of 'Java'* (1994). Pemberton offers a thoroughly researched and detailed account of how Javanese culture has been reinvented by the New Order government to suit its particular political needs. Although coming from a theoretical position that is perhaps closest to 'deconstructionism', Pemberton nevertheless refrains from using culture as a relativising factor, but rather shows how the shallow use of relativism is itself compromised. Here there is a close link between Pemberton's and Anderson's critiques of the construction of political culture.

Perhaps not anthropological, but certainly 'culturalist', William Liddle's *Leadership and Culture in Indonesian Politics* (1996) seeks to explain political development through a cultural and at times individual prism. Viewed as an added aspect of analysis, it is a welcome contribution, as issues of culture and personality play perhaps a more overt official role in Indonesian politics than elsewhere. However, viewed as an explanation alone or even as the main contributing factor, it is somewhat lacking.

An essential inclusion in any brief account of literature on Indonesian politics is the quarterly magazine *Inside Indonesia*. This specialist publication is arguably the world's best source of information on contemporary Indonesia, and while it is not exclusively about politics—art, literature and other reflections on culture are common—not surprisingly political matters do comprise most of its editorial content. *Inside Indonesia* draws on specialists in Indonesian affairs, both from Indonesia and abroad, and often leads the way with more scholarly articles on Indonesian issues. If there is a downside to *Inside Indonesia*, it is that, as a magazine, its contemporary contributions sometimes do not have the luxury of hindsight. Having said that, *Inside Indonesia* is remarkable for its ability to pick trends and highlight important issues before they are noticed elsewhere.

What is particularly interesting about these accounts is not their different disciplinary, methodological, or ideological distinctions. Rather, it is the way they demonstrate the tension between the exigencies of running a modern, heterogeneous state, the extraordinary levels of official corruption and political repression, and the influence of Javanese 'culture' and political 'tradition', which explains so much on one level and is reinvented to rationalise so much on another. Within the works of each of these authors, but especially between them, history, culture, and politics intersect. This confluence, located within and shedding light on the real, contemporary world, provides some extremely useful insights into the richly engrossing, sprawling, troubled, and troubling subject that is the politics of Indonesia.

REFERENCES

Abidin, I. 1993, Interview with the author, Jakarta, 20 December.

Alamsjah Ratu Periranegara, H. 1989, 'Social Justice as a Challenge to Today's Programme of Development' in I. Hadad, *Political Culture and Social Justice in Indonesia*, ed. A. Cominos, Southeast Asian Monograph series, no. 29, Centre for Southeast Asian Studies, James Cook University, Townsville, Qld, pp. 37–52.

Amnesty International 1994, *Power and Impunity: Human Rights under the New Order*, Amnesty International Publications, London.

Anderson, B. 1965, *Mythology and the Tolerance of the Javanese*, Monograph Series, Modern Indonesian Project, Cornell University, Ithaca, NY.

—— 1972, 'The Idea of Power in Javanese Culture', in C. Holt, B. Anderson, & J. Siegel, *Culture and Politics in Indonesia*, Cornell University Press, Ithaca, NY.

—— 1978, 'Last Days of Indonesia's Suharto?', *Southeast Asia Chronicle*, no. 63, July, pp. 2–17.

—— 1983, 'Old State, New Society: Indonesia's New Order in Comparative Historical Perspective', *Journal of Asian Studies*, vol. 42, no. 3, May, pp. 477–95.

—— 1990, *Language and Power: Exploring Political Cultures in Indonesia*, Cornell University Press, Ithaca, NY.

—— 1991, *Imagined Communities*, Verso, London.

Anderson, B. & McVey, R. 1971, *A Preliminary Analysis of the October 1, 1965 Coup in Indonesia*, Modern Indonesia Project, Cornell University, Ithaca, NY.

Anwar, D. F. 1997, *Indonesia's Strategic Culture: Ketahanan Nasional, Wawasan Nusantara and Kankamrata*, Centre for the Study of Australia–Asia Relations, Griffith University, Brisbane.

Asia Watch Committee 1990, *Injustice, Persecution, Eviction*, Human Rights Watch, New York.

Atkinson, J. 1987, 'Religions in Dialogue: The Construction of an Indonesian Minority Religion', in R. Kipp & S. Rogers (eds), *Indonesian Religions in Transition*, University of Arizona Press, Phoenix, pp. 171–86.

Austin-Broos, D. 1987, 'Clifford Geertz: Culture, Sociology and Historicism', in D. Austin-Broos (ed.), *Creating Culture*, Allen & Unwin, Sydney.

Australia, House of Representatives 1981, *Debates*, 1 April.

Australian Financial Review 1986, editorial, 11 December.

Aznam, S. 1992, 'Contested Closure', *Far Eastern Economic Review*, 26 November, pp. 20–1.

Bachrach, P. & Barartz, M. 1962, 'The Two Faces of Power', *American Political Science Review*, no. 56, 1962.

Baker, M. 1992a, 'A Timor Gap in Credibility', *Age*, 24 January, p. 13.

—— 1992b, 'What Price Australia's Principles on East Timor', *Age*, 16 April, p. 13.

—— 1993, 'Asia's Struggle for Success and Compassion', *Age*, 8 April, p. 13.

—— 1994, 'Keating and Indonesia: A Crisis of Credibility', *Age*, 25 June, p. 19.

Barton, G. 1994, *The Origins of Islamic Liberalism in Indonesia and its Contribution to Democratic Reform*, Working Paper series, no. 94–2, Centre for Asian and Middle Eastern Studies, Deakin University, Geelong, Vic.

Belo, C. 1993, Interview with the author, Melbourne, 17 November.

Berfield, S. & Loveard, K. 1997, 'A Split within the Ranks', *Asiaweek*, 13 September.

Bernstein, R. 1976, *The Restructuring of Social and Political Theory*, Harcourt Brace Jovanovich, New York.

Body for the Protection of the People's Political Rights Facing the 1992 General Election 1994, *'White Book' on the 1992 General Election in Indonesia*, trans. D. King, Publication no. 73, Cornell Modern Indonesia Project, Ithaca, NY.

Bourchier, D. 1987, 'The "Petition of 50": Who and What are They', *Inside Indonesia*, no. 10, April, pp. 7–10.

—— 1994, 'Solidarity: The New Order's First Free Trade Union', in D. Bourchier (ed.), *Indonesia's Emerging Proletariat: Workers and their Struggles*, Annual Indonesia Lecture series, Centre of Southeast Asian Studies, Monash University, Melbourne.

—— 1996, Lineages of Organicist Political Thought in Indonesia, PhD thesis, Department of Politics, Monash University, Melbourne.

Brandt Commission 1983, *Common Crisis, North–South: Co-operation for World Recovery*, Pan Books, London.

Branigan, W. 1986, 'Reagan Visit Turns into a Disaster for Suharto', *Guardian*, 11 May 1986, p. 17.

Bruton, H. 1985, 'The Search for Development Economics', *World Development*, vol. 13, nos 10/11, Pergamon Press, London.

Budiardjo, C. & Liong, L. S. 1984, *The War Against East Timor*, Zed Books, London.

Butler, S. 1996, 'A Tiger Stumbles', *US News*, 14 October.

Byrnes, M. 1986a, 'No Clear Motive behind Leaked Document', *Australian Financial Review*, 27 May.

—— 1986b, 'Jakarta's Army Lashes Out at the Threat from the South', *Australian Financial Review*, 3 June, p. 1.

—— 1986c, 'The Real Rulers in Indonesia', *Australian Financial Review*, 23 June, p. 10.

—— 1994, *Australia and the Asia Game*, Allen & Unwin, Sydney.

Byrnes, M. & Abueg, J. M. 1986, 'Suharto Scoops Marcos Assets', *Australian Financial Review*, 10 December, pp. 1, 4.

Caldwell, M. & Utrecht, E. 1979, *Indonesia: An Alternative History*, Alternative Publishing Co-operative Limited, Sydney.

Chomsky, N. & Herman, E. 1979, 'Benign Terror: East Timor', *Bulletin of Concerned Asian Scholars*, no. 11, April–June.

Church, G. 1995, 'The Forgotten Wars', *Time Australia*, 9 October, p. 39.

Clancy, A. 1992, 'In the Censor's Shadow', *Inside Indonesia*, no. 30, March, pp. 14–16.

Clegg, S. 1989, *Frameworks of Power*, Sage Publications, London.

Coman, J. 1987, 'Reporting Indonesia: An Australian Perspective', in P. Tickell (ed.), *The Indonesian Press: Its Past, Its People, Its Problems*, Monash Asia Institute, Melbourne.

Cribb, R. & Brown, C. 1995, *Modern Indonesia: A History since 1945*, Longman, London.

Crouch, H. 1988a, *The Army and Politics in Indonesia*, revised edn, Cornell University Press, Ithaca, NY.

—— 1988b, 'General Try Sutrisno', *Inside Indonesia*, no. 15, July, pp. 7–8.

—— 1994, 'Democratic Prospects in Indonesia', in D. Bourchier & J. Legge, *Democracy in Indonesia*, Monash Papers on South East Asia, no. 31, Centre of Southeast Asian Studies, Monash University, Melbourne, pp. 115–27.

—— 1986, 'Internal Power Jockeying Fans Indonesia's Jitters', *Age*, 16 September.

Dahl, R. 1971, *Who Governs?*, Yale University Press, New Haven, Conn.

Defence of Democracy Groups 1985, 'Suharto Challenges the Human Conscience', *Inside Indonesia*, no. 6, December, pp. 3–5.

Department of Foreign Affairs and Trade 1993, *Human Rights Manual*, AGPS, Canberra.

Dhakidae, D. 1992, Language, Journalism, and Politics in Modern Indonesia, paper presented to Democracy in Indonesia, 1950s and 1990s conference, Centre of South East Asian Studies, Monash University, Melbourne, 17–20 December.

Dharsono, H. R. 1986, 'Dharsono's Defence Plea', *Inside Indonesia*, no. 7, May, p. 8.

Donnelly, S. 1984, 'Human Rights and Development: Complementary or Competing Concerns?', *World Politics*, vol. 36, no. 2, January.

Drake, C. 1989, *National Integration in Indonesia: Patterns and Policies*, University of Hawaii Press, Honolulu.

—— 1991, 'Indonesia: Still Stamping on the Cockroaches', *Index on Censorship*, vol. 20, no. 7, July 1991.

Dunn, J. 1983, *Timor: A People Betrayed*, The Jacaranda Press, Brisbane.

—— 1995, *East Timor: The Balibo Incident In Perspective*, Australian Centre for Independent Journalism, Sydney, 1995.

Emerson, T. 1970, *The System of Freedom of Expression*, Vintage Books, New York.

Evans, G. 1993, *Asia's Cultural Mosaic: An Anthropological Introduction*, Simon & Schuster, Singapore.

Evans-Pritchard, E. E. 1969, *Social Anthropology*, Cohen & West Ltd, London.

Feith, H. 1962, *The Decline of Constitutional Democracy in Indonesia*, Cornell University Press, Ithaca, NY.

—— 1964, 'Indonesia', in G. Kahin (ed.), *Governments and Politics of Southeast Asia*, 2nd edn, Cornell University Press, Ithaca, NY.

—— 1978, *The Indonesian Student Movement of 1977–78*, Centre of South East Asian Studies, Monash University, Melbourne.

—— 1980, 'Legitimacy Questions and the Suharto Policy', in J. Fox, et al. (eds), *Indonesia: Australian Perspectives*, The Research School of Pacific Studies, Australian National University, Canberra.

—— 1989, 'Suharto under Pressure', *Inside Indonesia*, no. 19, April, pp. 2–4.

Feith, H. & Castles, L. 1970, *Indonesian Political Thinking, 1945–1965*, Cornell University Press, Ithaca, NY.

Foley, W. 1980, 'History of Migrations', in J. Fox et al. (eds), *Indonesia: Australian Perspectives*, The Research School of Pacific Studies, Australian National University, Canberra.

Fox, J., Garnaut, R., McCauley, P., & Mackie, J. (eds) 1980, *Indonesia: Australian Perspectives*, The Research School of Pacific Studies, Australian National University, Canberra.

Gadamer, H-G. 1979, *Truth and Method*, 2nd edn, Sheed & Ward Ltd, London.

Geertz, C. 1960, *The Religion of Java*, The Free Press, Glencoe, Ill.

—— 1963, *Agricultural Involution: The Process of Ecological Change in Indonesia*, University of California Press, Berkeley.

—— 1983, *Local Knowledge*, Basic Books, New York.

—— 1989, *Works and Lives: The Anthropologist as Author*, Polity Press, Cambridge.

—— 1993, *The Interpretation of Cultures*, Fontana Press, London.

Giddens, A. 1987, *Social Theory and Modern Sociology*, Polity Press, Cambridge.

Goodenough, W. H. 1970, *Description and Comparison in Cultural Anthropology*, Cambridge University Press, New York.

Goodin, R. 1979, 'The Development–Rights Trade-off: Some Unwarranted Economic and Political Assumptions', *Universal Human Rights*, vol. 1, no. 2, April–June.

Gramsci, A. 1971, *Selections from Prison Notebooks*, ed. & trans. Q. Hoare & G. N. Smith, Lawrence & Wishart, London.

Grant, B. 1996 (1964), *Indonesia*, 3rd edn, Melbourne University Press, Melbourne.

Gunawan Mohamad 1995, 'Opening Old Wounds', *Inside Indonesia*, no. 44, September, pp. 30–2.

Hadad, I. 1989, *Political Culture and Social Justice in Indonesia*, ed. A. Cominos, Southeast Asian Monograph series, no. 29, Centre for Southeast Asian Studies, James Cook University, Townsville, Qld.

Hadiz, V. 1994, 'The Political Significance of Recent Working Class Action in Indonesia', in D. Bourchier (ed.), *Indonesia's Emerging Proletariat: Workers and their Struggles*, Annual Indonesia Lecture series, Centre of Southeast Asian Studies, Monash University, Melbourne.

Hallpike, C. R. 'Some Problems in Cross-cultural Comparison', in T. O. Beidelman (ed.), *The Translation of Culture: Essays to E. E. Evans-Pritchard*, Tavistock Publications, London.

Heine-Geldern, R. 1942, 'Conceptions of State and Kinship in Southeast Asia' *Far Eastern Quarterly*, vol. 2, 1942, pp. 15–30.

Hettne, B. 1990, *Development Theory and the Three Worlds*, Longman Development Studies, Harlow, Essex.

Hidayat Djajamihardja 1987, Reporting Indonesia: An Indonesian Journalist's Perspective', in P. Tickell (ed.), *The Indonesian Press: Its Past, Its People, Its Problems*, Monash Asia Institute, Melbourne.

Hill, D. 1991, *The Press in New Order Indonesia: Entering the 1990s*, Asia Research Centre, Murdoch University, Perth.

Hill, D. & Sen, K. 1991, 'How Jakarta Saw the Massacre', *Inside Indonesia*, no. 29, December, pp. 6–8.

Hill, H. (ed.) 1994, *Indonesia's New Order*, Allen & Unwin, Sydney.

Hindley, D. 1964, *The Communist Party of Indonesia*, University of California Press, Berkeley.

—— 1967, 'Political Power and the October 1965 Coup in Indonesia', *Journal of Asian Studies*, no. 26, February.

Horne, J. C. 1974, *Javanese–English Dictionary*, Yale University Press, New Haven, Conn.

Howard, R. 1983, 'The Full Bellies Thesis', *Human Rights Quarterly*, vol. 5, no. 4, November.

Huus, K. 1997, 'Click Through the Suharto Clique: A Guide to the Family Empire', MSNBC (Microsoft/National Broadcasting Corporation) <http://library.msnbc.com/commerce.indonesia.31889:asp> 16 February.

Indonesia Resources and Information Programme News Service 1991, *Inside Indonesia*, no. 29, December, p. 4.

Indonesian Human Rights Forum 1991, *Background Report: Freedom of the Press*, LBHI, Jakarta.

Inside Indonesia 1992, no. 32, September, pp. 5–6.

—— 1993, no. 34, March, p. 5.

Institut Studi Arus Informasi 1995, *Bayang-Bayang PKI*, ISAI no. 01/95, Percetakan PT Intermasa, Jakarta.

IRIP News Service. See Indonesia Resources and Information Programme News Service.

—— 1995, *Inside Indonesia*, no. 45, December 1995, pp. 17–20.

'Jakarta Dismisses Torture Photos' 1997, *Sunday Age*, 23 November, p. 12.

Jenkins, D. 1984, *Soeharto and his Generals: Indonesian Military Politics 1975–1983*, Cornell University Press, Ithaca, NY.

—— 1986, 'After Marcos, Now for the Soeharto Billions', *Sydney Morning Herald*, 10 April, pp. 1, 7.

Jolliffe, J. 1978, *East Timor: Nationalism and Colonialism*, University of Queensland Press, St Lucia.

Kahin G. McT. (ed.) 1964, *Governments and Politics of Southeast Asia*, 2nd edn, Cornell University Press, Ithaca, NY.

Kingsbury, D. 1993, 'Looking After No. 1', *The Bulletin*, 6 April, p. 24.

—— 1994, 'Political Showdown', *Inside Indonesia*, no. 38, March, pp. 5–6.

—— 1997a, *Culture and Politics: Issues in Australian Journalism on Indonesia, 1975–93*, Australia–Asia Papers, no. 80, Centre for the Study of Australia–Asia Relations, Griffith University, Brisbane.

—— 1997b, 'Motor Industry in Indonesia Follows a Different Road', *Business Motoring*, May, pp. 33–7.

Koentjaraningrat 1985, *Javanese Culture*, Institute of Southeast Asian Studies, in association with Oxford University Press, Oxford.

Kohen, A. & Taylor, J. 1979, *An Act of Genocide: Indonesia's Invasion of East Timor*, Tapol, London.

Krisna 1995, 'Soldiering in Irian Jaya', *Inside Indonesia*, no. 45, December.

Lambert, R. 1993, *Authoritarian State Unionism in New Order Indonesia*, Working Paper no. 25, Asia Research Centre, Murdoch University, Perth.

Lane, M. 1986, 'Why Sinar Harapan Was Silenced', *Inside Indonesia*, no. 9, December, pp. 6–7.

—— 1988, 'Suharto Consolidates Ruling Clique', *Inside Indonesia*, no. 15, July, pp. 2–6.

—— 1989, 'Challenge to Suharto', *Inside Indonesia*, no. 20, October, pp. 2–3.

—— 1991, *'Openness', Political Discontent and Succession in Indonesia: Political developments in Indonesia, 1989–91*, Australia–Asia Papers, no. 56, Centre for the Study of Australia–Asia Relations, Griffith University, Brisbane.

Liddle, R. W. 1992, Can All Good Things Go Together? Democracy, Growth, and Unity in Post-Soeharto Indonesia, paper presented to Indonesian Democracy in the 1950s and 1990s conference, Centre of Southeast Asian Studies, Monash University, Melbourne, 17–20 December.

—— 1996, *Leadership and Culture in Indonesian Politics*, Allen & Unwin, Sydney.

Loveard, K. 1996, 'Suharto's Son Rises', *Asiaweek*, 12 April 1996.

Lowry, R. 1996, *The Armed Forces in Indonesia*, Allen & Unwin, Sydney.

Lukes, S. 1974, *Power: A Radical View*, Macmillan, London.

McCarthy, J. 1993, Australian Observer delegation, World Conference on Human Rights, Regional Meeting for Asia, Bangkok, 29 March–2 April.

MacFarling, I. 1996, *The Dual Function of the Indonesian Armed Forces: Military Politics in Indonesia*, Australian Defence Studies Centre, Canberra.

Mackie, J. 1996, 'After the Revolusi: Indonesia 1956–58', in A. Lucas (ed.), *Half a Century of Indonesian–Australian Interaction*, Flinders University Asian Studies Monograph series, no. 6, Flinders University, Adelaide.

Mackie, J. & MacIntyre, A. 1994, 'Politics', in H. Hill (ed.), *Indonesia's New Order*, Allen & Unwin, Sydney, pp. 1–53.

McIntyre, A. 1996, *Soeharto's Composure: Considering the Biographical and Autobiographical Accounts*, Working Paper, no. 97, Centre of Southeast Asian Studies, Monash University, Melbourne.

Mangunwijaya, Y. B. 1992, Some Notes about the Indonesia Raya Dream of the Indonesian Nationalists and its Impact on the Concept of Democracy among the Ruling Elites in Indonesia, paper presented to Indonesian Democracy in the 1950s and 1990s conference, Centre of Southeast Asian Studies, Monash University, Melbourne, 17–20 December.

Marx, K. 1977, *The Eighteenth Brumaire of Louis Bonaparte*, Progress Publishers, Moscow.

Mayall, J. 1978, 'International Society and International Theory', in M. Donelan (ed.), *Reason of States*, George Allen & Unwin, London.

Merleau-Ponty, M. 1964, *Signs*, trans. & preface R. McCleary, Northwestern University Press, Evanston.

McIntyre, A. 1996, In Search of Megawati Sukarnoputri, unpublished draft paper.

McMichael, H. 1987, *Indonesian Foreign Policy: Towards a More Assertive Style*, Australia–Asia Papers, no. 40, Centre for the Study of Australia–Asia Relations, Griffith University, Brisbane.

Milne, J. 1989, 'Australia Indonesia Media Relations: How to Bridge the Gap', *Pelongi*, vol. 5, no. 3, pp. 3–4.

Missen, G. 1972, *Viewpoints on Indonesia*, Nelson, Melbourne.

Moedjanto, G. 1993, *The Concept of Power in Javanese Culture*, Gadjah Mada University Press, Jogjakarta.

Moertono, S. 1981, *State and Statecraft in Old Java*, Monograph Series, no. 34, Modern Indonesia Project, Cornell University, Ithaca, NY.

Mortimer, R. 1971, 'Unresolved Problems of the Indonesian Coup', *Australian Outlook*, no. 25, April.

Muhammad Yamin 1970 (1945), 'Unity of Our Country and Our People' in H. Feith & L. Castles (eds), *Indonesian Political Thinking 1945–1965*, Cornell University Press, Ithaca, NY.

Murdoch, L. 1996, 'Suharto Fortune Expands with the Family', *Age*, 3 August 1996, p. 1.

Nasution, B. 1993a, 'Human Rights Have an Indonesian History', *Inside Indonesia*, no. 34, March, pp. 8–9.

—— 1993b, interview with author, Jakarta, 24 December.

Nono Anwar Makarim 1978, 'Indonesian Press', noted in K. D. Jackson & I. Proudfoot, 'The Early Indianised States of Indonesia: Religion and Social Control', in J. Fox (ed.), *Indonesia: The Making of a Culture*, Research School of Pacific Studies, Australian National University, Canberra.

Nuim Khaiyath 1992, personal conversation, Melbourne, 24 April.

OPM. See Organisasi Papua Merdeka.

Organisasi Papua Merdeka 1997, 'The West Papuan Case—Human Rights Abuses', *OPM Homepage* <http://www.twics.com/-boyjah/westpapua/human rights.html> 10 September 1997.

Organisation for Economic Co-operation and Development 1987, *Financing and External Debt of Developing Countries: 1986 Survey*, OECD, Paris.

'Overstepping the Mark' 1986, *Far Eastern Economic Review*, 8 May, pp. 44–5.

Palmer, R. 1969, *Hermeneutics*, Northwestern University Press, Evanston.

Pemberton, J. 1994, *On the Subject of 'Java'*, Cornell University Press, Ithaca, NY.

PERC. See Political and Economic Risk Consultancy Ltd.

Pirenne, H. 1936, *A History of Europe*, George Allen and Unwin, London.

Polak, J. 1989, *Financial Policies and Development*, Development Centre, Organisation for Economic Co-operation and Development, Paris.

Political and Economic Risk Consultancy Ltd 1997, *Country Risk Report: Indonesia*, 4 November, PERC, Hong Kong.

Press Act of Indonesia (n.d.), Department of Information, Republic of Indonesia, Jakarta.

Proudfoot, I. 1980, 'The Early Indianized States of Indonesia: Religion and Social Control', in J. Fox, et al. (eds), *Indonesia: Australian Perspectives*, The Research School of Pacific Studies, Australian National University, Canberra, pp. 151–62.

Pye, L. 1985, *Asian Power and Politics: The Cultural Dimension of Authority*, Harvard University Press, Cambridge, Mass.

—— (ed.) 1978, *Political Power and Communication in Indonesia*, University of California Press, Berkeley.

Raman, M. 1985, 'A New World Information and Communication Order—A Third World Perspective', paper to World Press Convention of the Confederation of ASEAN Journalists, Kuala Lumpur, 18–20 September 1985.

Rawls, J. 1991, *A Theory of Justice*, Oxford University Press, Oxford.

Reuter 1992, *Age*, 9 November, p. 8.

—— 1993, 'General Raps West's View of E Timor', *Age*, 9 November, p. 8.

—— 1995, 'Indonesia Rules Out New Probe', *Sunday Age*, 22 October, p. 11.

Rickard, D. 1988, 'Suharto's Human Rights Record', *Inside Indonesia*, no. 17, December, pp. 10–12.

Ricklefs, M. 1993a, *History of Modern Indonesia since c. 1300*, 2nd edn, Macmillan, London.

—— 1993b, *War, Culture and Economy in Java 1677–1726*, Asian Studies Association of Australia, no. 24, Allen & Unwin, Sydney.

Ricoeur, P. 1981, *Hermeneutics and the Human Science*, Cambridge University Press, Cambridge.

—— 1984, *The Reality of the Historical Past*, Marquette University Press, Milwaukee.

Robison, R. 1981, 'Culture, Politics and Economy in the Political History of the New Order', *Indonesia*, no. 31, April, pp. 1–31.

—— 1985, 'Class, Capital and the State in New Order Indonesia', in R. Higgott & R. Robison, *South East Asia: Essays in the Political Economy of Structural Change*, Routledge & Kegan Paul, London.

—— 1986, *Indonesia: The Rise of Capital*, Allen & Unwin, Sydney.

—— 1997, 'Politics and Markets in Indonesia's Post-oil Era', in G. Rodan, K. Hewison, & R. Robison, *The Political Economy of South-East Asia*, Oxford University Press, Melbourne.

Robison, R., Hewison, K., & Higgott, R. (eds) 1987, *South East Asia in the 1980s: The Politics of Economic Crisis*, Allen & Unwin, Sydney.

Rodan, G, Hewison, K., & Robison, R. 1997, *The Political Economy of South-East Asia*, Oxford University Press, Melbourne.

Rogers, P. 1982, *The Domestic and Foreign Press in Indonesia: 'Free But Responsible'?*, Australia–Asia Papers, no. 18, Centre for the Study of Australia–Asia Relations, Griffith University, Brisbane.

Said, E. 1991, *Orientalism*, Penguin Books, London.

Samson, A. A. 1978, 'Conceptions of Politics, Power, and Ideology in Contemporary Indonesian Islam', in K. D. Jackson & W. P. Lucian (eds), *Political Power and Communication in Indonesia*, University of California Press, Berkeley.

Schwartz, A. 1994, *A Nation in Waiting: Indonesia in the 1990s*, Allen & Unwin, Sydney.

Selochan, V. 1992, *New Directions and New Thinking in Australian–Southeast Asia Relations*, Australia–Asia Papers, no. 62, Centre for the Study of Australia–Asia Relations, Griffith University, Brisbane.

Serril, M. 1994, 'Limits of Tolerance', *Time*, 11 July, p. 43.

Sheridan, G. 1993, 'Suharto Steps into the Role of Statesman', *Australian*, 31 March, p. 9.

Sitompoel, H. 1993, *Sunday Observer*, Jakarta, 26 December.

Soejipto Wirosardjono 1992, Reform Agenda for the 1990s: Interpretation to [*sic.*] Current Turn of Events, unpublished paper, Melbourne.

Sri Bintang Pamungkas 1995, 'Demanding our Democracy', *Inside Indonesia*, no. 44, September, pp. 2–5.

Stackhouse, J. 1986, 'Anatomy of Australia's First Solo Foreign Affairs Crisis', *Bulletin*, 13 May, pp. 26–8.

Subrata 1993, Interview with the author, Jakarta, 23 December.

Suharto 1989, *Suharto: Pikiran, Upacan dan Tindakan Saya*, PT Citra Lantoro Gung Persada, Jakarta.

Supomo Suryohudojo 1970, 'Javanese Traditionalism', in H. Feith & L. Castles (eds), *Indonesian Political Thinking 1945–1965*, Cornell University Press, Ithaca, NY.

—— 1980, 'Rebellion in the Kraton World', in J. Fox et al. (eds), *Indonesia: Australian Perspectives*, Research School of Pacific Studies, Australian National University, Canberra.

Taylor, J. 1991, *Indonesia's Forgotten War: The Hidden History of East Timor*, Zed Books, London.

Thatcher, J. 1991, 'Indonesia Dispute Erupts as Try Rejects Debate', *Age*, 12 December, p. 9.

Tickell, P. (ed.) 1987, *The Indonesian Press: Its Past, Its People, Its Problems*, Monash Asia Institute, Melbourne.

—— 1992, Free From What? Responsible To Whom? The Problem of Democracy and the Indonesian Press, paper presented to the Indonesian Democracy in the 1950s and 1990s conference, Centre of South East Asian Studies, Monash University, Melbourne, 19 December.

Todorov, T. 1986, '"Race", Writing and Culture', trans. L. Mack, in H. Gates (ed.), *'Race', Writing and Difference*, University of Chicago Press, London.

Transparency International and Goettingen University 1996, *Internet Corruption Perception Index—1996* <http://www.transparency.de/> 23 May 1998.

Treasury & Australian International Development Assistance Bureau 1989, *Debt and the Developing World*, AGPS, Canberra.

Tsing, A. 1987, 'A Rhetoric of Centres in a Religion of the Periphery', in R. Kipp & S. Rogers (eds), *Indonesian Religions in Transition*, University of Arizona Press, Phoenix.

Tuckey, B. 1997, 'Orbital Cranks up for Indonesian Project', *Business Review Weekly*, 7 July, p. 35.

Turner, B. 1993, *The Management of Tensions: Relations between President Suharto, the Armed Forces and Muslim Groups in the Period February 1988 to May 1993*, research report, Deakin University, Geelong, Vic.

United Nations Educational, Scientific and Cultural Organisation 1978, *Declaration on Fundamental Principles concerning the Contribution of the Mass Media to Strengthening Peace and International Understanding, to the Promotion of Human Rights and to Countering Racialism, Apartheid and Incitement to War*, UNESCO, Paris.

United States Department of State 1997, *Indonesia Report on Human Rights Practices for 1996*, United States Department of State, Washington.

van Klinken, G. 1997a, 'Tinder-Box or Conspiracy?', *Inside Indonesia*, no. 50, April–June, pp. 6–8.

—— 1997b, 'Suharto Returns to Army Roots', *Inside Indonesia*, Internet Digest, no. 41 <http://www.pactok.net.au/docs/inside/index.htm> 13 September.

Vatikiotis, M. 1992, 'Party and Parliamentary Politics in Indonesia 1987–1993', paper presented to Conference on Indonesian Democracy in the 1950s and

1990s, Centre of South East Asian Studies, Monash University, Melbourne, 17–20 December.

—— 1993, *Indonesian Politics under Suharto*, Routledge, London.

Waddingham, J. 1987, 'Why the 1986 Executions', *Inside Indonesia*, no. 11, August, pp. 11–12.

Walters, P. 1997, 'Indonesians Halt $55bn in Infrastructure Development', *Australian*, 24 September, p. 8.

Waters, B. 1993, 'The Tragedy of Marsinah', *Inside Indonesia*, no. 36, September, p. 12.

Weber, M. 1964, *The Theory of Social and Economic Organisation*, ed. T. Parsons, The Free Press, New York.

Wertheim, W. (n.d.), 'Indonesia's Hidden History of 1965: When Will the Archives Be Declassified?', *Kabar Seberang Sulating Maphilindo*, nos 24–5, pp. 284–306.

Whorf, B. 1956, *Language, Thought and Reality: Selected Writings of Benjamin Lee Whorf*, ed. J. Carroll, The MIT Press, Cambridge, Mass.

Widjojanto, B. 1993, Interview with the author, Jakarta, 20 December.

Williams, H. 1992, *International Relations in Political Theory*, Open University Press, Milton Keynes.

Williams, L. 1997a, 'Indonesian Troops Out in Force for Poll', *Age*, 29 May, p. 13.

—— 1997b, 'Jakarta Police Free Australian Unionists', *Age*, 22 September, p. 3.

—— 1997c, 'Strife-Torn Indonesia Goes to Polls', *Age*, 30 May, p. 11.

Willner, A. R. 1970, 'Indonesia', in L. W. Pye (ed.), *Cases in Comparative Politics in Asia*, Little Brown & Company, Boston.

Winters, J. 1996, *Power in Motion: Capital Mobility and the Indonesian State*, Cornell University Press, Ithaca, NY.

Wittfogel, K. 1957, *Oriental Despotism*, Yale University Press, New Haven, Conn.

Woodman, D. 1955, *The Republic of Indonesia*, The Crescent Press, London.

Wright-Neville, D. 1993, *Asian Culture, Asian Politics and Asian Diplomacy: Problems in Theorising*, Working Paper no. 3, Centre for International Relations, Politics Department, Monash University, Melbourne.

Zainud'din, A. 1975, *Indonesia*, Longman Modern Times series, Longman, Melbourne.

INDEX

ABRI: *AB* (newspaper), 115, 116; administrative structure, 52–3; and industrial disputes, 189–90; and militant wing of Indonesian Islam, 143–5; and the Petition of Fifty, 110; anti-PKI killings over attempted coup, 57–8, 63, 103; as guardian of the state, 52; bans state lottery, 122, 222; books on, 261; 'corrupt generals' within, 102, 104; coup plans, 240–1; criticism of Australia, 116; crushes PRRI–Permesta rebellion, 55; dislike of Habibie, 244; dispute with Suharto and Habibie over warship purchase, 157, 158; dissatisfaction with Suharto, 74, 103, 108, 111, 113, 118–19, 121–2, 123–6, 201, 222; distrust of PKI, 56, 59; dual function, 7–9, 52; factional manœuvring, 219–20; factions and 'clusters' within, 123–6; financial enhancement, 79; foundation, 35; 'functional groups', 51; generals, split with Suharto, 103–6; 'green' faction, 123, 251; nominates Try Sutrisno as vice-president, 121–2; opposition to Sudharmono, 73–4, 113, 118; political groupings and leaders, 224–7; political tensions within, 82; presidential succession candidates, 219, 220, 221; reassertion of authority, 120–3; 'red and white' faction, 123, 126, 184, 219, 220, 221, 230, 253; representation on MPR and DPR, 120–2; response to East Timor protesters, 119; response to student protests, 250–1; role in

government, 110, 113, 118; Social and Political Affairs office, 226; support for Megawati Sukarnoputri, 122, 224; support of Suharto, 7–8, 99
absolute poverty, 89, 92, 179
Aceh Merdeka, 165, 184, 185
Aceh Province, 27, 28, 33–4, 39, 143; human rights violations, 166, 184–5; separatist movement, 9–10, 128, 165–6
Alitas, Ali, 100, 179
All-Indonesia Workers' Union (SPSI), 187
Amnesty International, 166, 168, 183, 185, 191, 192, 195, 196
Anderson, Ben, 24, 41, 261, 262
Anglo-Dutch Treaty 1824, 31
animism, 18–19, 20, 23, 28, 43
anti-corruption measures, 200–1
anti-government criticism, 190, 191, 195
anti-government rioting, 251
anti-Javanese sentiment, 39, 174, 248
Anti-Subversion Law, 195
Apkindo, 206
Ariwibowo, Tunky, 216
armed forces, 3, 6; business activities, 101; dual function, 7–9; internal tensions within, 60; oust Sukarno loyalist forces, 66; policy differences to PKI, 59; political role, 5; size of, 69; strengthening of power, 1957, 52; unease over Suharto's grab for power, 66–7; *see also* ABRI
ASEAN, 5, 101, 113
Asia Watch, 155

Asia-Pacific Economic Cooperation (APEC), 216
'Asian values' debate, 178, 247
Association of Private Radio Stations, 151
Association of South East Asian Nations (ASEAN), 5, 101, 113
Australia, diplomatic dispute with, 26, 85–6, 111, 114–16, 150–1, 200
Australian journalists, expulsion, 85–6, 117
Australian tourists, cancellation of visa-free entry, 115
Australian troops, 44

Bahasa Indonesia: additional 'social realism' words, 41; as national language, 40–1
Bahasa Melayu, 41
Baker, Mark, 157, 158
Bakin (State Intelligence Coordinating Body), 66, 115
Bali: Dutch occupation, 34; Hinduism, 20–1, 28
Bambang Trihatmodjo, 96, 151, 152, 204–5, 207, 213, 230, 233; Golkar treasurer, 224; Hyundai car production, 211–12
Bank Alfa, 96
Bank Andromeda, 96
banking, 50, 207, 214; deregulation, 86; lack of controls on, 92, 95
Bantuan Presiden, 83
Batak peoples, 174
Belo, Bishop Carlos, 169
'Berkeley Group' influence, 78–9, 82, 86, 97
Bimantara Cakra Nusa car company, 211–12
Bimantara Group, 204, 212
Bintang Indonesia, 152
Bourchier, David, 36
bribery, official, 78
British troops, 44
Brown, Colin, 260
building development, 131; Jakarta, 88
Bush, George, 85, 117

Cabinet: appointed by president, 72; powers, 36–7; 'reform', 252, 253
Caldwell, Malcolm, 260
cannibalism, 165

car industry, 209–12, 213, 214; car sales, 215; international objections, 215–18
Castles, L., 260
censorship, 147, 153, 154–5
Central Javanese traditions: and national culture, 40; as guidance for Indonesian government, 37–8, 68–9
Central National Committee, 36
Centre for Information and Development Studies (CIDES), 131
Centre for Strategic and International Studies (CSIS), 131, 141
Chinese community, see ethnic Chinese community
Christian-animism, 28
Cipta Lamtoro Gung Persada, 151
civil and political rights, 177, 186
Code of Criminal Procedure, 195
colonialism, and religious influence, 27–9
communism: definition, 190–1; suppression of, 181; see also PKI
company tax-payers, 208
Confucian values, 178
consensus politics, 50–1; under Suharto, 68–9
conspiracy theories, 114–20
Constitution (1945), 4, 36, 72, 158; and Pancasila, 42–3; freedom of the media, 148; presidential and Cabinet powers, 36–7; readoption in 1959, 37, 194
Constitution (1950), 193
corruption, 3, 15, 84; anti-corruption campaign and the Indonesian economy, 235–6; anti-corruption measures, 200; in Indonesia, 198; in legal system, 194; Indonesian response to Sydney Morning Herald report, 85–6; institutionalised, 68, 78, 92, 95, 97, 198–9; Javanese interpretation, 199; poverty and Islam, 111–12, 201–2; public concerns over, 103, 107–8; public service, 200–1; Suharto, 85–6, 103, 109, 114, 115, 116, 117, 118, 199–202; Suharto business/financial friends, 15, 81; Suharto first family, 15, 200, 201, 202, 208, 209–13, 218
cost of living, 91
coup, alleged (30 September 1965): Suharto's knowledge of, 61–2; theories, 57–61
Cribb, Robert, 260

criminal law codes, 190, 195
criminals, 192–3
cronies, *see* Suharto business/financial friends
Crouch, Harold, 124, 261
cultural politics, 4
cultuurstelsel, consequences, 32–3
currency collapse, 88, 92, 95, 97, 205, 208, 218, 235

Dar'ul Islam rebellion, 47–8, 54, 130, 143
Darusman, Marzuki, 217
Dayak people, and Madurese, 163–5
death squads, 192
defamation (of the president), 191, 195, 222; definition, 190
defence, 111, 140, 157, 158, 228
democratisation, 247–9
Deutero-Malay people, 18
development projects, 11
Dewan Perwakilan Rakyat (DPR): ABRI representation, 121; and the MPR, 72–4; elections, 72, 98, 108, 108–9, 128, 130, 132, 139, 173, 240; restrictions on political parties, 108; structure, 72
Dhakidae, Daniel, 149
Dharsono, Lt General Hartono Rekso, 104, 108; criticism of Suharto, 113–14
Dili massacre, 114, 119–20, 121, 157, 170, 172, 181, 182–3; Santa Cruz Cemetery, 156, 170, 173, 182
Diponegoro, Prince, 31, 42
dissidents, 190–2
Dita Indahsari, 138, 190, 191
Djody, Setiawan, 211
Djojohadikusomo, Hashim, 205, 226
Djojohadikusomo, Sumitro, 226
domestic politics, division in, 99–126
DPR, *see* Dewan Perwakilan Rakyat
Drake, Christine, 93
dry-field rice growing, 18
Dutch colonialism, 17–18, 28, 29, 30–5
Dutch military forces, 44, 45
Dutch property, nationalisation of, 52, 54
Dutch United East India Company (VOC), 30, 31
Dutch: administration, 35, 39; agree to formation of RUSI, 46; and the *prijaji*, 32; debt passed onto new

Republic, 46; 'Ethical Policy', 34; exploit divisions between Javanese royal households, 30–1; influence of the, 30–5; introduce *cultuurstelsel*, 32–3; military attacks, 45–6; political hegemony, 33–4; postwar negotiations, 45; retain sovereignty postwar, 44; trade routes, 30, 31

East Asian economic boom, 87
East Indies: Dutch administration, 35; Dutch domination, 30–4
East Timor, 39, 108, 169–74; armed conflict, 170, 171, 183; high military presence, 170–1; human rights violations, 170, 180–4; Indonesian dominance of local economy, 172–3, 183; Indonesian interest in, 26; Indonesia's occupation of, 9, 10, 169; International Committee for the Red Cross office, 196; military response, 119–20, 181–3, 184; planned invasion of, 106–7, 119–20; rioting, December 1994, 183–4; tourism, 173; *see also* Dili massacre; Fretilin
economic decline: under Suharto, 84, 85; under Sukarno, 6, 56; *see also* currency collapse
economic development: and Pertamina scandal, 79–81, 82, 84; banking and taxation reform, 86; based on oil revenue, 6, 77, 81, 83, 84, 85, 86; 'Berkeley Group' influence, 78–9, 82, 86; buying support, 77–81; IMF and World Bank credits, 78; IMF rescue package, 96–7, 217; investment crisis, 1984, 85; nationalistic approach, 81–5; private investment, 78; roller coaster ride, 85–8; under Suharto, 68, 77–98
economic growth, 15, 88, 91–2; post-Sukarno, 6–7
economic indicators, 91–3
economic performance, analysis, 88–93
economic policies, as ideological perspective, 93–8
economic problems, 1949–57, 49–50
Edi Sudrajat, General, 158, 167, 230, 233
education, 11, 89
election campaigns, regulation, 71–2, 108, 129

elections 1978, 108
elections 1982–83, 108–9
elections 1997–78, 72, 98, 128, 130, 132, 139, 143, 173, 219, 240
electoral system: overhaul, 108; protests over, 132–3
ethnic Chinese community, 83, 143, 229; dislike of, 12, 235; Muhammadiyah criticism of, 142; riots aimed at, 49, 82, 104, 164, 250
Expo, 154
exports, 51, 84

Falintil guerillas, 170, 171, 173, 182, 184
Fatwa, Haji A. M., 112
Feisal Tanjung, General, 123, 135, 224–5, 226, 232
Feith, Herb, 50, 260
Five Power Defence Arrangement, 111
foreign debt, 92, 95, 97
foreign influence, on Indonesia, 5–6
foreign investment, 50, 77, 81, 87, 156, 167; and crony business practices, 208; and economic growth, 15; and economic instability, 235; cessation of, 52; 'Timor' car concerns, 212, 216
foreign media, 85–6, 117, 150–1, 156, 160
foreign ownership, riots over, 82, 104
foreign relations, 85–6, 100–1, 111, 114–16, 150–1; and human rights issues, 176–7
foreign reserves, 84
Forum Demokrasi, 123, 135
'Fosko', 108, 109
Free Papua Movement (OPM), 10, 166–9, 185, 186, 227; and ABRI, 167, 168
Freeport mine, Irian Jaya, 167, 208
Fretilin, 10, 107, 120, 170, 171, 172, 181, 184
'functional groups', 51; *see also* Golkar

GDP, 92, 93, 215
Geertz, Clifford, 11, 19–20, 56, 262
generals, death of (alleged 30 September coup), 58, 60, 61, 102
Golkar, 51, 67, 89, 140, 146; advantages over 'rival' parties, 71; as the effective party of government, 70; Bambang

Trihatmodjo elected as treasurer, 224; executive board, 224; Habibie elected to board of management, 224; loss of ABRI support, 222; Suharto control of, 74, 112, 224; Tutut elected as vice-chairperson, 224
Golkar leaders, media ownership, 151–2
government employees, voting requirements, 71
government, definition, viii
government-directed enterprises, economic support, 83–4
Grant, Bruce, 54, 259
Great Britain, colonial expansion, 31
Guided Democracy, 35, 43, 52–6; and martial law, 52; and readoption of 1945 Constitution, 37, 194; introduction, 52; *mufakat* 53; Sukarno's idea of, 51; suppression of the media, 153
Gumelar, General Agum, 231, 232
Gus Dur, 123, 137, 233, 239, 254; as leader of NU, 133–5, 140, 141; criticism of government, 139–40; criticism of Megawati, 140–1; supports Suharto in 1998 election, 234
Gusmao, Xanana, 172

Habibie, Bucharuddin, 74, 101, 122, 134, 221; as head of ICMI, 142, 143; as president, 228, 243, 244, 246, 252; as presidential candidate, 220, 228; as vice-president, 228, 229, 234, 242, 244, 252; high-technology projects, 228–9, 253; management of Golkar board of management, 224; nuclear reactor proposal, 228; political survival, 254; purchase of East German warships, 140, 157, 158, 228; reform credentials, 254; unpopularity of, 244, 252, 253
Hamengkubuwono, Sultan of Yogyakarta, 200
Hamid, Syarwan, 252
Harmoko, 101, 134, 140, 151, 154, 157, 221, 225, 229, 251, 252; party chairperson, 224
Hartono, Lt General Raden, 134, 221; ABRI factional group, 225; political aspirations, 242–3
Haryanto, Petrus, 138, 191
Hassan, Bob, 206, 216, 252

Hatta, 36, 46
head-hunting and cannibalism, 165
Hendropriyono, Major General A. M., 224, 230, 231, 232, 253
Hill, Hal, 90–1, 93, 95
Hinduism-Buddhism, 23
Hinduism, 20–1, 28
Hoegeng, General, 110
Horta, Jose Ramos, 169, 172
human rights; and diplomatic relations, 177; and Indonesian rights, 176, 178–9, 196–7; and right to development, 177, 179–80; as civil and political rights, 177; cross-cultural interpretation, 177–8; government initiatives, 195–6; United Nations interpretation, 179; human rights violations, 176, 180, 192; Aceh Province, 166, 184–5; East Timor, 170, 180–4; Irian Jaya, 168, 185–6
Humardhani, Sudjono, 82, 206
Hutomo Mandala Putra, see Suharto, Tommy

Ikatan Cendekiawan Muslem se Indonesia (ICMI), 14, 123, 131, 139, 142
imports, 5
income: and corruption, 202; and income distribution, 90, 92, 93, 201–2, 248; minimum wage, 187, 189
independence: Japanese preparations, 36; post-proclamation moves, 1945–49, 43–6
Indocement, 208
Indonesia Raya (newspaper), 150
Indonesia: anthropological view, 262; as a 'nation', 10–11; critiques on, 257–60; cuts defence links with Australia, 111; democratisation, 247–9; economic polices, ideological perspectives, 93–8; foreign relations, 100–1, 111; liberalisation under Habibie, 254–5; most corrupt country in Asia, 198; name origins, 35; national unity, 40, 163, 174–5, 248–9; political opposition within, 127–46; political structure, 72–4; regional role, 5, 101, 111
Indonesian Centre for Labour Struggle (PPBI), 138, 190
Indonesian Communist Party, see PKI

Indonesian economy, 259; after Suharto, 245; and oil-price boom, 6, 77, 81, 83, 84, 85; and Pertamina scandal, 79–81, 82, 84; and regional economic development, 87–8; IMF bail-out, 96–7, 217; ordinary Indonesians concern over, 98; performance analysis, 88–93, 95; roller coaster ride, 85–8; Suharto friends and family, influence, 74–5, 83–4, 235–6; World Bank report, 84–5; see also foreign investment
Indonesian Journalists' Union (PWI), 161
Indonesian Labour Union for Prosperity (SBSI), 188
Indonesian Legal Aid Foundation (LBHI), 139
Indonesian politics, as 'either–or' political style, 68–9
Indonesian Socialist Party, 226
Indonesian state, conception of, 39–42
Indonesian Times, 154
'Indonesianisation', 50
Indosat, 208
industrial relations, 187–8, 189–90
inflation, 56, 88, 91–2
Inside Indonesia, 263
Institute of Constitutional Awareness (LKB), 108, 109
institutionalised corruption, 68, 78, 92, 95, 97, 198–9
intelligence organisations, 66, 232
International Committee for the Red Cross, 196
International Monetary Fund (IMF), 78, 80, 92; economic bail-out, 96–7, 217
international recession, 84
Investigating Committee for the Preparation of Independence, 36
investment crisis, 1984, 85
Irian Jaya, 39; hostage release, 227; human rights violations, 168, 185–6; separatist movement, 10, 166–9; Sukarno's plan for occupation of, 61, 102, 106; tension between ABRI and Papuan people, 168–9; transmigration policy, 166–7
Islam, 23, 100; corruption and poverty, 111–12; role of, 12–14; spread of, 27–9; see also Muslims

Islamic organisations: non-political, 13–14, 35, 133–5, 139–43; political divisions, 49, 129–33
Islamic rebellion, 47–8, 130, 143–4
Islamic scholars, 133–5
Islamic terrorism, 144

Jakarta government, distrust of, 48
Jakarta Jakarta, 156, 157
Jakarta: as centre of power, 46–7, 249; building development, 88; newspaper closures, 154; riots, 82, 137, 191, 240, 247, 250–1; student protests, 251; wealthy elite, 241
Japan's economic growth, 87
Japanese occupation, 35–6
Japanese ownership, concerns over, 82, 104
Japanese: coopt proto-nationalist leaders, 36; establish Independence Committee, 36; training of auxiliary army, 35
Jasin, General, 109, 110
Java War (1825–30), 31
Java: Muslim groups, 13; pre-colonial, 4, 33; royal houses, 30–1
Javanese auxiliary army, 35
Javanese economy, and *cultuurstelsel*, 33
Javanese rulers, 14, 23
Javanese traditions, and government thinking, 37–8, 68–9
Javanese: centralism, 249; conception of appropriate political and social behaviour, 11; conceptions of power, 24–7, 101, 110; culture, 19–20, 21–2, 256; *halus* (behavioural form), 6, 19, 20, 37, 75, 100, 101; mythology, 21; religious influences, 18–19, 21; traditional influences, 17–18
Jenkins, David, 85, 109, 110, 111, 114–15, 116, 117, 118, 200, 261
Joedono, Satrio Budihardjo ('Billy'), 216
Jongkie Sugianto, 212
journalism, *Pancasila*, 147–9, 153, 157
journalists: and the *Press Act*, 160–1; sackings and arrests, 154, 156–7, 161
judiciary, ABRI/government interference in, 9, 194
Jufri, Fikri, 158
Jurnal Ekuin, 154

Kahin, G., 260
Kartasasmita, Ginanjar, 228, 229, 254
Kartosuwirjo, 48
kasekten, 25, 26, 75
Kemal Idris, 104, 113
Kia-Timor ('national' car) project, 209–12, 213, 214–15, 216, 217
Kim Woon Keun, 217
Kompas-Gramedia Group, 151
Kopkamtib, 65, 82, 105, 192
Kostrad: headed by Prabowo, 221, 226; headed by Suharto, 61–2, 102
Kotjo, Johannes, 204

Lampung incident, 144–5
Language: as unifying factor, 40; Bahasa Indonesia, 40–1; market Malay, 36, 40
Latief, Colonel Abdul, 61, 254
Law on Mass Organisation, 112
League of Upholders of Indonesian Independence (IPKI), 135
Legal Aid Foundation, 189, 196, 222
legal process, 192, 193
legal system, 193–5; ABRI/government interference in, 9, 194; and the Constitution, 193–4; political 'crimes', 195; Suharto fails to reform, 78
liberal Indonesia 1949–57, 46–52; differences between centre and periphery, 51; economic problems, 49–50; Islamic revolts, 47–9; political difficulties, 50–1
Liddle, William, 262–3
Liem Sioe Liong, 203, 204, 206–7, 229
literature review, 256–63
living costs, 93
looting, 251
Lowry, Robert, 69, 167, 168
Lubis, Mochtar, 150

MacFarling, Ian, 59, 261
Machmud, Amir, 104
McIntyre, Angus, 236
Mackie, J., 91
Madiun affair, 45, 113
Madurese transmigrants, and Dayak people, 163–5
Majapahit empire, 20, 23, 28, 34
Makarim, Major General Zacky Anwar, 232
Malacca, 23, 27, 30

Malari riots, 82, 104–6, 153
Malay Peninsula, 31
Malaysia, hostility towards, 26, 60
Malik, Adam, 135
mandala, 25, 26, 37
Marcos, Ferdinand, 203
market Malay; as national language, 36, 40; spread of, 34, 40
Marsinah case, 189–90
martial law, and Guided Democracy, 52
Maryadi, Eko, 161
Masyumi, 35, 44, 49, 50, 130, 141
Masyumi–PNI coalition, 45
Masyumi–Socialist–NU coalition, 50
Mataram empire, 23, 28–9
Mayall, John, 47
Medan, student protests, 250–1
media business: government involvement, 151; Suharto first family ownership, 151–2
Media Indonesia (publishing group), 151
Media Indonesia, 152
media: censorship, 147, 153, 154–5, 156; foreign, 85–6, 117, 150–1, 156, 159, 160; freedom of expression, 148–9, 155; government control over, 147–8, 149–51, 152–5, 228; loosening under Habibie, 254; newspaper closures, 154–5, 157–8; 'openness' ends, 157–8, 223; 'openness' period, 155–7, 222; *Pancasila* journalism, 147–9, 153, 157, 177, 223; precedents for control, 152–3; *Press Act of Indonesia*, 148, 149, 158–62; publishing licence, 149–50, 154, 157, 160; Radio Australia broadcasts, 150–1; role and requirements, 147–62; self-censorship, 150; suppression of the, 153; taboo topics, 156, 161; telephone culture (government control), 150, 153
Megawati Sukarnoputri, 14, 71, 106, 122, 128, 132, 139, 140, 191, 219, 231, 240, 254; ABRI support for, 136, 137, 237; as PDI leader, 136, 137, 224, 230, 231, 237; as political alternative, 236, 237–8; ousting of, 136, 238
Mejelis Permusyawaratan Rakyat (MPR), 66, 112, 128; ABRI representation, 120, 121–2; and Habibie

presidential appointment, 244; calls for Suharto resignation, 251, 252; structure and function, 72–4
Meliala, Major General Sembiring, 222
Mentawai of Siberut Island, 174
middle class, 11–12, 88–9, 93; car purchases, 214–15
military intelligence, 232
Minangkabau people, 174
minimum wage, 187, 189
mining policy, 142, 167
Moedjanto, G., 262
Moertono, Somarsaid, 262
Mohammad, Mar'ie, 157
Mokoginta, General, 110
MPR, *see* Mejelis Permusyawaratan Rakyat
mufakat, 53
Muhammadiyah, 13, 35, 139, 141–3; intolerance of ethnic Chinese and Christians, 142
Murdani, General Benny, 66, 73, 105, 106, 121, 139, 142, 192, 201, 220, 232, 233; and the *Pendawa Lima*, 234; as defence minister, 119, 201, 234; East Timor invasion, 107, 119; engenders diplomatic dispute with Australia, 114–16; in ABRI anti-Suharto camp, 123, 125, 126, 244; power of, 234; sacked by Suharto, 122, 201; tension with Suharto, 112–13, 114–15, 118, 125, 157, 223
Murtopo, Ali, 82, 105, 144, 192; planned invasion of East Timor, 106–7
Muslim United Development Party, 138
Muslims, 5, 6, 12, 121; concerns over marriage and divorce laws, 104–5; loosening of restrictions on, 238; political parties, 13, 130; tension with non-Muslim communities, 131
Musso, 45
mysterious killings, 192–3

Nahdatul Ulama (NU), 13, 35, 49, 123, 130, 139, 233; Gus Dur as leader, 133–5, 139, 140, 141; leaves PPP coalition, 134, 135, 239; liberalism, 134
Nasakom, 56, 130
Nasution, Adnan Buyung, 196, 222

Nasution, General Abdul Haris, 52, 54, 58, 61, 79, 102, 108, 110, 135, 206
nation, definition, viii
'National Council', 51
'national' culture, 40, 41
National Human Rights Commission, 195–6, 217
national unity, 40, 163, 174–5, 248–9
nationalisation of Dutch property, 52, 54
nationalism, 41–2, 50, 81–5
Negara Islam Indonesia, 48
nepotism, 92, 198, 208, 213
New Order government, 18, 22, 35, 51; and Islamic parties, 129–33; and Petition of Fifty, 109–10; and standard of living, 88, 90–1; and the media, 147–62; and unionism, 187–90; anti-communism stand, 181; attracts foreign investment, 77; austerity campaign, 97; constraints on free political organisation, 112; control over the media, 147–8, 149–51, 152–5, 158–62; discontent with, 67–70; disputes within ABRI and Golkar, 127–8; divisions within, 101–3, 109; domestic opposition, 127–9; economic direction, 77–98; economic performance analysis, 88–93; economic policies as ideological perspectives, 93–8; election campaign regulation, 71–2, 108, 129; military and intelligence bodies, 65–6; need for succession from Suharto, 100; political opposition, 127–46; proclaimed by Suharto, 57; reliance on tradition, 68, 69; repression of dissidents, 69, 114; seizes power, 57–75; shift of power, 63–7
newspaper closures, 154–5, 157–8
newsprint suppliers, 152
Nitisastro, Widjojo, 79, 83
non-government organisations (NGOs), 145
non-Javanese regions, and unity, 163
NU, see Nahdatul Ulama

October 17 (1952) affair, 50
oil: price decline, 85–6, 117, 208; wealth from, 6, 77, 81, 83, 84
Operation Mandala, 102, 106
OPM, see Free Papua Movement

opposition parties, 70, 108, 128–9; divisions between, 146; insurmountable obstacles, 146; non-government organisations, 145; non-political Islam, 139–45; NU, 133–5; PDI, 135–8; PPP, 129–33
'Opsus' (Special Operations), 65, 66, 104, 144

Padang, West Sumatra, demand for full autonomy, 54
Pakpahan, Mochtar, 138, 188–9
Pancasila, 4, 25, 131, 195; and 1945 Constitution, 42–3, 109, 146; and Petition of Fifty, 109; and political organisations, 112; principles, 42, 163; Suharto and Sukarno government interpretations, 42
Pancasila journalism, 147–9, 153, 157, 177, 223
Pangestu, Prajogo, 207
Panjaitan, Major General Sintong, 120
Papua New Guinea government, 168
Partai Demokrasi Indonesia, *see* PDI
Partai Kristen Indonesia, 135
Partai Murba, 135
Partai Muslimin Indonesia, 130
Partai Nasional Indonesia (PNI), 44
Partai Persatuan Pembangunan, *see* PPP
Partai Rakyat Demokrasi, *see* PRD
Partai Sarekat Islam Indonesia, 130
Parti Katolik, 135
patronage, system of, 79, 82, 83, 84, 103, 225
PDI, 14, 70, 71, 100, 108, 112, 120, 128, 129, 219, 222; as opposition to New Order, 135–8; destruction of, 132, 135, 136; formation, 135–6; influenced by ABRI and government, 71, 136; join PPP in demonstrations, 132, 238; Megawati elected as leader, 136, 137, 224, 230, 231, 237; *see also* Megawati Sukarnoputri
PDI headquarters, attack on, 137, 191
Pelita, 151, 152, 154
Pemberton, John, 262
Pendawa figures, 232–3
Pendawa Lima, 230–3, 246; and Murdani, 234
penembaken misterius (petrus), 192–3
personifying the state, 26–7

Pertamina (state-owned oil company), 79, 80, 82, 86; debt, 81, 84
Perti, 130
Petition of Fifty, 109–10, 114
PKI: and 30 September 1965 attempted coup, 57–8, 63–4; arms shipment from China, 58–9; democratic ideals, 55; influence in Sukarno government, 59; massacred by the army, 57–8, 63; re-establishment, 44; *santri* Muslims violence against, 144; suppression of, 12, 14, 69, 103; tension with army, 56, 59
political authority, concept of, 4
political dissent, government attitude towards, 190–2
political economy model, 3–4
political groupings and succession: ABRI contenders, 221–7; beyond ABRI, 228–9; factional manœuvring, 219–20; *Pendawa Lima*, 230–3, 246; pro-democracy movement, 236–9; strategic alliances, 233–4
political leadership, post-Suharto, 245–6
political parties: constraints on, 112; election campaign regulation, 71–2, 108, 129; electoral success since 1971, 70; post-War, 44; under Suharto, 70–4
political prisoners, release of, 254
political process, people's lack of access to, 8, 245
political structure, 72–4
Pontoh, Coen Hussein 191
population, 5, 17
Portuguese, colonisation of Malacca, 27, 30
poverty, 7, 89, 90, 92–3, 111, 179, 241
PPP, 13, 70, 71, 108, 112, 128, 129; as Islamic party, 129–33, 238–9; as opposition to Suharto and Golkar, 132; join PDI in DPR elections, 132, 238; lack of cohesion and purpose, 130–1, 239; Muslim party components, 130; NU withdrawal from, 134, 135, 239; policy alternatives to Golkar, 133; rallies over DPR structure, 132–3, 240; renegade members, 138; support from young people, 238–9
Prabowo Subianto, General, 119, 120, 205, 221, 231, 251, 253; ABRI fac-

tional group, 226–7; military performance, 227; political aspirations, 242, 243
PRD, 14, 190; affiliations, 138; blamed for PDI attack and riots, 137–8
Press Act of Indonesia, 148, 149, 158–62
Press Council, 160
prijaji, influence of, 32
print media, 150
private banks, 96, 97
Probosutedjo, 206, 212
pro-democracy groups, 6, 8–9
pro-democracy movement, 14–16, 236–9
protesters, 190–2
Proto-Malay people, 18
Proton Saga (Malaysia's 'national' car), 2121
PRRI–Permesta rebellion, 48, 53–4, 130, 141, 143, 174; ABRI crushes, 55, 113; USA and UK support for, 54–5
public health campaigns, 11
publishing licence, 149–50, 154, 157, 160
Purwopranjono, Major General Muchdi, 253

quality of life, 90–1

Rachmawati, 237
Radio Australia broadcasts, 151–2
radio, domestic, 152
Rais, Amien, 142, 143, 254
RCTI (television station), 151
Reagan, Ronald, 85–6, 117–18
rebellious provinces, 128; *see also* Aceh Province; East Timor; Irian Jaya
'reform' Cabinet, 252, 253
regional economic development, 87–8
religions, and *Pancasila*, 42–3, 131
religious groups, 5, 6
religious influences, 18–22, 23, 27–9
Renville Agreement, 48
Republic of Indonesia; 1945 Constitution, 36, 37; proclaimed, 36, 43
Republic of the United States of Indonesia (RUSI), 46; commitment to multi-party system, 49; constitution, 193; federal structure, 46
Ricklefs, Merle, 260, 261
right to development, 177, 179–80, 186

riots: 1996–98, 14–15, 90, 98, 202, 240, 248; East Timor, 183–4; Jakarta 1974, 82, 104–6, 153; Jakarta 1996, 137, 191, 247; Jakarta 1997, 240; Jakarta 1998, 250–1; Sumatra and Java 1995–98, 48–9; Tanjung Priok, 111–12, 114, 143, 191

Robison, Richard, 111, 115–16, 260

Royal Netherlands Indies Army, 31

Rudini, 181

rupiah decline, *see* currency collapse

Sadikin, Lt General Ali, 108

Sailendras, 23

Saleh, Ismail, 115, 116

Salim, Anthony, 207

Salim, Emil, 254

Salim Group, 206–7

Salosa, Melkianus, 168

Sanusi, H. M., 112

Sarekat Islam, 13

Sarwo Edhie Wibowo, Lt General, 104, 105, 113

Sastroamidjojo Cabinet, 50, 51, 52

Satelindo (satellite service), 204

Schwartz, Adam, 257–8, 259

Second World War: Allied operations, 44; Japanese occupation, 35–6

Sekneg (government procurement), 83–4

separatist movements, 9–10, 128, 165–6, 166–9

September 30/October 1 1965; coup theories, 57–61, 102; Suharto's knowledge of Untung/PKI plan, 61–3

shadow play (fiction), 1–3

shipping, 50, 52

Sigit, Ari 205

Sigit Harjojudanto, 204

Sinar, 152

Sinar Harapan, 154

Sinar Mas group, 207

Siregar, Major General Syamsir, 231

Siti Hardiyanti Rukmana, *see* Suharto, Tutut

Siti Hediati Herijadi, *see* Suharto, Titiek

Siti Hutami Endang, 205

Sjahrir, Major General, 253

Sjahrir, Sutan, 45

Sjarifuddin, Amir, 45

Socialist Party, 44

South Sulawesi rebellion, 48

Sri Bintang Pamungkas, 138

Srivajaya empire, 23, 34

Stackhouse, John, 116

standard of living, 88, 90–1, 93, 202

State lottery, banning of, 122, 222

State: competing conceptions of, 39–42; construction of the, 10–12; definition, viii; mandalic view, 26; personifying the, 26–7; 'rights', 29

strategic alliances, 233–4

street marches, 191

street names, 41–2

strikes, 187, 188, 189, 190

student newspapers, closures, 154

student protests, 107–8, 222–3, 250–1

Student Solidarity for Indonesian Democracy, 138

Subrata, 159, 223

subversion, 138, 191; Anti-Subversion Law, 195; definition, 190

succession to Suharto, contenders, 100, 219–29

Sudharmono, Lt General, 105, 119, 152, 201, 229, 242, 252; ABRI opposition to vice-presidential appointment, 73–4, 113, 118; Sekneg (government procurement), 83–4

Sudharsono, Juwono, 253

Sudwikatmono, 151, 152, 203, 206, 208

Suharto: ABRI dissatisfaction with, 74, 108, 111, 118, 119, 121–2, 123–6, 201, 222; ABRI support of, 7–8, 99; accumulation of wealth, 75; and East Timor invasion, 106–7, 119–20, 121; and favourite son, Tommy, 213–14, 217; and 'super-rich' Chinese, 12, 49; and the office of the monarch, 27; and the state lottery, 122, 222; announces new presidential elections, 252; appointed as Kostrad commander, 61–2, 102; appoints Habibie as president, 252; appoints Sudharmono as vice-president, 73–4, 113, 118–19; as 'father of development', 11; *Bantuan Presiden*, 83; comparison with Ferdinand Marcos, 203–4; consolidation of power, 118–19; corruption allegations, 85–6, 103, 109, 114, 115, 116, 117, 118, 199–204; courts Muslim vote, 142–3; early life, 76; early opposition to, 67–70; economic development, 68, 77–98; fall of, 250–5; generals split with, 103–6; Gus Dur (NU leader) as ally, 234–5; imperious style, 110; increases political authority, 68; insults military commanders, 108; joint business ventures, 199, 200; kingly role, 70, 72; knowledge of Untung/PKI coup plan, 61–3; 'Kopkamtib' letter from Sukarno, 64, 65; named as acting president, 67; opposition to, 99–101, 125, 128, 175; party system, 70–4; personal wealth, 202, 203, 253; political strengths, 74–6; proclaims New Order government, 57; resentment of, 82; resignation calls, 251, 252; resignation greeted with enthusiasm, 252, 253; seizes power, 61, 63–4, 65, 102–3; shift in power from Sukarno, 63–7, 102; successor contenders, 100, 219–29; suppression of the media, 153; system of patronage, 79, 82, 83, 84, 103, 225; tension with Murdani, 112–13, 114–15, 118, 125, 157, 223; transition from, 241–2; unease over grab for power, 66; unofficial funding source, 79–81; uses reconstructed traditional political history, 68; *yayasans* (charitable foundations), 199–200, 202, 203–4, 206, 207; *see also* New Order government

Suharto, Tien, 108, 109, 203, 213, 233

Suharto, Titiek, 205, 243

Suharto, Tommy, 75, 198, 208, 236; clove market enterprise, 212–13; Lamborghini purchase, 211; Timor 'national' car project, 96, 209–12, 213, 214, 217

Suharto, Tutut, 134, 139–40, 151, 152, 204, 207, 225, 233, 236, 252; as possible vice-president, 242; Golkar vice-president, 224; Proton car imports, 212

Suharto business/financial friends, 76, 81–2, 206–9, 216, 229; corruption, 15, 81; influence on Indonesian economy, 74–5, 235–6; monopolistic business interests, 208; wealth, 207–8

Suharto first family, 83, 134, 139–40, 198, 204–6; and the 'national' car, 209–12, 213, 214, 217; corruption among, 15, 200, 201, 202, 208, 218,

222; DPR appointments, 112; enterprises, 96, 97, 151–2, 204–6, 212–13; influence on Indonesian economy, 235–6; power of, 75; sibling alliances, 233; wealth, 204, 217, 223; wealth redistribution following Suharto's fall, 236; *see also specific Suharto children*

Sujatmiko, Budiman, 138, 191

Sukarno: adopts traditional Javanese symbols, 56; and the *Gestok* (attempted coup), 62; and the office of the monarch, 27; as charismatic leader, 64; as Republic's first president, 36, 46; attempts to save his position, 64–5; belief in *mufakat*, 53; children, 236–7; endorses socialist/communist ideologies, 55–6; gives Suharto letter to restore order, 64; Guided Democracy, 51, 52; language borrowed from Soviet Union, 41, 56; nationalist aspirations, 47; ousted as president, 57; PKI influence, 59; proclaims Republic of Indonesia, 36; shift in power to Suharto, 63–7; suppression of the media, 153; syncretism, 43, 56, 130; views on Dutch colonial occupation, 34–5; vision for the state, 47

Sukarno, Guntur, 237

Sukarno, Guruh, 237

Sukarno administration, economic decline, 6, 56

Sukarno–Hatta government, 36, 45, 54

Sulawesi, bloodless coups, 53–4

Sumarlin, Johannes, 79

Sumatra, bloodless coups, 51, 53

Sumatran peoples, 174

Sumitro, General, 82, 104, 105

'super-rich', 12

Surat Izin Usaha Penerbitan Pers (SIUPP), 149–50

Surya Citra Televisi, 151

Suryadharma, Air Force Commander, 54

Suryadi, 136, 137, 237

Sutowo, General Ibnu, 79, 80, 81, 113, 217

syncretism, 18, 43, 56, 130

Tanaka, Kakuei, 82, 104, 105

Tanjung Priok riots, 111–12, 114, 143, 191

Taufik, Achmad, 161
tax concessions, 96
tax contributions, highest payers, 207–8
tax reform, 86
'Team 10' group, 83–4, 229
television, domestic, 152
Tempo, 152, 157, 158
Ternate, 28
timber industry, 206, 207
Timor 'national' car project, 96, 209–12, 213, 214; car sales, 215; international objections, 215–18
Titiek, *see* Suharto, Titiek
Tommy, *see* Suharto, Tommy
Try Sutrisno, 74, 120, 121, 135, 157, 230, 252; as presidential candidate, 220, 244; vice-presidential nomination, 121–2, 222, 242; views on Dili massacre, 170, 184
Tutut, *see* Suharto, Tutut

UDT (Uniao Democratica Timorese), 107
unemployment and underemployment, 89–90, 93, 187
unionists, 161, 186–90, 254
United Nations, 45, 52, 169, 177, 186
unofficial funding, 79–81
Untung, Lt Colonel, 58, 60, 61
Utrecht, Ernst, 260

Vatikiotis, Michael, 67, 148, 203, 258
vice-president: appointment, 9, 36, 73–4, 113, 118–19, 228, 229; as Suharto's successor, 234; nominations, 121–2, 222, 242–3
village, influence in social and political life, 29

Volunteer Army of Defenders of the Fatherland, 35
vote-rigging, 72
voting irregularities, 70

Wahid, Abdurrahman, *see* Gus Dur
Walters, Patrick, 158
Wanandi, Sofyan, 253
Wanita Indonesia, 152
Warouw, Brigadier General Rudolph, 120
wealth distribution, 90
wealthy civilian elite, 3, 7, 12, 202, 241
West Kalimantan, violence, 163–5
West Timor, 107, 173
wet-rice agriculture, 18; influence of, 23
White Group ('Golput'), 70
Widjaya, Eka Cipta 207
Willner, A. R., 56
Winters, Jeffrey, 259
Wirahadikusumah, Umar, 252
Wiranto, Lt General, 225–6, 230, 231, 232; as possible vice-president, 242, 243; power of, 252, 253; Suharto retirement call, 251, 252
Wismoyo Arismunandar, Major General, 120, 221
working conditions, 186–7
World Bank, 78, 84–5
World Trade Organisation, 216

yayasans (charitable foundations), 199–200, 202, 203–4, 206, 207
Yosfiah, Major General Yunus, 231, 253
Yudhoyono, Major General Susilo Bambang, 226, 230, 232, 251

Zainuddin, Farid, 231–2